*Jesuit Ranches and the Agrarian Development
of Colonial Argentina, 1650–1767*

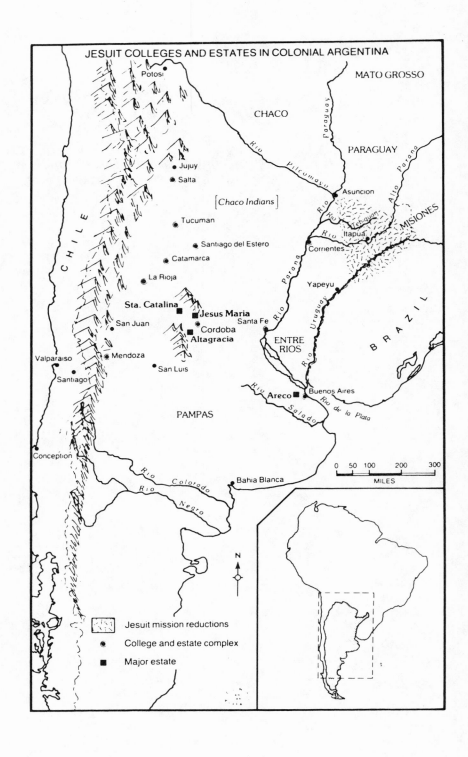

JESUIT COLLEGES AND ESTATES IN COLONIAL ARGENTINA

MATO GROSSO

CHACO

Potosi

PARAGUAY

Jujuy

Salta

[Chaco Indians]

Asuncion

MISIONES

Tucuman

Itapua

Santiago del Estero

Corrientes

Catamarca

Yapeyu

La Rioja

BRAZIL

Sta. Catalina

Jesus Maria

San Juan

Santa Fe

Cordoba

Altagracia

ENTRE RIOS

Valparaiso

Mendoza

Santiago

San Luis

Buenos Aires

Areco

Rio de la Plata

PAMPAS

CHILE

Conception

Rio Colorado

Rio Negro

Bahia Blanca

0 50 100   200   300

MILES

N

Jesuit mission reductions

College and estate complex

Major estate

Jesuit Ranches and the Agrarian Development of Colonial Argentina, 1650–1767

Nicholas P. Cushner

State University of New York Press
ALBANY

ALSO BY NICHOLAS P. CUSHNER

Landed Estates in the Colonial Philippines

Lords of the Land: Sugar, Wine, and Jesuit Estates of Coastal Peru, 1600–1767

Farm and Factory: The Jesuits and the Development of Agrarian Capitalism in Colonial Quito, 1600–1767

Published by State University of New York Press, Albany

© 1983 State University of New York

For information, address State University of New York Press, State University Plaza, Albany, N.Y., 12246

Library of Congress Cataloging in Publication Data

Cushner, Nicholas P.
  Jesuit ranches and the agrarian development of colonial Argentina, 1650–1767.

  Bibliography: p. 195
  Includes index.
    1. Agriculture—Economic aspects—Argentina—History. 2. Agriculture—Economic aspects—Argentina—Tucúman—History. 3. Jesuits—Argentina—History. 4. Ranches—Argentina—History. I. Title.
HD1862.C87   1983   338.1'0982'43   82-19503
ISBN 0-87395-707-5
ISBN 0-87395-708-3 (pbk.)

Contents

CONTENTS

vi

Illustrations and Tables

Map

Figures

Tables

Preface

I have been singularly fortunate in receiving a great deal of quality assistance in the preparation of this and my previous book (*Lords of the Land*) that touched on colonial Argentina. The late Guillermo Furlong, S.J., guided me as only he could through the maze of rich archives in Argentina, pointing me in the direction of the National Archives, the archives of Córdoba, and the Jesuit Province of Argentina archives located just outside of Buenos Aires in the suburb of San Miguel. Valentín Torres, the director of the Museo Nacional de Jesús María, was my gracious host and guide during my stay at the former Jesuit estate of Jesús María. The library staff of the Jesuit Casa de Escritores (Pablo Aranda 13, Madrid) allowed me to consult the Pastells Collection of AGI transcripts during the sacred month of August when the library is normally closed to researchers. Carmelo Saenz de Santa María, S.J., of the Instituto Gonzalo de Oviedo, C.S.I.C., was very helpful with suggestions and providing me with offprints of his own work on the economics of Jesuit colleges in Guatemala. Jonathan C. Brown read the manuscript and made extensive comments and suggestions. His advice has resulted in a substantially improved book. I am also indebted to Daniel Mulvey, S.J. for the genuine interest, as well as sympathetic but exacting criticism he gave of key portions of the text. The encouragement, courtesy, and assistance I received from fellow Jesuits in Europe and Latin America when I was a member of the Society of Jesus made the process of research much more enjoyable and challenging.

A grant from the American Philosophical Society allowed me to pursue essential research in the Archive of the Indies, Seville, in the summer of 1981. The Research Foundation of the State University of New York, which had generously contributed to the research and publication of my three books on the agricultural history of colonial Latin

ix

America, provided funds for the preparation of the manuscript. And lastly, I must record a special word of thanks to Mr. William Eastman, the director of the State University of New York Press, and to Nancy Sharlet, Production Editor, for having resolutely seen this and my other two volumes to press. It has been a pleasure to work with the SUNY Press's highly competent staff.

Nicholas P. Cushner
Empire State College, Buffalo
State University of New York

Abbreviations

AGBA Archivo General de la Nación (Buenos Aires)
AGI   Archivo General de las Indias (Seville)
AHC   Archivo Histórico de Córdoba
APA   Archivum Provinciae Argentinensis (San Miguel)
ARSI Archivum Romanum Societatis Iesu (Rome)
BNC   Biblioteca Nacional de Chile (Santiago)
BS   Biblioteca de Salamanca (Jesuit residence, San Antonio)
CA,1 Cartas Anuas (1609–1614)
CA,2 Cartas Anuas (1615–1637)
FG   Fondo Gesuitico (in ARSI)
LC   Libro de Cuentas. Candelaria 1718–1767 (in APA)
LCC   Libro de Cuentas de este Colegio de Córdoba de la Compañía de Jesús, 1711 (in APA)
LOPP Libro de Oficio del P. Procurador de Provincia, 1711 (in APA)
MJM   Museo de Jesús María (Estancia de Jesús María)
SL   St. Louis University, Vatican Microfilm Collection

Introduction

This book is the third and last in a series that has examined Jesuit economic activity in three major geographic regions of colonial Spanish America. The first, *Lords of the Land,*[1] focused on Jesuit sugar and wine production on the Peruvian coast primarily from the viewpoint of the agricultural geographer. The second, *Farm and Factory,*[2] looked at the complex of Jesuit farm, wool, and textile production in Interandine Quito insofar as it contributed to the beginnings of agrarian capitalism in Latin America. The present book examines the agropastoral development of colonial Argentina, primarily Tucumán, its farms, its ranches, and its trade connections with Alto Peru. Three major geographical regions are thus studied, each specializing in a distinct complex of economic enterprises, but each linked by trade routes that crossed snowy mountains and traversed barren deserts. Within the unity there was specificity.

These three books were never intended to be an institutional history of the Jesuits, even though most of the data used pertained to their economic activities. Rather I proceeded on the assumption that the economic activity of the Society of Jesus could tell us something about the economic history of colonial Spanish America. Given the relative absence of economic data from the private sector that spanned long time periods, perhaps the institutional owner could supply answers to some important questions. This does not mean that a blind leap could be made from the specific to the more universal, only that certain types of data drawn from institutional holdings could suggest certain lines of development. They might even suggest trends in colonial economic history requiring of course further verification.

The farms and ranches studied in this book were for the most part owned by colleges of the Society of Jesus. As in Peru and Andean Quito, the major thrust of Jesuit work was in the urban colleges. The

1

original foundation grant or endowment funds, required by the Society before a college could open, were invested in land on which were usually small functioning farms or ranches. The American innovation, not practiced by Jesuit colleges in Europe but started in Mexico, saw Jesuits themselves administering and managing landed estates instead of simply receiving accrued revenues.[3] The practice was extended from Mexico to Peru, Quito, New Granada, Chile, and Paraguay. So the sons of Ignatius Loyola found themselves growing sugar cane, producing wine, managing sheep and textile mills, raising mules and cattle, and turning wheat into flour. Attendant and associated activities were even more numerous. The physical plants for these rural activities consisted of massive (for that time and place) constructions of churches, farmsteads, ranch houses, barns, and bunk houses. The largest Jesuit constructions in colonial Argentina were of those enterprises belonging to the College of Córdoba, Jesús María and Altagracia, and to the Jesuit province as a corporation, Santa Catalina. All of these figure prominently in this book.

This does not mean that the Jesuits were the sole owners of large farms and ranches in Córdoba. Spanish colonization of the region far antedated the arrival of the Society. Land was distributed, the soil plowed, and cattle raised long before the first Jesuit set foot in Tucumán. The agro-pastoral origins of the region responded to both internal and external circumstances. Land, soil, and climate were eminently suitable for certain types of crops, and the grasses of the northern pampas equally suitable for raising and fattening cattle. Northwest of this area, high in the Andes, the mining centers of Potosí and Huancavelica, and the Andean communities of Cuzco, La Paz, and Oruro needed what Tucumán could produce. The confluence of need and the ability to produce what was needed dominated the political economy of colonial Tucumán.

Contrary to popular opinion, the agrarian history of Argentina did not begin with the gaucho. Nor did it begin with the development of the pampas, even though the politics of wheat and cattle have defined the economic structure of Argentina in modern times. Long before the gaucho became the symbol of the Argentine cattle range and the southern pampas were cleared of troublesome Indians, a tradition of cattle raising and cereal farming had taken root. This agro-pastoral tradition had several early foci: the Río de la Plata area, just west of Buenos Aires; the Asunción, Corrientes, and Entre Ríos triangle that focused on cattle; and the Córdoba-Tucumán region. In this book, I have attempted to explore this early tradition, to examine its component parts, to lift the veil at least partially on a segment of the rural world of colonial Argentina by concentrating on the Tucumán region. The view is mainly through Jesuit spectacles, but hopefully the vista is not too far out of focus.

The geographical and temporal parameters of this study are fairly clear. In general, the old Jesuit Province of Paraguay which included all of modern Argentina, Paraguay, and Uruguay forms the outer limit. However, the major focus is on the colonial *gobernación,* later the province, of Tucumán and the region around Córdoba. For comparative purposes, other areas within the Jesuit province of Paraguay have been brought into the picture because they specialized in different economic enterprises (e.g., wines of Mendoza and La Rioja, or *yerba mate* production in the missions of Paraguay). The region's similar physical features (soil quality differs but climate is uniform), make it a fairly homogeneous and unified subject area.

The time frame, 1650–1767, coincides with the gradual development and apogée of Jesuit properties. Again a word of explanation. The origins of Tucumán's agro-pastoral development precede 1650 by more than half a century, and the intense interest and concentrated agricultural effort there continued long after 1767. In the 1780s and 1790s, the Consulado of Buenos Aires requested monthly reports from Tucumán and other provinces on crop production, prices, cattle raising, and climatic conditions. The time frame falls into the wider framework of agricultural development, and the Jesuit data are most meaningful for this period. Prior to 1650, Jesuit ranches and farms either had not yet been purchased, or if they had been, income from them was minimal. Unexamined in this study, but a theme which I hope to examine at some future time, is the relationship or correlation between the rise of the large institutional ranch or farm and fluctuations in the money and credit market, Peruvian mine production, and the slackening of privately owned landed property in Tucumán. This would require a much deeper knowledge of colonial Tucumán's business and commercial history than we now possess. Long term fluctuations in prices, credit, and business transactions would have to serve as the backdrop and gauge for a serious economic study of the large colonial ranch and farm. Until this could be accomplished, we have to content ourselves in a sense with a series of tableaux of the seventeenth and eighteenth centuries. They are not offered in place of a more sophisticated examination of colonial Tucumán's economy, but as a preliminary effort with a view to developing a number of useful working hypotheses on the colonial period. The time frame used here,

3

1650–1767, offers a more than adequate period during which to identify and articulate the main lines of colonial rural development in the region.

The general plan I used in *Lords of the Land* and *Farm and Factory* is also used in this book. A brief survey of major geographical features serves as background for chapters on land acquisition and land use. Man-made physical structures and specific enterprises, especially mule and cattle raising, are followed by chapters on labor and financial implications. Some general conclusions follow. Thus, in several succinct chapters we see how the Spanish settlers reacted to their new environment, how they shaped it to meet their specific social and economic needs, and how previous occupiers of the land were either coopted as laborers in the new economic and social order, or stood outside it as direct active opponents.

The socioeconomic effects of this active opposition have not been fully explored. Between the 1580s and 1790s, periodic flare-ups occurred on the frontier, or the four frontiers as the Spaniards called them, and a number of these flare-ups continued for years with devastating effects on lives and property.[4] In 1589 the town council of San Miguel de Tucumán described an especially brutal Indian raid on their town that destroyed the settlers' houses and cattle.[5] In 1664 Governor Alonso de Mercado y Villacorta wrote that the Mocobies and Chaco Indians had been active for the past thirty years, attacking with impunity the frontier towns of Esteco, Salta, Jujuy, Tarija, and Santa Cruz de la Sierra long before Bojorques, the pseudo-Inca, had successfully roused the natives to armed protest.[6] Almost twenty years later, Governor Fernando de Mendoza lamented the sorry state of Tucumán occasioned by Indian raids and the expenditures made to resist Calchaquí incursions.[7] Fighting with the Mocobies continued through 1700 and well beyond. During the period 1740–1780, the conquest of the Chaco became almost an obsession. The provinces of Tucumán, Buenos Aires, and Paraguay joined forces to subdue the common menace.[8] In ensuing battles the Spaniards gave no quarter, took few prisoners, and slew all Indians under arms.[9] Apparently it was only in 1776 that some degree of peace was obtained. Speaking for the Spanish government, local officials assured the Mocobies Indian leaders of gifts of clothes, a fort for themselves, houses, ranches, farms, and cattle in a *reducción* (reservation) to be called Remolinos.[10] A period of peace followed.

The major effects of the Indian wars were disruption of economic links with Peru and an unstable agrarian development. This led directly to what governors José de Harro and Fernando de Mendoza described as the "extreme poverty of Tucumán's Spanish population."[11] Although conflicts with the frontier Indians is not a major theme of this book, what is presented here should be considered with the Indian wars forming a background. Their precise effect on the mule trade, livestock production, and wheat raising has not been measured, but when it is, I suspect that there will be a high correlation.

The role of Jesuit ranching and farming must be placed within the context of the expanding Spanish frontier. The Society's activity was more participatory than innovative. Their massive landholdings helped to provide a bulwark against encroaching and marauding Indians, and their continual trading activity helped to cement and advance economic and commercial ties with other colonial centers.

Nevertheless, the chief importance of detailing Jesuit activity lies in throwing some light on the process of farming, ranching, and product distribution in colonial Argentina. The management of property, the employment of types of laborers, and accounting systems were very similar on both institutional and private estates. The major differences must have been the way land was used and the availability of capital for a labor supply. But even assuming these differences, an examination of the institutional ranch or farm in colonial Tucumán can still be of great interest and considerable importance in lifting the veil ever so slightly from the commercial and rural world of colonial Latin America.

In addition, two underlying themes that run through the book should be pointed out. One is the recurring notion that essentially medieval concepts of business practice were gradually giving way to more modern views. Certain credit mechanisms that had once been considered evil by nature were beginning to emerge as standard—if not totally accepted, they were at least tolerated. A second theme is the frequent use of European religious models for comparison rather than other Latin American or Mexican prototypes. This bias is deliberate primarily because both Mexican and South American religious communities used European monasteries as archetypes. This does not mean that regional variations did not emerge, determined by diverse physical and ministerial circumstances. As Herman Konrad has so clearly shown in his splendid work on Santa Lucía hacienda, the Jesuits in Mexico did not hesitate to adjust their rural economic activity to local circumstances, even though it meant abandoning traditional European practices. But it does mean that the way the Latin American religious institutions related to the frontier should be compared to their predecessors' experience on the European frontier. It is apparent that even the large Jesuit cattle ranches of Sinaloa on Mexico's Pacific coast played quite a different role from Jesuit sugar estates of coastal Peru, or Jesuit mule ranches of Córdoba.[12] But granted these differences, institutional estates tended to demonstrate a common personality that bears more fruitful comparison with their European antecedents.

CHAPTER 1

The Lay of the Land

The Physical Environment

The origin of Spanish colonial settlements and the related acquisition of large landholdings in Tucumán had as much to do with physical geography as with the trajectory of Spanish military conquest. The Spanish exploratory thrusts from Peru and Chile terminated on the fertile plains of what is today central Argentina. East of these plains were the floodplains of the Paraná; west were the Andes Mountains, and to the north was the barren Chaco. Directly north were the rocky mountain passes leading to Alto Peru.[1] The first century-and-a-half of Spanish colonial life centered on these plains of the northern pampas and its major city, Córdoba. Smaller towns sprouted to the west of Córdoba on the vineyard oases of La Rioja, San Juan, and Mendoza; east were the important cities of Asunción and Santa Fe, the latter a little to the southeast on the Litoral, the area immediately to the north of Buenos Aires.

Córdoba was part of a wider geographical and political unit, called the Gobernación of Tucumán, whose official boundaries were never exactly determined. They extended somewhat north to the Chaco and south to the other major political subdivision of the region, the Río de la Plata. The only clear and exact physical boundary was the eastern rim of the Andes Mountains. In general, the jurisdiction of Tucumán covered the present provinces of Córdoba, Jujuy, Salta, Tucumán, Santiago del Estero, La Rioja, and Catamarca.

Córdoba was superbly located on all of the key commercial routes and so played a major role as economic intermediary between coast and interior. A large city developed from the original inauspicious settlement mainly because of its location and its delightfully pleasant, temperate climate with a more than adequate rainfall that attracted numerous Spanish settlers. The fertile land of the northern pampas, on which Córdoba was situated, was eminently suitable for both ranching and agriculture. The soil in general is fertile, but near Córdoba, stretching on an east-west axis, are the Córdoba Hills, the Sierra de Córdoba. At the base of these hills in the long low-lying intermountain valleys were located some of the largest of the Jesuit cattle ranches. The city of Córdoba was located near the base of this range at about 390 meters above sea level. Except near the hills, the soil is entirely free from stones and large rocks.

The region has generally mild winters (June–September) and hot summers (December–March). Buenos Aires has about the same temperature in January (22°C) as does New York City in July. However, winter in Córdoba and Buenos Aires is much less severe. The average temperature of the coldest month in Córdoba is about 10°C. But there are few days of extreme heat or extreme cold in Córdoba; the little rain that does fall between October and March does so in the south and southeast portions of modern Córdoba Province. The irrigated pastures around Córdoba were eminently suitable for ranching. River systems that generally drain eastward towards the Atlantic flow through Córdoba. Five notable streams flow from their headwaters in the Córdoba Hills called simply the Primero (First) through Quinto (Fifth). The largest, the Tercero (Third) and the Quarto (Fourth), unite before joining the Paraná River above Rosario.

The felicitous combination of climate and soil was used to great advantage by early Spanish settlers. By 1584, not only were the fertile plains around Córdoba described as such, but by means of a system of irrigation canals, wheat, corn, barley, and other European grains were harvested in abundance.[2] Twenty years later, the city had sixty Spanish householders with over 4,000 Indians in *encomienda,* and by 1670, the city was described as one of the most populous and illustrious outside of Peru.[3] Each of the religious orders prominent in the evangelization of Mexico and Peru had adequate residences and churches and the Jesuits administered the University of Córdoba. The affluence of the city was a reflection of the wealth accumulated through farming, ranching, and commerce.

Acquisition of Land

The acquisition of land and the development of the large estate complex around Córdoba occurred very differently from the way it took place in coastal Peru or Interandine Quito. In Lima and Quito, Francisco Pizarro and his lieutenants established absolute control in a relatively brief period of time. There was no doubt that they intended to

8

stay and rule. On the other hand, initial Spanish occupation of Tucumán was sporadic. In 1537 the Mendoza–Irala expedition advanced to Asunción and Buenos Aires but did not return to the latter until 1580. The Rojas expedition of 1542–1544 into northwest Argentina resulted in no permanent settlement.[4] Spanish advances from Peru and Chile ran into stiff Indian resistance. Towns were founded and *encomiendas* granted but often they were left unattended. The first Jesuits arrived in 1585 but the Jesuit Province of Paraguay was not established until 1604. All this indicates a state of flux in the early years of Tucumán's settlement that had not been present in Peru or Quito.

The region south of Bolivia and Brazil seemed almost too vast to settle. Probing expeditions were mounted which were too small to control effectively the wide spaces lying below Alto Peru. This piecemeal approach to conquest affected the way the land was divided and settled. In Peru and Quito, a major spatial focus was established, whether Lima or Quito, and from these two nuclei almost all of the contiguous arable land in the surrounding valleys was distributed among the settlers within a matter of decades. In Tucumán and Paraguay, three major foci were established, Asunción, Córdoba, and Buenos Aires; from these three points occupation and settlement of arable land took place. But the land was so vast that complete Spanish occupation of available land was impossible, and even many land claims could not possibly have been worked, let alone effectively controlled. In Peru, land was measured by the *fanegada* (about three hectares); in Quito by the *caballería* (about the same), whereas Tucumán and Paraguay measured their holdings by the league, in six kilometer units! Settlers were relatively few and the land was abundant.

The main thrust of Spanish settlement came from Peru across the Altiplano, leaving a string of Spanish towns from Salta to Córdoba. Santiago del Estero was the principal town in this chain until 1573 when the provincial governor, Jerónimo Luís de Cabrera, and the Archbishop of Tucumán, Fernando de Trejo y Sanabria, moved to Córdoba which then assumed the role of pre-eminent settlement. But Córdoba in the early days was not much to speak of. In 1585 the city had about 150 Spaniards living in one-story, mud brick houses, and an Indian population of about 6,000 did their manual work.[5] But plenty of surrounding land was available.

Between 1573 and 1600, over 400 grants of land from Córdoba south to the Río Quinto were made to Spanish settlers by the governors of Tucumán.[6] The family with the largest landholdings in colonial Tucumán was the Cabreras, the descendents of the founder of Córdoba. On November 24, 1574, Jerónimo Luís Cabrera received a royal order that made him the encomendero of the Indians of Córdoba, a vague jurisdiction that stretched indeterminately as far south as Buenos Aires. Cabrera distributed many of these Indians to his soldiers but he retained 2,000 for himself, "to serve me and my haciendas all the days of my life and my successor's life."[7] Unfortunately, Jerónimo did not live long enough to enjoy the fruits of conquest. He died in 1574.

In 1617 an official visit was made to the major estates of Jerónomo's heir, Luís de Cabrera. The lands were called San Francisco de Buena Vista, located about twenty-four leagues south of Córdoba, with houses, corrals, outlying ranch houses, and grazing and agricultural land. Luís owned four other major estates in addition to San Francisco de Buena Vista. In 1681 the Cabrera family's ownership of their lands was confirmed. They then consisted mainly of what was lightheartedly called "The Lands of the Río Quarto," lands that stretched from the Río Quarto south to the Río Quinto, and "North to the Saladillo River, and these lands are ten leagues wide and ten long, to the pampa up to Melincue, and from here north ten leagues and south to the Sierra and jurisdiction of the Punta."[8] The land was owned "with all watering holes, rivers, streams, mountains, and pastures."

However, by the 1680s the family holdings were showing signs of breaking up. The enormous amount of land was almost unmanageable and the lack of laborers acute. The owner in 1681, José de Cabrera, complained that he could not manage the estates because the pampa Indians were continually raiding his holdings and threatening to kill him. "The Indians," said José, "will not subject themselves to an encomendero; they live in paganism; they pay no tribute and they attack travelers on the roads to Córdoba."[9] So instead of willing all of his lands to the eldest son as tradition required, José divided his lands in 1689 among four heirs in the following manner: to José, Hac. Río Quarto; to Francisco, Hac. San Bartolomé, Las Peñas; to María, ½ Hac. Langunilla; and to Fernando, Hac. Costasacate, lands of Santa Fe, Hac. of Paraná, Lajas, and Achiras.[10]

Each of these were sizeable pieces of property in their own right. The major estate, the hacienda of the Río Quarto, measured ten leagues east to west and twenty leagues on a north–south axis. Three large herds of horses, mares, and their offspring grazed on the land. However, as mentioned above, there were bitter feelings between the local pampa Indians and the ranch, the causes of which one could only suspect. Nor were they mitigated by the ranch's subdivision; nor did the Indians have only the Cabrera's ranch to contend with. By this time (1681), there were about 700 Spanish-owned estates scattered throughout the province of Tucumán, with most south of Córdoba around the Río Tercero and Río Quarto. The Indians bitterly resented the Spanish presence on and absorption of what had been their hunting and grazing lands.

The large chunks of land which the conquerors of Tucumán generously granted to themselves were not necessarily typical of the size of landholdings awarded to ordinary settlers. The grant usually included a house plot *(solar)* within the town limits, a small field *(chácara)* outside of the city, and often a much more extensive piece of rural property further removed from the city. For example, in 1600 Guillermo de Asurde received a land grant "for an *estancia* of one league in extension, thirty leagues from Córdoba on the road to Mendoza."[11] The official designation of size, however, meant very little. The size of the *estancia* in early Tucumán was limited only by the amount of labor available to work the land and care for the cattle. Also of little meaning was the official regulation prohibiting granting land already occupied by Indians. Attempts were rarely, if ever, made to verify a settler's claim that the desired land was unoccupied. His word was taken at face value and it should not have been. Much of the native population had been "reduced" to the towns of Córdoba, Santiago del Estero, or La Rioja and made to serve the Spaniards, so Indian traditional lands were vacant.

In coastal Peru, the decline of the Indian population was closely related to the continual rise of Spanish landholdings. Disease and resettlement of villages frequently opened wide the door to Spanish occupation. Interandine Quito was not so acutely affected by an Indian population decline, so at first Spaniards and Indians squeezed into the same little mountain valleys and basins. But there is little hard data available on the Indian population of Córdoba and Tucumán at the time of the Spanish conquest. Governor Cabrera's description of the area south of Córdoba in 1573 points out that most of the Indians were farmers, but he makes no calculation of their numbers.[12] Between 1573 and 1600, dramatic changes took place affecting the native population. Large numbers of Indians fled to Peru to escape the burdens of estate labor; a considerable number were pressed into domestic service in Córdoba, Buenos Aires, and Santiago del Estero; others fled to the mountains west of Tucumán. In 1596 Governor Juan Ramírez de Velasco estimated that the *gobernación* of Tucumán had 50,000 Indians, but apparently this figure included those working in Córdoba and Santiago del Estero. Since there were over 6,000 Indians in Córdoba around 1582, about 2,000 in Buenos Aires and environs brought down from Tucumán, and a slightly lower number in Santiago del Estero, an original figure of around 60,000 Indians for northwest Argentina at the time of the Spanish conquest seems not unreasonable. The most recent population estimates for Córdoba vary between 12,000 and 15,000.[13] There might well have been some connection in the Indian population shifts that occurred in northwest Argentina, Upper Peru, and the coast. During the seventeenth century, the declining or shifting Indian population of Peru was increasingly unable to supply Potosí and other mining regions with workers. This might have triggered increased Spanish settlement in Tucumán.

However, it is unlikely that the Indian population and the origin of the large estate were as closely related in Tucumán as they were in Quito and Peru. The relationship does become critical in the analysis of availability of a labor force. But land was so plentiful that neither an Indian population decline nor a systematic resettlement plan was required to make suitable arable land available to Spanish settlers.

Jesuits acquired land in Tucumán in much the same way that they acquired it in Lima and Quito (by purchase and donation), only they acquired more of it. Most of the largest Jesuit college acquisitions in the seventeenth and eighteenth centuries came from original grants by the local government and additional purchases.

Jesuit Lands

Although the Jesuits entered Córdoba in 1599, it was not until 1610 that a college was established.[14] In order to support students and faculty, as well as begin some necessary construction, four estates were acquired: Caroya, Jesús María, Altagracia, and Santa Catalina. Caroya, just north of Córdoba in the Guanusacate river valley, was originally a grant made to Bartolomé Jayme in 1574. It passed to several successive owners and in 1616 it was sold to the college for 450 pesos. At the same time surrounding vacant land measuring two leagues wide "from the Caroyapa to the city" was given to the college by Governor Luís de Quiñones.[15] The estate had a circumference of five leagues, and in the early days of its use—in the 1620s—mostly cattle grazed on it. Jesús María, directly north of Córdoba adjacent to Caroya, was purchased from its owner, Gaspar de Quevedo, as a functioning farm. The college purchased the vineyard of 20,000 vines, a mill, 250 head of cattle, pigs, goats, and twenty oxen for 8,000 pesos in 1618. And for good measure Governor Quiñones threw in two square leagues of contiguous land. The cattle ranches and farms acquired by the Jesuit novitiate, the

12

house where applicants to the Society studied and lived, became among the most productive of the entire Jesuit Paraguay Province. The novitiate was attached to the College of Córdoba, so early seventeenth-century land acquisitions tended to be confused with the college's. However, the novitiate's major holding, the ranch of Santa Catalina, was purchased in 1622 for 4,500 pesos. The land was originally a grant awarded to Juan de Burgos in 1614, and when he sold it, the ranch he developed had only 237 head of cattle, 1,800 sheep, and 180 goats.[16] The soil was of high quality, hence the stiff purchase price. Added to the list of Córdoba estates in 1643 was the ranch and textile mill of Altagracia (southwest of the city of Córdoba). This was in a sense donated to the college by Alonso Nieto, who on becoming a widower entered the Society of Jesus as a lay brother and brought his estate with him.

The most famous Jesuit estate located in present-day Argentina was that of Jesús María, if only because its colonial structures have been meticulously preserved as a national monument by the Argentine government and are now visited each year by thousands of tourists. The purchase of Jesús María in 1618 was intended to supply the fifty-two Jesuits (twelve priests, twenty-nine seminarians, and eleven brothers) in the Córdoba residence with fresh vegetables and farm produce. Wheat, corn, and wine from the vineyard were its chief products. The ranch at Caroya supplied beef, mutton, and goats, and both the farm and the ranch were considered sufficient by the Jesuit superior, Pedro de Oñate, to provide easily for the material needs of the college.[17]

Both Jesús María and Caroya were located at the foot of the Córdoba Hills, so much of their land was hilly and some even mountainous. In 1767, only one square league out of the total ½ league by 5½ leagues were considered suitable for grazing cattle.[18] The vineyard was the most valuable asset of the farm, as it was in 1618 when the original purchase was made. The lands of Jesús María had been acquired by Pedro de Deza soon after the founding of Córdoba. He was awarded one league of land near the Río Guanusacate (now Río Ascochinga) in 1576. Other grants and purchases, in 1588, 1599, 1605, and 1609 were made to Deza who sold all of his holdings to Alonso de Camara in 1617. Within a year, the lands were resold to Gaspar de Quevedo who in turn sold them to the Jesuit College of Córdoba on January 15, 1618, for 8,000 pesos. Quevedo may well have played the role of Jesuit agent in the purchase. Over the following years, the farm increased its landholdings through grants, donations, and purchases. Major transactions took place in the following years:

1628—purchase of land from Diego Negrete de Cámara, fifty pesos
1631—purchase of land of San Cristobal
1640—donation of ½ square league
1640—estate extended to Indian settlement of Ministalalo
1678—vineyard of Luis Ponce in Guanusacate added
1683—Nintes and Cabinta, to Northeast, purchased.[19]

Nor did purchases and additions cease in the 1680s. They continued through the early eighteenth century.

Changes in landownership were often accompanied by shifts in siting. The local Indians were the ones chiefly affected by these changes, so much so that a visitor to Jesús María in 1637 could not locate an *encomienda* held by his grandfather, Miguel de Ardiles, in 1618. Ardiles had land bordering Jesús María that was part of his *encomienda*. In 1637 these Indians were living on Jesuit lands; whether they were enticed as paid laborers or required to move because of "land development" is unknown.[20] In any case, there were many Indians living on and around the lands of Jesús María when the estate holdings were purchased. Building clusters on a range, originally cattle corrals and a few bunk houses (called *puestos*), developed into full-scale Indian settlements, such as Nintes, Cabinda, Sinsacate, San Pablo, San Cristobal, and Camta. But not without some tension. A good deal of litigation occurred involving local Indians with claims on estate land and water. The Indians rarely won.

About 40 km southwest of Córdoba was the Jesuit estate of Altagracia, likewise preserved today in its colonial splendor by the Monuments Commission of Argentina. Located at the foot of a ridge of hills called the Sierra Chica, the cattle ranch and its associated enterprises extended over an extraordinarily large area. The original owner, Juan Nieto, was one of the first conquistadors of Córdoba. The land grant made to him in 1578 was passed on to his son, Alonso, in 1609, but Alonso entered the Society of Jesus as a lay brother in 1643 and donated the land to the Jesuit province at the time of entrance. Throughout the rest of the seventeenth century, adjoining estates were added to Altagracia, like that of the Carmelite nuns, and smaller pieces of property were annexed by purchase and donation. By 1767 the estate measured 1,050 square miles (fifteen leagues by ten leagues)! Land had been acquired principally for herds of horses, mules, cattle, and sheep that altogether numbered about 15,000 head. But the ranch also had fruit groves and farmland for wheat, corn, and barley. One of Altagracia's land transactions, and this type was not infrequent, was the simple exchange of property. The College of Córdoba gave Capt.

Francisco de Ledesma, a neighbor, lands "for a ranch, cattle breeding, and vegetable farming," called Tras la Sierra near the town of Salsacate, in exchange for grazing land for Altagracia that Ledesma purchased from the Convent of Santo Domingo.[21] Both properties were deemed of equal value and so were swapped without much formality.

The Jesuit ranch of Santa Catalina was a little northwest of Jesús María, Caroya a little west, and Altagracia was a little southwest of the city of Córdoba. These estates with their outlying ranges became the nucleus of the College of Córdoba's landholdings, and, as will be seen in Chapter 6, provided the lion's share of the college's income.

The College of Santa Fe's major estates were San Miguel de Carcaraña near Rosario, which was purchased in 1719 with the proceeds from the sale of 1,500 mules.[22] The estate ran along one side of the Carcaranal River for about ten leagues (eight leagues in depth) and for about eight leagues (six in depth) on the other. As can be guessed, the estate was never measured exactly nor laid with boundary markers. There was no need to since land in the vicinity was so plentiful. What was called the "Entre Rios" estate, likewise belonging to the College of Santa Fe, was rather cavalierly described as measuring ten leagues from north to south and an equal number west to east.[23] This rich cattle land was under continual dispute in the late seventeenth and eighteenth centuries by the Garay family, but from the time of its acquisition in 1669 the Jesuits retained legal possession.

The College of Asunción's (also called the College of Paraguay) largest estate, San Lorenzo in the Valley of Tapuyperi, was composed of several contiguous pieces of land purchased by the college in 1679 from Don José Cypriano Delgado for 1,000 pesos. The ranch of Paraquari, about 100 km from Asunción, was originally a grant given by Fernando Arias to Don Francisco Gonzalez in 1615.[24] In 1620 Gonzalez, whose brother Roque was to become a saint of the Society of Jesus, donated the land to the college. But it was not until 1674 that the college took an active interest in developing it.

As early as 1618–1619, when there was sixteen Jesuits resident in the College of Asunción, the land and real estate holdings were basically three: a fairly large farm donated to the college as an alms, some houses in the city from which rents were realized, and a smallish plot of land which the city of Asunción gave to the Jesuits.[25] The region around Asunción quickly developed as a ranching and farming region, so in 1627 the Jesuits erected a church about two leagues from the city dedicated to San Lorenzo Martyr that served as a parish church for the many haciendas in the vicinity.[26] The church with its associated dwellings eventually developed into the modern town of San Lorenzo.

Both the large farm and the smallish plot expanded with additional acquisitions, and it is no coincidence that a major transportation route was close by. Suffice it to say (more will be said about estate and farm proximity to major roads in the next chapter) that the estates of the College of Asunción, i.e., Paraquari, San Lorenzo, and the Tierras de la Frontera, were connected by a good road to the major Jesuit reductions of San Ignacio Guazu, Nuestra Señora de la Fe, and Santa Rosa to the southeast; and to the capital city of Asunción to the northeast. This, of course, greatly facilitated commerce and economic relations between the Jesuit reductions, the college's estates, the college itself, and the Asunción commercial community.

Through purchases the boundaries of these estates had become contiguous by the eighteenth century. On the south, San Lorenzo faced the Tierras de la Frontera; on the east were lands formerly owned by Don Francisco Angelos, but by 1760 they were part of a capellanía administered by the parish priest of Encarnación, Don Pedro Martinez. On the western boundary of San Lorenzo were the lands that formerly belonged to General Joseph Avalos and afterwards to his son-in-law, Antonio Ruiz de Arellano. In the 1760s Arellano's children, Francisco and Joseph, occupied the land. However, exact demarcation of land west of San Lorenzo was dubious because boundary markers had never been put into place. Not to have markers was unusual, but one of the corners of a piece of San Lorenzo land sold to the college by Pedro Rodríguez de Villaformo had a "boundary marker with two sides, on one of which was the college shield."

South of San Lorenzo were the Tierras de la Frontera in the valley of the same name. In 1599 a cleric, Don Rodrigo Ortiz, first donated to the college a vineyard with 30,000 vines. In 1611 Doña María Obobari donated a water source for a mill. In 1621 the husband of Beatriz García de Castro sold two cuadras of land to the college and in the following years additional pieces of land were purchased. In 1638, 1654, and 1686 smaller parcels were added to the Tierra de la Frontera by purchase and others were purchased from a cleric named Molgavigo, from a widow, Juana Arevalo, and from Francisco Medina. In 1765 the compiler of a summary of sales and donations lamented that exact sizes and location of these lands were not given in the original sales and transferal documents. This was a most unusual omission, but given the circumstances of place and time perhaps understandable. The available grazing and farming lands were so vast and the usually standard physical boundary markings so imprecise to begin with, that it was likely that estate boundaries were so blurred and imprecise as to be meaningless. This, of course, opened the door to future litigation and squabbling.

16

The lands of Paraquari were the third set of holdings acquired by the college of Asunción. In 1612 the land called Yarigua Quazes was purchased by the college and added to the land acquired by a grant in 1615. The total size was given as three leagues by three leagues, but an eighteenth-century chronicler estimated that the estates, called San Isidro de Yarigua, was in reality much larger, probably closer to five leagues. In 1642 a grant from Governor Gregorio Inistros, measuring an additional league, was added and in 1652 Francisco de la Rotivo sold to the college another two leagues contiguous to those already owned by the college. Soon after, in 1653, a fifth addition was made, a portion of land called Yarigua, land originally granted in 1605 by Governor Hernando Arias de Saavedra but afterwards given to Martín Suárez de Toledo, who in turn donated them to the college. This addition was substantial, three leagues by two leagues, extending the boundary of the college lands to the foothills of the cordillera on the east, probably the range of hills indicated on contemporary maps just north of the Caañabe River.

The Jesuits of Asunción were also the recipients of what we would call today "deferred giving," a fairly common form of bequest. Don Juan Gonzalez Melgarejo, Dean of the Cathedral, kept usufruct rights and ownership of a small cattle ranch and farm about two leagues from Asunción. Upon his death, the house, farm, and ranch would pass to Jesuit ownership to be used for giving the Spiritual Exercises of St. Ignatius. The Jesuit rector of the college, Juan José Rico, accepted the donation on August 17, 1737.

It is apparent that the methods of acquisition of these lands, a mix of government grants, purchases, and donation, were very similar to the way Jesuit lands were acquired in Tucumán and in other parts of Latin America. Only here there were more lands to acquire.

The smaller Jesuit colleges which sprouted in the late seventeenth and throughout the eighteenth century also acquired much of their land by purchase from and donation by private citizens. In 1691 Don Felipe Ruíz de Aguero donated two leagues of land for the College of Corrientes.[27] In 1627 the founder of the College of Tucumán donated 4,000 pesos to found the College of Salta as a center for mission activities in the Chaco. But continual battles between Indians and Spaniards, theft of cattle herds, and even a flood kept the six Jesuits who were posted to Salta from establishing any stable apostolic or associated economic activity for many years, up to about 1710. In 1631 the College of Esteco had no income, rents, or lands, but lived solely on alms until the early 1700s.[28] The College of La Rioja purchased the vineyard of Nonagasta (in Argentine wine country) to insure a steady income. The report from Juan Nicolás de Araoz in 1700 advising purchase waxed eloquent about the pleasant climate and weather, quality of the soil, and "the fame of Nonagasta wines . . . better even than the wine of Jesús María of Córdoba."[29] The vineyard was purchased but 5,000 pesos had to be spent for draft animals, cattle, and equipment. The vineyard never became "the right arm of the college," as Araoz predicted. Poor harvests, poor administration, and a lowering of wine prices left the enterprise and the college in debt for the last twenty-five years of its existence as a Jesuit estate.[30] The College of San Pedro in Buenos Aires was founded in the mid-eighteenth century with a mixed endowment of land, real estate, and funds totalling 46,000 pesos. Around the same time, Catamarca was founded, the last of the Jesuit colleges established in present-day Argentina.[31] In 1743 the town council donated two cuadras of town land and ample grazing land in order to entice the Jesuits to open a college. They did.

In 1754, the Jesuit residence of Catamarca purchased from a group, *de mancomún,* headed by Sergeant Melchor Suárez, a *suerte de tierras* that bordered the college lands of Pozo.[32] For 200 pesos in goods the Jesuits acquired the land in the Charcaras de Catamarca.

In keeping with the early pre-eminence of the city of Córdoba, the major Jesuit College of Buenos Aires (Belén) got off to a rather slow economic start in the seventeenth century. In 1614 the small residence of Jesuits was supported by a few small vineyards and plots of farmland. By 1619 the annual letter written by Pedro de Oñate reported that the economic base of the college had been substantially widened by the purchase of a "cattle ranch which will support most of the needs of the college."[33] This ranch, about 100 km west of Buenos Aires, developed into the largest and most productive of the Jesuit ranches, the Estate of Areco, that measured in 1767 fifteen leagues by six leagues, or about 810 square miles.[34] On its lands grazed over 40,000 head of cattle. Also administered by the College of Buenos Aires was the estate of Areca that started functioning in 1726. Don Pedro de Echegarraga gave 52,158 pesos to the college from which an estate was to be purchased to support a house in which the Spiritual Exercises of St. Ignatius were given, in other words, a Retreat House. Excess interest from the investments was to be distributed to the other colleges for the same purpose. Either Don Pedro or the Jesuit procurator, I suspect the former, divided the original endowment thus:

10,791 pesos—to be invested in Cádiz, Spain
18,267 pesos—to be invested in Buenos Aires in land

7,000 pesos—to be given in cash to the College of Buenos Aires
10,000 pesos—to be invested in the College of Córdoba
6,000 pesos—in coin in possession of Don Pedro.[35]

This type of donation, i.e., a sum of money with precise conditions of its use laid down by the donor, was not uncommon, but it had to meet the approval of at least two layers of Jesuit bureaucrats: the college rector and his advisors, and the provincial and his advisors. In this case, the donation was accepted but other offers with pre-conditions deemed disadvantageous to the Society were rejected.

There was a similarity among the sizes of the Jesuit colleges found in Peru, Quito, and Tucumán. In each region a very large college or university was established in which resided a relatively large number of Jesuits, anywhere from seventy to one-hundred. This was the focal point of regional activity. Gradually, smaller colleges were founded, staffed by no more than five to ten Jesuits. The estates owned by the major college or university were greater in size and substantially more productive than the smaller college estates. These smaller colleges and estates appear to have been almost an afterthought, although they did serve a distinct educational purpose in smaller towns. Usually they were opened at the behest of local elite groups who wanted the prestige of a "college" in their town with themselves as founders. However, it is clear that the major effort and energy went to the support and development of the major college or university. This was certainly true of Tucumán (Córdoba University), Lima (University of San Marcos), and Quito (Colegio Máximo of Quito).

Jesuit acquisition of land was also influenced by how soon after the initial conquest the Jesuits arrived. In Mexico, Peru, and Quito, they were relative late-comers. Much of the best land had already been distributed. They arrived in Tucumán from Peru not too long after the initial Spanish penetrations. But it is doubtful whether even this had any serious effect on acquiring land since there was so much of it. Writing sometime during the second quarter of the seventeenth century, Ignacio de Frias stated that "all the Spaniards of Tucumán have a great number of ranches and even lands to hunt wild cattle."[36] Acquisition of land in Tucumán and in the Río de la Plata offered little difficulty.

The place where land was acquired and its quality affected the use to which the land was put. Types of land use were also determined to an extent by the proximity, presence, or absence of a laboring population. The area around Córdoba became predominately a farming region. The climate was appropriate for it; the soil of the northern pampas was highly suitable, and in the vicinity were sedentary Indians capable of being organized for labor service on farms and ranches. The same was more or less true for the region around Asunción, only here a substantial part of the laboring Indian population became part of the Jesuit reductions of Paraguay, much to the chagrin of local farmers and landowners, while vast herds of cattle developed in the nearby areas of Entre Ríos. This partially explains the viciousness with which landowners in the early 1600s opposed Francisco de Alfaro and his Jesuit supporters who waged a vehement campaign against the practice of personal service on Spanish-owned farms and ranches. Deprived of Indian labor, the vast tracts of farm and grazing land were well-nigh useless to the Spanish colonist. For this reason, the farmers around Córdoba and Asunción never quite forgave the Jesuits for campaigning so actively on the side of Alfaro. They felt that the Jesuits were acting hypocritically because the fathers retained all the labor they needed in the reductions while denying the same to the lay farmer or rancher. There was some truth to this but of course the Jesuits never admitted it. They argued that the Indian reductions were mission stations where Indians remained voluntarily, while at the same time working for their own support and for the support of their spiritual tutors. The organization of Indian labor on the reductions and the distribution of its fruits were in missionary hands, argued the Jesuits, lest rapacious white traders cheat the Indians by underpaying them for their principal product, *yerba mate.*

While Córdoba and Asunción were primarily focused on farming in early colonial days and through the seventeenth century, the region of the Buenos Aires estuary became predominately a ranching area. Soil suitability and the lack of Indian laborers militated against farming. In fact, there were so few laborers available even in the eighteenth century that soldiers frequently had to be sent from Buenos Aires to help in the grain harvesting lest the city suffer food shortages. But settlers were attracted to the Río de la Plata primarily by the relative ease with which one could obtain meat products and the valuable by-products (e.g., grease, hides) of cattle that could be sold locally or exported for a handsome profit.[37]

Once land was acquired (and a labor organization assured), the landowner could exercise several options. The land could be worked for a predetermined use; it could be rented or leased, allowed to lie fallow, partially cultivated, or sold to a third party. Jesuit colleges exercised all of these options at one time or another on their landholdings around Córdoba, Asunción, and Buenos Aires, in order to obtain maximum productivity. Ancillary enterprises associated with the major farms or ranches provided services and goods for personnel and for sale outside of their place of origin. How land was used and organized were major factors determining settlement patterns.

Distribution of Farm/Ranch Units

When Jerónomo Luís de Cabrera first saw the broad expanse of Tucumán in 1572, he marveled at the skills of its native farmers. He envisioned the fertile, rolling countryside as one large pasture "on which to raise great numbers of cattle like those in Spain and on which to build farms and mills for the prosperity of those who come here."[38] Over time Cabrera's vision became a reality. Just ten years later, Pedro Soltelo Narvaez reported to the Audiencia of Charcas that the Indians were gradually being conquered, the climate was delightful, and Córdoba's settlers were growing on the province's fertile plains the corn, wheat, vineyards, barley, and vegetables that they were so used to in Spain.[39] Cabrera's original group had clearly come to settle.

Two opposite tendencies affected the way Spanish colonists settled lands around Córdoba, and for that matter, in Asunción and Santa Fe as well. The social advantages of city, town, and village life were balanced against the prestige or "lord of the manor" mentality accompanying the ownership of large tracts of land fairly far removed from populated settlements. This latter tendency or attraction was the dream of many Spaniards who emigrated to America. The notable exceptions were the artisans who remained in the cities and towns to ply their trades. For the most part "making it" in sixteenth-century Tucumán meant owning and operating a farm or ranch unit, which in turn meant the organization, disposition, and control of a labor force. It was this capacity to organize human resources that carried the prestige; to command men had always been the Spanish ideal of (or substitute for) work. Nevertheless, the pull towards town life was likewise present. The town was the hub of commercial and economic activity. Here money was often made and spent. It was in the town or village that the largest churches were found, usually staffed by the secular clergy. Church organizations, *cofradías,* and the religious provided a bit of color to an otherwise humdrum existence in the form of processions and holidays, which were always religio-social affairs and in which the entire town participated as actors or observers. The proximity of friends, associates, and neighbors provided opportunities for swapping news or gossip. And the formal education that was available

21

was always found in the town and city. In other words, the social and cultural advantages of town life were highly prized. But apparently not enough to attract everyone. The pull to opposites resulted in compromise.

Although the city governments, with authority from the central government, approved the size of government-granted plots (*mercedes* mentioned in Chapter 1), no government authority actually determined before settlement how the land would be divided, nor did it decide on the layout of the roads. In other words, there was no settlement plan. The result was a dispersion of not-too-widely scattered farmsteads in which units arranged themselves according to natural or man-made features. In the latter seventeenth century, Jesuit missionaries estimated a total of about 600 to 700 Spanish-owned farms and ranches scattered about the area from Córdoba south to the Río Primero. And around 1700, the Jesuit, Ignacio de Frias, reported that "all of the Spaniards of these provinces have a great number of ranches and farmsteads, some twenty to thirty leagues from towns. Most live all year round with their families on these estates. Those who live in the cities have workers on their ranches, blacks, Indians, mulattoes, and some mestizos, to keep guard over the cattle and to cultivate the farms."[40] The missionary estimate of about 700 ranches and farms in 1700 seems feasible in the light of the 400 government land grants made to settlers up to 1600. Since the area of the present province of Córdoba is about 174,610 square km (1/6 of which is mountainous and another 1/6 unfit for cultivation), it seems that the central zone, with rich vegetation and abundant pasture, held one farm/ranch unit per 140 square km. This is not as dispersed or isolated as one might imagine. It meant that there was another farm or ranch ten or twenty km away, or a horse ride of less than one hour.

Proximity to other settlers was especially important at times of Indian raids which intensified in the late seventeenth and eighteenth century and affected settlement. The town of Esteco moved twice because of Indian raids and the farms in the district were frequently burned by the Mocobies, Abipones, and the Guycurus, who also attacked the Camino Real to Peru in 1701. The Valley of Chomoros, about seventy leagues northwest of Tucumán, was totally abandoned by ranches and farmers because of intense Indian raids, thus halting a substantial flow of corn, wheat, and cattle for neighboring towns. In 1701 the northern town of Santa Cruz de la Sierra and towns in the Corregimiento of Tarija were described as being "under siege."[41] Of course, limited markets and scarce labor supply hindered Spanish settlement in the area north of Córdoba, but also Indian raiding parties made Spaniards think twice about becoming "lords of the manor" in rural Tucumán. Living on not-too-isolated farmsteads made collective action a bit easier.

However, the frequent references made to individuals living in towns (Córdoba for example), while at the same time maintaining farms or ranches, indicate another type of rural arrangement whereby an absentee landlord drew income, not from the rental, but from the operation of a rural enterprise. It would be difficult to quantify this but one does get the impression from the quantity of land grants awarded by the city council of Córdoba that the number of house plots far removed from farmsteads was considerable. The problem lies in determining whether the owner-farmers actually resided on the city house plot or moved to the countryside, leaving the town plot for relatives. If we were to believe Ignacio Frias in this, cited above, then it seems that permanent rural residents far outnumbered those who left farms and ranches in a surrogate's care while maintaining permanent residence in the city. This might have been because few could afford the large ranch required to support an appropriate urban house. It also appears that the economic disadvantages of scattered farm plots, which meant clearing fields far from a distribution or consumption center, thus impairing the efficiency of farm operations, as well as the danger of Indian attacks, were outweighed by the apparent social advantages of patterned isolation.

The settlement pattern both in Córdoba and in Asunción was affected by two major features, one natural—streams or rivers—and the other, man-made—roads. The rivers Segundo and Tercero were not only convenient boundaries, but they also attracted numerous settlers to their banks. All of the major ranches and haciendas of the College of Córdoba, Altagracia, Jesús María, Santa Catalina and Candelaria, were located near rivers or streams, and both Altagracia and Santa Catalina had man-made reservoirs constructed near the main building complex in order to insure a steady, abundant supply of water for the ranch's enterprises. Eighteenth-century maps show clearly that these estates were connected by road not only to Córdoba and the large Jesuit enterprise there, but also by path with each other. The Asunción estates were likewise connected by major roads with the college and town as well as with the major reduction villages southeast of the estate of San Lorenzo. The Paraná and Caañabe rivers were supplied with abundantly flowing streams. It is clear that roads and rivers were major factors in selecting sites for farms and ranches.

23

Lawsuits and Litigation

There was no clear pattern to the types of lawsuits and squabbles engaged in by Tucumán's landowners. *Pleitos* or lawsuits involving individual Jesuit farms and ranches occurred in the seventeenth and eighteenth centuries, and they spanned the entire spectrum of possible disputes. Land, land use, water rights, boundaries, and donations were the chief subjects, usually with other Spaniards but at times with Indian groups.

In 1680 a long standing dispute ended between the College of Santa Fe and the prestigious family heirs of Hernando Arias de Saavedra.[42] The litigation was over the right to claim the wild cattle in an area "on the other side of the Paraná River." It seems that a relative of Doña Angela Blanca de Murgia took possession of an expanse of lands near the Corrientes River but the Jesuits of the College of Santa Fe claimed that she left her estate to them. A court decided that the college should receive ten leagues of land and all the cattle on it; in return the college would give the Caprera family (the other litigants) lands "from Punta Gorda up to the Riachuelo."

Another dispute involved the estate of Jesús María in the 1660s and the Indians on the neighboring estate of Don Diego Solis de Burgos (Estancia de Buenosacate) over land and water rights.[43] The squabble was centered on the "lands and waters of Guanasacate," purchased by Solis who owned nine or ten leagues of land nearby (he did not know exactly how much he had). The Jesuits were accused of supporting Solis and allowing the cattle of Jesús María to wander indiscriminately over the Indian cornfields, doing great damage to Indian patches. The estate was awarded an *amparo,* or government statement of ownership, for water from the Guanasacate River. Possession of a canal was in dispute with Luís Ponce de León. Ponce had allowed his cattle to destroy the Jesuit estate's canal that brought water from the river. The case went all the way to the courts in Buenos Aires which declared in favor of the Jesuits in 1672.[44] Similar disputes involving the estate of Jesús María, especially about boundaries and boundary markers, occurred with frequency between 1640 and 1670.

Different in nature was the squabble between the Jesuit owners of Areco and not so friendly neighbors from Las Palmas, Pesquería, and Cañada de la Cruz. The neighbors claimed that their cattle had inadvertently wandered onto Areco pasturage and were now mixed with the estate cattle. The neighbors wanted to enter estate ranges and round up their cattle, which the Jesuit administrator, Collado, resolutely opposed because it would permit them to round up and make off with their own cattle in addition to the ranch's. A court order prevented them from doing so, and the Areco administrators themselves rounded up what they said was non-estate cattle, much to their neighbor's disappointment.[45]

Disputes with Indians occurred more frequently than perhaps has been supposed. Land encroachments, water rights, and jurisdiction over Indians were the chief causes of litigation. In 1712 the Indians of Maligaste near La Rioja brought suit against the College of La Rioja over "ownership of the lands and water of Matagasta."[46] A royal order declared in favor of the Indians, leaving the Jesuits "the right to draw water from one well." The Jesuit rector of the college, Martín García, appealed to the higher court of the Audiencia of Charcas. He argued that when General Gabriel Sarmiento of La Rioja received an *encomienda* in the Valley of Famatina, only two Indians lived in the vicinity. For fifty years his heirs worked the lands until they passed to one of the sons, Joseph, who inherited them when Doña Leonora de Ibarra died. Joseph entered the Society of Jesus and gave the Jesuits his portion of the land. The Jesuits built farmhouses on the land and planted corn and wheat. The Indians were attracted to the estate as potential laborers and lived on the fringes of the college lands which were so cultivated for twenty-five years with no Indian protest. Martín paraded a galaxy of witnesses to uphold the Jesuit position, most of whom declared in one way or another that the protesting Indians originally lived leagues away from the estate; that the town of Maligasta was composed of many different outside Indian groups who gradually insinuated themselves into the Calchaquí families, "as is easily shown by the *padrones* of the town."[47] The Jesuits must have won the case because they owned the estate at the time of their expulsion in 1767 (or no court decision had ever been made). A major contributing factor to the victory was that the Judge Baygorri who originally ruled against the college was removed from the case and forbidden to hear any future cases dealing with the Jesuits.[48] We do not know why.

This sample of cases gives the idea of the type of litigation engaged in by Jesuit colleges to defend the perceived integrity of their lands.[49]

The lush physical environment of the northern Pampas encouraged Spanish settlement. Because of the scarce Indian population, rural reorganization did not take place to the degree that it did in Charcas or in other sections of Peru. Jesuit estates sprouted up, linked by road to their own colleges and to major commercial and trade routes, and numerous smaller ranches and farms spread throughout northwestern Argentina. Landholding patterns emerged that reflected land availability, with size restricted only by the number of laborers available. Once land was acquired and the settlement made, the process of building began; not only in the physical sense but also in the sense of constructing a relationship between dwelling and farmland. A close-up view of the farmstead and ranch enables one to explore the complex intricacy of this relationship.

CHAPTER 2

Farmsteads and Ranches

The kinds of enterprises developed and the amount of land or space available were reflected in the farmstead structure. The structures of the large Jesuit estates of coastal Peru (San Xavier, Villa, or Huaura), for example, give the impression of ample lands available; the structures, although nucleated, were separated and widespread. On the other hand, the farmsteads of Quito reflecting a mixture of farming, sheep raising, and a textile industry appear more compact, more close-spaced. This is, no doubt, due both to the physical, inter-mountain nature of landholdings that often appear squeezed between two ranges in a thin ribbon of a mountain basin and to a denser population. In sharp contrast, Tucumán's spatial arrangement of farm and ranching units reflects an abundant amount of available land. The close-up view of residence, associated farm/ranch/industrial buildings, and other facilities reveals not only a physical arrangement of units occupying considerable space but also a variety of approaches to serve economic needs in a specific physical environment.

The Structures

There is a good deal of similarity in the ground plans of the central structures of the two major Jesuit-run haciendas in Tucumán: Altagracia and Santa Catalina. This is due in great part to the fact that the kinds of enterprises engaged in by both were roughly the same. (See figures 1 and 2.) Both farmsteads were dominated by large, expansive churches alongside, connected to which was the major residence looking out onto a large patio. In this residence lived the Jesuit superior of the group, the religious instructor, the *estanciero* and usually a Jesuit lay brother or two. Both Santa Catalina and Altagracia had large orchards enclosed by an outer wall, but only Altagracia is mentioned as having orchards outside of the walls as well. The walls, which were of stone and adobe, were not only boundary markers but served to keep out undesirable farm or wild animals as well as to keep in slaves and to maintain a high degree of privacy. It is unlikely that they were built to withstand Indian raids, none of which occurred in any case, even though they were threatened in the 1740s. A *tajamar* or man-made reservoir was necessary for operating mills. It was located near the outer walls of each. In Altagracia a fairly well-developed textile industry required supplies of water for the milling apparatus. On Santa Catalina the water was needed for a small textile mill and for irrigation ditches. Local rivers and streams were tapped for construction of the reservoirs. The slave labor force on Santa Catalina was housed in the *ranchería* that still stands today (1979), located in what must have been near the orchard. The slave population of Altagracia must have been housed in the building within the walls (see figure 2). Storage rooms and carpenter shops were located in the large structure within the outer walls. Ancillary farm or ranching enterprises were often located within the walled complex. On the lands of Altagracia, its 4,000 head of cattle were kept in ranges called *puestos,* a good distance from the main complex of structures. The mule breeding farm (*cría de mulas*) was also far removed. The wheat fields (119 *fanegas* were harvested in 1746) were closer. On the lands of Santa Catalina the ranges were referred to as *parajes* rather than *puestos,* but often the terms were interchangeable.

Santa Catalina and Altagracia were very similar to what one usually imagines a hacienda to be. Present was a major focus or enterprise with several other minor or supportive enterprises. Slightly different in structure were the plans of two other "types" of estates: one, the combination of vineyard/ranch, and the other, the rural ranch. The first type is exemplified by the hacienda of Jesús María, the second by Candelaria. The major enterprise of Jesús María was a vineyard which in the 1740s had over 48,000 vines. The major hacienda structure, still preserved today in its colonial splendor, held both the winery (*lagar*) and storage area (*bodega*), with at least five large casks and four medium-sized ones. Ovens for baking bricks and tiles, carpenter and tool shops were located on the lower floor. The fact that there were upper and lower floors was in itself somewhat unique and underlines the presence of a certain architectural sophistication. The entire non-church structure was L-shaped, giving a compactness to the farmstead. As with the other two structures discussed, one hesitates to say that Jesús María was oriented towards a road, river, or some natural or man-made feature. There was a road and a river nearby, but one cannot say that the estate was oriented toward it. Nevertheless, they were major factors in siting.

The last construction type to be mentioned was that of the ranch, Candelaria. There was an agricultural component associated with the major ranching focus, but the latter was by far the major activity. The ranch buildings were snuggled close together in one contiguous unit high in a little valley between ridges of the Sierras Chicas and Sierras Grandes, in a place called the Rincón de Ocampis. The origin of the ranch dates back to the beginnings of the seventeenth century when the land was given to García de Vera y Mujica. His son, Francisco, inherited and then donated it to the Jesuits of Córdoba around 1673. From that time on, the property was used primarily as the college ranch, both for beef cattle and for mules. All of the ranch buildings formed a square. The chapel, interior patio, and arched cloister for the two or at most three resident Jesuits, tool sheds and storage rooms—all give the impression of having been constructed to withstand Indian raids. The construction materials—stone, tiles, and no wood—also suggest this. The animal barns and the nine ranges with at least 6,000 head of cattle were separated from the main complex of buildings, or *casco,* of the estate. A grinding mill with a large stone occupied one of the main connected structures, called *dependencias.* Wheat grown on estate land was ground into flour. A bunk house (ranchería) for over 200 black slaves was located a short distance from the main complex. The range lands owned by Candelaria were extensive, about ninety-seven km south to north and about thirty east to west. It was hilly land, difficult to measure accurately.

These four types of major structures found on the estates of Altagracia, Jesús María, Santa Catalina, and Candelaria represent four different approaches to farmstead/ranch/hacienda construction. It should be emphasized that these four types were not representative of the size of most farmsteads or structures in Tucumán, but only of the form or kind of construction. Most farmstead structures were much smaller.

Construction Materials

The construction materials used on Jesuit estates reflected utility and convenience.[1] Latin America in general provided abundant construction materials. Some kind of stone was always available; adobe or limestone was not scarce, brick could easily be made. Lumber for rafters, beams, and columns was readily available from well-stocked forests. Jesuit buildings in Tucumán used all of these construction materials. The main portals or doorways of the major house and of the adjoining

Figure 1. Estate of Santa Catalina.

Figure 2. Estate of Altagracia.

church were of stone, as were the corridor floors. The corridor floor of the one story slave ranchería in Santa Catalina was made of well-spaced rectangular stones. The pillars, even their bases, were made of brick. Usually heavier stone was used as a foundation pedestal, but possibly because this ranchería building was only one story, a heavier base was not needed. A mixture of adobe, bricks, and stone was used in the construction of the main residence and portico of Jesús María. Here also the corridor floors were of heavy stone and the present crumbled exterior cover of the wide cloister (called the *Patio de los Naranjos*) arches reveals the original brick. Curved roof tiles were common on the slanted roofs, clearly evident in Jesús María, Candelaria, and on the smaller one-story rural dwellings that were often located on puestos. The square-shaped pattern of Candelaria's structures was almost completely roofed with tiles.[2] The interior doorways and even the major doorways of Candelaria were made of a wood skeleton base and in a major portal, carved into the broad beam that stretches over the doorway are the words "AÑO 1695" and the Jesuit anagram, IHS.

All of the Jesuit enterprises in and around Córdoba had facilities for making construction materials. Jesús María had two ovens and forges for tiles and bricks. The roof tiles so commonly seen on colonial and modern constructions were made in the College of Córdoba. Altagracia had an oven for preparing limestone. Lumber and wood was carted in from Jesuit-owned stands. Since construction often lasted for decades, the brick, tile, and limestone operations were often continuous. There always seemed to be something to be built or repaired.

The construction material available and used by local builders affected architectural styles.[3] Of the three major forms examined here, church, attached residence, and farmstead and rural ranch, only the first actually reflected architectural styles, and even here there was no definite "Jesuit" style in America, let alone in Tucumán. Colonial buildings could have been classified within the framework of European architectural forms. The Jesuit haciendas of Tucumán—large, substantial structures built of stone and brick and almost always employing masonry vaults—were imposing structures on the drab rural landscape that for the most part was dotted only with one-story brick, adobe, and thatched-roofed homes.[4] Within the imposing Jesuit complex, the church stood above all other structures, both in height, size and quality of decorative arts. Kelemen and others before him have pointed out how the two Italian Jesuits, Andrés Blanqui and Juan Bautista Primoli, were influential in regional construction.[5] A somewhat protruding portal stands between the two-towered facade of Santa Catalina

Church. The central pediment is characterized by graceful, undulating lines, echoed in the belfry above it. An imposing approach leads to the atrium. There is an emphasis on rounded shapes—in the finials, balustrade, the decoration on the belfry, and on the deep quatrefoil windows in the towers.[6]

The church at Altagracia was based on designs of Blanqui. Curving stairways provided a dramatic approach and the nave is covered with barrel vaulting. The dome is massive with large windows. Undecorated pilasters extend the full height of the facade. The gateway has a flaring stairway.

The hacienda residence attached to the church was often two stories that enveloped one, sometimes two, enormous patios. One of the major features of both Altagracia and Jesús María was massive high arches surrounding the interior cloisters. It was at least fifteen feet from the floor to the arched ceiling on the second-floor portico of Altagracia. Individual rooms (called *piezas*), likewise with extraordinarily high ceilings, looked out onto a corridor that surrounded the patio. The massively high arches were also used in the slave quarters in Santa Catalina. In Altagracia and Jesús María, their use gives the aspect of great majesty and affluence, especially to the white-walled corridors and to the whole construction, whereas the naked brick vaulting and square pillars of the slave quarters in Santa Catalina reminds one of a medieval dungeon, which is of course what it was. The patio was a major construction feature of cultural significance since it reflected an Andaluz influence. "Make me a patio, and if there is space left, some rooms," went the sixteenth-century Spanish saying. A patio surrounded by cloister-like corridors was a European architectural form common to the great religious monasteries of the continent.

The Spanish colonial buildings of Tucumán, and the Jesuit hacienda structures in particular, were rather simple in design. In contrast to the elaborate facades of Quito, Cuzco, and Lima, they were also simple in decoration. This was probably due to a lack of native craftsmen. Traditional crafts of pre-Columbian times created a reservoir of these artisans who abounded in the capital cities of Cuzco, Quito, and Mexico City. Such a reservoir did not exist in Tucumán and this affected church and civil decoration. Pillars, balustrades, walls, pediments, and facades are lacking the decorative touches that are present in Andean churches and civil architecture. In Tucumán emphasis was put on design rather than decoration.

The major Jesuit structures in Tucumán were eminently baroque in style. In answer to protestant iconoclasm, interiors were filled with paintings, frescoes, statues, gilt, marble, lapis lazuli, and precious

32

metals, many interwoven with emotional themes. They were designed to astound and instruct an illiterate populace. European Jesuits were divided about the extravagance of some of their churches, and the Spanish Superior General, Vicente Carafa, even removed all paintings from his quarters and refused a donation to decorate the chapel of St. Ignatius. On the other hand, another Jesuit General, Oliva, promoted almost all types of artistic enterprises and argued that a careful distinction should be made between Jesuit residences, which should reflect holy poverty, and Jesuit churches, which should "try to reach up to the sublimity of God's eternal omnipotence with such appurtenances of glory as we can achieve."[7]

One real function of Jesuit structures on the Tucumán landscape was that of a "power house"—a show case, an image maker displaying concrete evidence of wealth and power.[8] This was the church militant and triumphant. Perhaps structures were not seen precisely as such by the Jesuits themselves but surely they were by other Spanish settlers and native Indians. The sprawling hacienda complex, composed of a large church, main ranchhouse or farmstead, and associated buildings were obtainable only by the wealthy, the ruling class. The religious institution participated in this elite power because it possessed the symbols of the wealthy: large houses, servants, slaves, and massive properties as well as control of trade and commercial networks. The local Jesuit provincial, under pressure from Rome, tried to moderate the tendency toward erecting massive structures. In 1710 the Jesuit official visitor, Antonio Garriga, actually put a stop to all construction, "in order to avoid the excesses introduced in these times of overly large buildings and other signs of excess wealth that should be foreign to our profession of religious poverty."[9] Three years later Garriga had to repeat his order, this time with the added constraint of Holy Obedience. He even specified the size of patios and individual rooms. But this had little or no effect on future church construction and none whatsoever on additions to buildings. Size meant power and power was the basis of the Spanish-Amerindian relationship.[10] In this the Jesuit builders in Tucumán had the massively ornate churches of seventeenth-century Spain and Italy as models. In those days the unquestioned goal was to transport European Catholicism and all of its appurtenances, physical as well as attitudinal, to America.

While the major farms and ranches were immense, simplicity was the characteristic of the smaller Jesuit ranches and houses whose floor plans and farmstead layouts are available today. The College of Salta, for example, had six Jesuit residents in 1638, a very small income, and a debt of 4,000 pesos.[11] The college had one cattle ranch from which its income was derived. By 1710 nine Jesuits lived in the residence and a wheat farm was a major enterprise. An eighteenth-century map, drawn with no attention to scale, shows that the Jesuit residence in Salta was a two story structure with no separate church. The house was near the granary *(perchel)*.

This type of farmstead structure placed the fields and orchards (presumably the clumps of bushes in the map indicate orchards) close to and in front of the residence with the granary alongside. The cattle and mules were kept in the hills on their respective ranges. The fields, bordered by two rivers running roughly in an easterly direction, were about three km by one km. The imposing aspect of grandeur and affluence is missing in the rural farmsteads such as Salta's. This is a reflection of the modest resources available in the Salta Valley and also a reflection of the more usual type of farmstead construction seen in rural Tucumán.

As in Salta, all farmsteads were on a single tract of land. The farm house, its outbuildings, and the farmland were all on farm property. It seems that the only noncontiguous land was the cattle ranges usually found separated in more remote mountain valleys, or farmland that was rented out by the Jesuit owners. The farmland, on which was often grown grains, vegetables, and beans, for the slave population, or orchards of fruit trees for commercial sales, was close to the nuclear farmstead cluster of buildings called the *casco*. This reduced extensive transportation of laborers to the field sites and facilitated the movement of men to produce, and equipment between fields and the tool/repair/and storage center.

The organization of farms and ranches, their physical parts, and their location was geared to production. Livestock, grains, or vegetables supportive of a major enterprise or grown for sale on the market were the enterprises engaged in on such massive haciendas and ranches as Santa Catalina and Altagracia, or on the more modestly constructed estates of Salta, Santiago del Estero, or La Rioja.

Enterprises

The major enterprises engaged in by Jesuit estates in Tucumán were beef cattle raising, mule breeding, grain production, winemaking, and fruitgrowing. Secondary enterprises included brickmaking, tile production, and vegetable farming. Ancillary enterprises or those required for and supportive of major or secondary enterprises were carpentry, tool repair, or blacksmithing. Each college had a pattern of

34

these enterprises in operation on its estates. The degree of investment in them depended on desired financial returns.

Each of the major estates of the College of Córdoba focused on a distinct enterprise that filled a specific financial or economic function.[12] Jesús María focused almost equally on cattle raising (220 head in 1746), general farming, and viticulture, supplying the College of Córdoba up to the 1740s. Corn, wheat, fruit orchards, and a vineyard of 48,000 vines were developed in the early eighteenth century. However, frequent Indian raids originating from the Chaco had reduced cattle holdings, and it appears that the vineyard became the focus of estate activity from the 1750s on. The slave labor force increased from 114 in 1746 to 244 in 1767, an indication that the labor-intensive vineyard became more predominant. The estate of Jesús María, bordering both Caroya and Santa Catalina, measured one-half league north to south and five-and-a-half leagues east to west.[13] This proximity of Jesuit-owned estates was very similar to the pattern of San Pablo's holdings in the Huaura Valley, Peru, and the College of Quito's estates in Interandine Chillos. Contiguity meant that the estates could cooperate in a variety of ways yet remain physically and financially independent. Caroya, in fact, was administered for the benefit of a college residence, Santa Catalina for the novitiate of the Jesuit province of Paraguay, and Jesús María for the benefit of Córdoba college.

The combination of vineyards and cattle raising was unusual if not unique, certainly for that section of Tucumán. Even in the eighteenth century, viticulture was associated more with the cooler hilly areas of Mendoza and La Rioja than with the drier flat region of the northern Pampas. Nevertheless, the wine production of Jesús María was highly successful, and the other Jesuit viticulture attempts were compared to it. It has been claimed that the vine was introduced to Argentina in Santiago del Estero around 1557 and that the climate, fertility, and irrigation patterns were favorable for its development.[14] In La Rioja, about 23,000 vines covered nine to ten hectares; the Jesuits of San Luís had a vineyard but used too much of the Chorillo River to suit the local townsfolk. One night they sharpened their hatchets and cut down the vines. Since then there has been no vineyard in San Luís. The type of grape, the *mollar de América*, which was extensively cultivated in Alto Pero, was the type cultivated in Tucumán and Catamarca.[15] This particular type of grape flourished in the sandy soil, the kind present around Jesús María.

No records exist that would explain the process, machinery, utensils, or types of wine produced from the vineyard of Jesús María nor from other Jesuit vineyards in Catamarca or La Rioja. However, from instructions left by visiting provincials and from partial production re-cords, one can gather a number of interesting details pertaining to the estate's wine production.

Yearly production on Jesús María in the middle of the eighteenth century was close to 600 *botijas,* a large earthenware jar for storing wine, with a capacity of nineteen to twenty-three gallons.[16] This was about double the production of Nonagasta in 1754, the vineyard of the college of La Rioja, that produced 300 botijas with sixty black slaves.[17] This vineyard (called the Estancia de Nonagasta) was about six km out-side of the town proper in the foothills of the local mountains. In 1754 the size of the vineyard was 147 *varas* by 100 *varas,* or 134 m by 91 m; it had 1,750 vines or *cepas,* considerably fewer than Jesús María's but apparently highly productive.[18] Around the same time, in the 1750s, the hospice of Catamarca's vineyards, called La Toma, and Alpa-tuaca, the former with 6,000 vines and the latter with 600, were pro-ducing a limited amount of wine. The College of Mendoza's vineyards produced about 300 *botijas* a year in the last decade of Jesuit owner-ship that were sold for 7/8 pesos each. From June through August of 1765, which was the period just following the *vendimia* or grape har-vest festival, the college received from the vineyards about 240 *botijas* of wine and aguardiente, mostly the former.[19]

The grapes of Jesús María were planted in traditional rows, pruned in July, weeded and irrigated. Grapes were harvested, pressed and al-lowed to settle in the immense estate *bodega,* or wine storage room, still present today as a tourist attraction. The wine was stored in five gi-ant *cubas,* and also in the twelve *tinajas* or large jars that served for fermenting. The harvest usually filled all of these storage vats unless a frost destroyed the grapes. In 1747 the harvest was forty *botijas* of *la-grimilla* and botijas of wine "enough for the yearly needs even though almost half of the vineyard that occupies lower land was dam-aged by frost."[20]

Almost all of the wine produced in Jesús María was consumed by the Jesuit community of the College of Córdoba both at meals and at lit-urgy. In 1739 the provincial, Antonio Machoni, warned that "the wine on deposit in Jesús María should not be disposed of until this year's grape harvest is assured. Otherwise, the community supply may be lacking and the brethren will have to be served *lagrimilla* like last year and that is more harmful than good."[21] It was the custom in Tucumán not to sell wine from Jesús María to taverns or to individuals. Not that there was something intrinsically wrong in doing so; it was "inappro-priate to our state." However, wine could be sold to other Jesuit colleges, but only, as was customary with wine and all other products that were sold between Jesuit houses, at cost price.[22]

More extensively grown than grapes was wheat. This was the "ideal" European crop, ground into flour and used for baking European type bread. The fields of Jesús María produced 500 *fanegas* of wheat a season, besides what was put aside as seed for the following years' sowing. Bread was baked in the college's ovens. The harvest in Altagracia was smaller: 50 *fanegas* in 1697 used almost entirely for the sick and for the administrative officials of the estate; and this was harvested from about 23 *fanegadas* of wheat fields in 1695 and considerably more in 1746.

Corn was also an estate product for which Santa Catalina and Jesús María had large storehouses. The latter produced 400 *fanegas* annually in the 1740s. All of the colleges in Argentina in the eighteenth century had farms that supplied corn and wheat. The wheat was turned into flour for bread and the corn was usually distributed in some form to Indian and slave workers. Extensive irrigation works on the estates of the college of Córdoba[23] (the reservoirs, an aqueduct in Santa Catalina, and *acequías* in Jesús María and Candelaria) helped provide adequate grain and vegetable supplies for the college, but occasionally, when other regular providers experienced crop failures, as in 1762, the college had to look elsewhere for supplementary supplies.[24]

The fields of corn and wheat were usually far removed from farmstead or college grounds. Closer to the college or farmstead was the *huerta* which was either a fruit orchard, or, as in the case of the College of Córdoba, a rather large vegetable garden called the Huerta de Santa Ana. This was located about four city blocks from the college. It had a little well and an irrigation canal leading to it. The Huerta de Santa Ana had over 2,000 fruit trees planted, 125,000 onion plants, watermelons, and other vegetables. The proceeds from this paid the salaries of *peones* and *conchabados,* which seem to have been around 2,000 pesos a year. The Huerta de Santa Ana was in reality a small farm. On the grounds were a fairly large-sized shed, a chapel, two mules, four plow-oxen, and a horse, besides plows and other farm tools. Three black slaves constituted the permanent work force. Another field near the college, called simply the *huerta,* produced onions, peppers, and cauliflower for the college kitchen. Only about 100-pesos-worth of this supply was sold each year. The major part supplied house-pantry and kitchen.

Many, if not most, colleges in Tucumán had these small *huertas* closeby. The largest estates, e.g., Altagracia, Jesús María, and Santa Catalina, had them on their grounds, either dedicated to fruit or to vegetables. Altagracia sent most of its fruit to the college; Jesús María's grew large quantities of apples, pears, melons, duraznos, and peaches.

All of these associated enterprises were modest compared with the estate's major enterprises, but in a time when self-sufficiency was often more convenient and far less expensive, they played an important role in the dynamics of the economic life of the institution. Their unique aspect is that they were located right on college grounds rather than far removed on rural estates. The textile mill on the College of Córdoba compound had five looms producing fine woolens, shawls, serge, and baize. Fourteen workers as well as several officials produced clothing for the hacienda slaves (522 in 1744) and Indian salaried laborers. After clothing the workers, what remained was sold and from these sales the college realized about 3,000 pesos annually. "It would be much more if there were more spinners," said the college economic report of 1746. The soap was made from waste fats and lye. Two slaves worked the repair shop for iron tools and slaves also manned the carpenter shop in which were repaired wagons and coaches. About 27 km from the city was a lime deposit and two large ovens. Limestone and bricks were made here. In fact, the college buildings were constructed with stones made from this deposit. Chapel, eighteen oxen, fifteen cows, and 162 sheep were corraled for the use and food of the workers. A *puesto* or range was about ten km outside of the city. It was really a small estate, complete with watering place, corrals, ranch house, and resident cowboys. Here were kept the draft animals for college use, as well as beef cattle and sheep brought from Altagracia and Candelaria for the community and slaves of the college.

With the exception of the range and the Calera, the other enterprises of the college were grouped together in the college compound. The three major estates of the college were located at some distance from the college proper. These, of course, were the major income producers. But associated enterprises, such as the textile mill that used estate- produced wool and the soap factory that used estate animal fats, were grouped closely together within a single, related, compound.

By way of contrast and of an entirely different nature was the large ranch of Areco owned by the College of Buenos Aires. The ranch, about 100 km northwest of Buenos Aires, was dedicated exclusively to raising cattle and mules.[25] The grazing land of the estate was enormous, stretching sixty-five km by thirty km. The grazing land alone was valued at 42,000 pesos. A bunk house for about 100 black slaves and an

38

unimposing house with rooms for a Jesuit administrator, chaplain, ranch officials, and dining rooms, kitchen, and storerooms formed the nucleus of the ranch. The large herd of cattle (42,500 head in 1767) was dispersed on ranges apart from mules (4,700), horses (1,700), and the mares (9,500), that were crossbred with donkeys to produce a mule. Much of the farmland owned by the college was rented out for payment in cash or in produce (wheat or corn), and this represented a significant departure from traditional Jesuit land use practice in Spanish America. Other enterprises were developed on other holdings represented in Figure 3.

Figure 3: Enterprises of College of Buenos Aires in 1750s

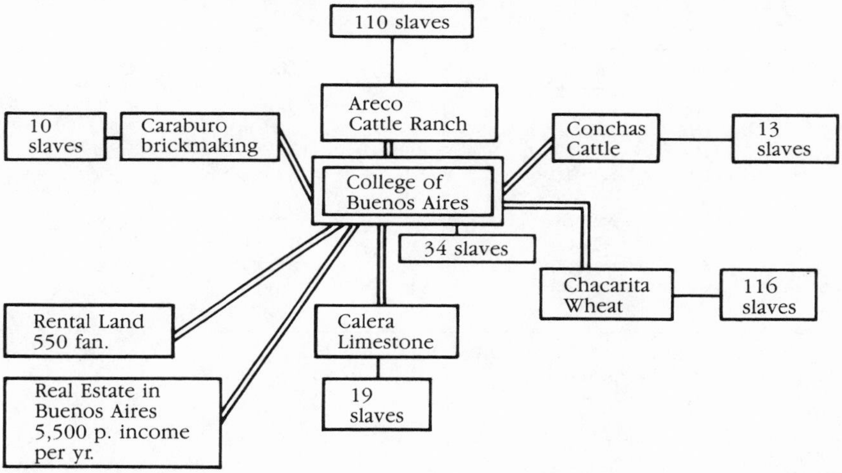

Source: AGBA, Compañía IX, 6-10-5

What is strikingly different about some of the enterprises owned by the College of Buenos Aires is the capitalistic nature of their most productive efforts. Real estate holdings alone produced more than the yearly income of many colleges in Peru or Paraguay. And instead of working all available farmland as was usually done by Jesuit colleges, much of Buenos Aires's farmland was rented out. As will be pointed out below, the maintenance for the 326 college slaves and 200 *peones* divided among these enterprises, amounting to 6,250 pesos annually (to say nothing of the original cost of the slaves, which must have been around 150,000 pesos), was a significant drain on college resources. But it was an expense necessary in order to continue the productive activity of the enterprises.

Cattle, mules, and horses were the three major ranching enterprises of Jesuit colleges in Tucumán and the Río de la Plata. They will be treated in more detail in the next chapter. Suffice it to say that the livestock on Córdoba's ranches was not insignificant even though this was the only college that had major agricultural efforts. Raising mules for sale in Salta and Peru was a major and profitable activity engaged in principally by the Jesuit Colleges of Córdoba, Buenos Aires, Santa Fe, and Corrientes. Every year, thousands of mules with Jesuit college brands would make the long drive to Córdoba and north to the lush pastures of the Valley of Lerma in Salta for fattening. The livestock holdings on the College of Córdoba estates are given in table 1.

Table 1. LIVESTOCK ON COLLEGE OF CÓRDOBA'S ESTATES

Year	Mules	Horses	Cattle	Sheep
1710		4,500	9,000	18,000
1718	2,932	8,384	6,181	7,011
1719	1,517	10,509	10,993	6,866
1720	710	6,920	3,000	5,975
1723	2,684	10,148	20,331	11,202*
1724	2,961	9,380	22,000	11,108*
1740	2,000	4,530	11,500	8,751
1744	2,000	8,331	8,000	9,359
1753	1,500	7,000	20,000	7,000
1760	5,395	16,375	33,450	11,952

SOURCE: LCC; Catalogus Tertius, ARSI, Paraq. 6
*not including Jesús María

Organization and Management

The organizational structure of Jesuit estates in Peru, Quito, and Tucumán was in theory the same. However, regional differences, both geographical, topographical, and internal, prevented exact duplication. For example, some of the largest ranches in Tucumán or Paraguay, where distances were vast, were 200 km away from the owner college. Jesuits were not allowed to live on estates so far removed from other Jesuit communities but were appointed to ranches or haciendas fairly close to the owner college. Jesús María or Altagracia were considered "close" to Córdoba; Candelaria was not.[26] So a lay administrator or majordomo was hired. In fact, only on the largest ranches and farms were there Jesuit administrators or chaplains. An interesting progression is evident for the number of Jesuits assigned to Córdoba's estates.[27] In

1710 two were assigned; in 1720 three; in 1739 nine; and in 1744 there were eleven. Of these eleven, Andrés Astina is listed as an administrator, *(administrator exercitationis praedii),* five are chaplains *(curat spiritualia in praediis),* and the other five are Jesuit brothers who are listed simply as farmers *(curat temporalia in praediis).* But most of the other colleges had very few resident Jesuits (even Santa Fe never had more than fifteen, nor Asunción eighteen) and could not afford the luxury of assigning Jesuits to their farms and ranches.

Although a resident administrator who might or might not have been a Jesuit was appointed, ultimate responsibility for the financial success or failure of the enterprise rested with the rector of the owner college. The rector was advised to visit the estates frequently, to see that they were well administered and that their slaves and workers were decently fed, clothed, and housed. Every three years or so the Jesuit provincial superior of the Province of Paraguay would visit each college and its estates and leave a memorandum of his visit. In it the rector or administrator was advised in very specific terms either to improve herds, build or repair certain buildings, or to correct this or that problem. The specificity of the memoranda (many of which are still preserved in AGBA) vary according to the familiarity of the provincial with farms and ranches. Judging by these memoranda, at least several provincials of Paraguay were very familiar with how to run ranches or farms, long and short term investments, and personnel administration. I have not found memoranda for visits of provincials to Peru's or Quito's establishments, so one cannot compare them.

The organizational structure of the Jesuit province place the provincial over rectors of colleges, and the rectors over estate administrators. The intermediary between rector and administrator was frequently the business manager of the college, and if the estate were exceptionally large, the business manager of the estate. In 1663 estate administrators and Jesuits who were assigned to estates were given guidelines by the "Visitor" of the Province, Andrés de Rada. They became more than guidelines. They were a yardstick for the future relations with estate workers as well as reminders of certain basic Jesuit principles. So important were these *"Ordenes"* considered that they were to be read monthly by Jesuit brothers working on estates. They are here given in full because they express a noneconomic dimension of the estates and formulate what might be called the personnel policy of the Jesuits in Tucumán and the Río de la Plata.

"Orders of the 'Visitor' Andrés de Rada for Estates of our Colleges":

1. You must first attend to the things of the spirit, never omitting morning meditation or other spiritual exercises for temporal matters, persuading ourselves that for this reason we joined religious life. In this way we will bring down the blessing of Our Lord on our work, as the gospel says: "Seek first the kingdom of God,"—by seeking first the spiritual; by doing this, favors in the temporal order will follow.

2. On workdays mass will be said after morning meditation. It can be delayed a little if the brothers have some important work to do. On holy days the celebrant will wait for the workers and neighbors before beginning services.

3. On holy days no work is to be done. We should be an example in this to others, as Ignatius Loyola so often enjoined us. On workdays our laborers shall work from dawn to sundown. The workday is not to be extended under any circumstance except in extreme necessity, for the development of the hacienda depends on the good treatment given to slaves and other workers. By not pushing them too much and exercising a bit more love they will work better.

4. Take special care to teach christian doctrine on various occasions to our workers, as our Fathers General have so often recommended. They should be taught how to go to confession and communion. For this the priest on the estate should hold classes thrice weekly: after Sunday mass when he should deliver a brief talk exhorting them to keep the Ten Commandments and to honor Our Lady; the other two times should be Wednesday and Friday evenings, when the catechism is explained and the rosary recited. Take special care with the sick so that they do not die without proper acknowledgement of the mysteries of the faith or without the Last Sacraments, preparing them in time as best as possible.

5. The piety and benignity proper to our calling should temper the administering of punishments. Punishments should never be administered by a Jesuit but only by the majordomos or another slave or Indian. Ours should not even be present at the punishment of women but the majordomo or an aged trustworthy slave (to eliminate the possibility of indecency) should be present, with the actual punishment administered by a trustworthy black woman. The pregnant or nursing mothers should not be subject to corporal punishment or to verbal abuse. Make sure that unmarried men do not sleep in the houses assigned to married people, but alone and apart.

6. Male and female slaves should receive each year a new set of clothes preferably at the beginning of winter time.

7. Only in absolutely necessary situations, e.g., in time of sickness or confession, should Jesuits visit the houses of slaves or Indians, and then only with another Jesuit or trustworthy slave or Indian. Nor should they visit the neighboring farms.

8. No priest or brother in charge of a hacienda should begin a construction project without explicit permission of the rector.

9. No Jesuit, either by himself or indirectly though majordomos or another party should be involved in contracts that smack of usury (so often condemned in divine and human law), such as buying for the sake of reselling. See to it that our dealings are sound both in conscience and in the external forum. To this end do not sell even fruits of our farms and ranches little by little so that it seems we have inns or shops; nor should majordomos or slaves from our haciendas do any selling because it will be said that we have shops and inns.

10. Not only will such illicit dealings be avoided, but Jesuits can neither sell nor buy anything without the express order of the superior or advising the procurator of it. The procurator should see to it that those who are in charge of estates should have what they need so that they do not have to buy and sell.

11. No Jesuit should distribute to Indian women or to female slaves their food rations but it should be given through their husbands or another person. Children, not women, should be allowed to bring food from the kitchen to our residences; nor should Jesuits enter the kitchen except in an urgent case.

12. Fathers who go from the colleges to the estate to say mass should be reminded that they cannot administer the sacrament of matrimony without the local priest's permission or that of the rector. Those who do administer the sacraments of matrimony or baptism should record it in the estate church record books.

13. The chaplain of the estate should not conduct missions in a town or farm more than three leagues distant without express permission of the provincial or rector. The provincial or rector will determine whether or not to do so, with which other Jesuit, and whether it is possible to administer the sacrament of matrimony to those who are not from our estate even though their parish priests have given permission.

14. The church door should be locked except at the time of mass and confession.

15. The rule of cloister should be kept most exactly. Under no

circumstances or pretext should women be admitted to our estates as overnight guests no matter what their condition or quality, whether they are on a journey or accompanied by their husbands or not. The kitchen and bakery should be in a building separate from the Jesuits.

16. Laypersons should not be allowed to stay in the chapel. They should not be allowed to stay overnight there with their families because that would violate the reverence and decency owed to the place where mass is said. To this effect a room should be arranged outside of our house, where people of quality who should not be turned away can stay as guests.

17. Our Father General has determined that a priest who is in the estate should be superior to the brothers and so respected. This should be observed. And if the priest should overstep his bounds, the rector should be told.

18. The priest should be advised that although he is superior, he should not meddle in the running of the estate. He should correct with suaveness what he thinks needs correction. If he needs an Indian or a horse to go to hear confessions, the brother should supply them immediately, because roles should not be confused. The father can also give the Indians and slaves meat and bread in moderation; and also offer the hospitality they deserve to friends and associates, attempting to balance with religious kindness whatever may be offensive on the part of the brothers.

19. The hacienda must keep its book in order.

20. Lastly, I charge the fathers and brothers to let the provincial or rector know if anything is lacking in the estates. On this depends the stability and development of the estates in their temporal and spiritual dimensions. In order that these precepts be observed, I order the fathers on the estates to read them to the brothers once a month.[28]

Rada's precepts were directed primarily at Jesuits (both priests and brothers) resident on farms, their workers, and only secondarily at Jesuit transient guests. Of primary importance was the reminder of the hierarchy of priorities, the spiritual over the temporal. This underlined the frequently-stated position that ranches and farms were simply means to an end. They provided the financial base for the Jesuit corporate urban ministry. The rural ministry existed only in the form of periodic mission sweeps through the countryside, important but surely not the major focus of activity. No social visiting of neighbors was to occur, a precept intended to force the Jesuit residents to seek friendship and support from within their own group, a little difficult in a community of two, and psychologically unhealthy if they happened not to get along. The resident Jesuits were also enjoined to treat workers and slaves well, a precept that sprung as much from christian charity as from an enlightened self-interest. In fact, the latter was the stated reason, the former being implicitly understood. The length of the work day was fixed, new clothes prescribed, and orders given that punishments were never to be administered by the religious themselves. Jesuits on estates were forbidden to purchase anything for resale. This would smack of business; nor were residents even allowed to sell their own farm or ranch products without express permission of the superior. Even in the 1680s sensitivity to charges of business dealings was evident. Although in the religious life priests were considered socially superior to the lay brother, they were not to meddle in the routine decisions about farming and ranching. Nor were they to lord it over the brother, indirectly implied in numbers 17 and 18. Rada touched on what were then considered basic personnel relationships on the farm and ranch. But they were general precepts with the built-in flexibility so characteristic of Spanish law.

Rada's precepts were by-and-large carefully observed over the next hundred years (more will be said about them below). They were fairly clear about how to manage Indian and slave personnel but said nothing about who managed the managers. In the 1730s this was the major concern of the Jesuit Superior General in Rome, Francis Retz. In his letters to the Jesuit provincial of Paraguay, Retz repeatedly criticized rectors for not appointing to haciendas administrators who really knew what they were doing.[29] Retz failed to see in them the "zeal and application for estate development" that was necessary if the ranches were to succeed. Most of the colleges of the Jesuit Province of Paraguay were operating at minor deficits, and Retz thought that this was inexcusable. He also thought he put his finger on the cause: the unnecessary purchase of contiguous, adjacent land (especially for Jesús María and Santa Catalina), so in 1734 he forbid for ten years the purchase of any land by a college.

Retz's letters, all of which are still carefully preserved in the Jesuit Archives in Buenos Aires, are a striking example of how dangerous it is to issue directives for a situation 10,000 miles and two years away. I strongly suspect that the Paraguay provincial agreed with Retz (and said so in his return letters) but continued placing men he considered appropriate. The local provincial best knew the quality and mind of subjects. These provincials must have found themselves in much the same position as the Spanish colonial governors when faced with an order from Madrid that they knew was inappropriate, disruptive, or ill-advised. Only the Jesuit provincial had no "obedezco pero no cumplo"–mechanism to employ. Consulation and advice should have been available. But frequently provincials were left to their own devices to solve a problem or to choose a mode of action. This was done by attempting to act according to a vision of the Society, the church, and the world, which Jesuit superiors were expected to possess as part of their intellectual baggage.

World Vision and Commercial Venture

There are several levels or dimensions at which one can view the group of buildings, the farmland, and the grazing land that made up the Jesuit colonial estate in Tucumán. One level is that of colonial architectural style. Enough remains of the old structures to enlighten us about construction forms and their artistic embellishments. To what degree did indigenous elements shape this particular form of Latin American art and architecture? Or were they transplanted forms totally European in concept and design? A further step on this level would be the interpretation of these cultural features to arrive at deeply felt convictions; buildings were constructed in a period when convictions were often expressed in visual representation. Another level of assessment could view the estate as a specific response to economic needs. How and how well did the constellation of structures function? What if anything does it tell us about social organization? Still another level could ascertain whether the man-made pattern of buildings, worked fields, dammed and diverted rivers, and other natural but modified features responded to some inner need or vision—even world view if you will. In other words, was the large, religious-owned estate on the northern pampas an agricultural experiment, an economic phenotype, a rural commercial venture managed but not staffed by a few members of a religious order, or was it a unique blending of elements from all of these interpretations?

The large Jesuit farms and ranches—particularly Jesús María, Santa Catalina, and Altagracia—combined elements of the medieval monastic estates and the more commercially oriented businesses. The compound of church, cloister, workshops, and slave quarters, all surrounded by a wall, suggests a monastic vision of the world—an orderly, integrated, self-sufficient world capable of housing and feeding hundreds of people. By contemporary Latin American standards the individual buildings rising upwards for stories were imposing, massive testimonials to the permanence of Spanish settlement. It was a clear message to Indian America that the Spaniards and their religion had come to stay. Liturgy and work life were complementary, but prayer and religious services came first in the stated order of importance.

The Jesuit (and other religious) farm and ranch establishments were unlike the old medieval abbeys and monasteries in that they did not contain entire religious communities. Nor were they totally isolated or self-sufficient, but on the contrary, they maintained fixed social and economic ties with surrounding estate owners and local markets. They were likewise dissimilar to the monastic grange, pioneered by Cistercians, in that the grange was unencumbered land on the margins of existing settlements. But the Jesuit estates were similar to the independent monastic farm or grange that was controlled by a team of lay brethren assigned to the purpose by the monastery, each subject to supervision of an official based in the abbey. Sited within easy reach of the abbey to which the grange returned its produce, survival of the unit depended on the profits it brought. These granges were the basis of the Cistercian agricultural economy during the twelfth to fifteenth centuries, just as Jesuit colleges depended for income on their ranches and farms in the seventeenth and eighteenth centuries.

Another characteristic shared by Jesuit establishments and earlier monastic foundations was the rather close association with local people.[30] Toward the later Middle Ages the local peasantry eventually managed the grange and staffed the farms with plowmen, carters, herdsmen, cowherds, and general laborers. The same was also true of Jesuit estates. Local Indians provided labor, and just as in medieval times, land donations were often accompanied by entitlement to labor services, so the *yanaconas* and Indians on purchased lands often remained as permanent laborers. Similar also was the monks' and Jesuits' direct responsibility for large-scale production for a market. On monastic granges, small units of monks directed and participated in farming operations;[31] on Latin American estates, one or two Jesuits acted as administrators and managers. As is clear, the Jesuit rural establishments of seventeenth- and eighteenth-century Latin America shared a number of important characteristics with their monastic cousins of an earlier age.

The major characteristic shared by both was the commercial nature of the enterprises. A close examination of farm buildings and land acquisitions shows how calculating and empirical were the actions of both abbot or *procurador* in developing estates and consolidating lands.[32] And it might not be too farfetched to draw the parallel even further. Just as the monks, especially in England, reached their "limit of ambition" before the dissolution of the monasteries or reform in the sixteenth century, so too the massive Jesuit estates of Tucumán and Latin America reached their apogee in the middle of the eighteenth century, a decade or two before the expulsion of the Jesuits from the Spanish domains.

The economic base of the Jesuit colleges in Tucumán was the mule. Córdoba and Salta became the gateway to the vast mule market of Peru. Proceeds from sales enabled colleges to construct residences, churches, farmsteads, and barns. What wheat and corn were to the medieval monastery, the mule was to the Jesuits of Tucumán and the Río de la Plata.

CHAPTER 3

The Mule Trade

After an inspection of the Jesuit ranch of Altagracia in 1747, the provincial of the Jesuit Province of Paraguay, Manuel Querini, strongly recommended that the rector of the college "spare no effort to build up the ranch's mule-breeding enterprise, because this is the college's major source of income"[1] He specifically advised the rector to put at least 6,000 mares in the mule production center and a proportionate number of male donkeys for breeding purposes. Querini had become something of an expert agronomist and rancher, so his suggestions were not lightly dismissed. Raising mules for sale *was* the college's single most important source of income, accounting at the time for forty to sixty percent of the institution's running expenses. Mules were big business, engaged in by some of the wealthiest ranchers and traders in Tucumán and the Río de la Plata. The Jesuit College of Córdoba more than held its own in this lucrative business that supplied the mines and ranches of Alto Peru and the haciendas of the Peruvian coast.

Mules and Donkeys

The mules shipped from Tucumán to Peru were raised on the vast, fertile breeding areas of the northern pampas. Peruvian mines and haciendas created great demand for mules, but fixed land use priorities and insufficiently large pasturage militated against mule raising. The closest potential breeding ground was several hundred miles southeast of Peru, interrupted by treacherous mountain terrain. The mule trade between Peru and Tucumán was a natural concomitant of normal trading activity. The string of settlements that stretched from Jujuy to Buenos Aires maintained close commercial relations with Peru. In the sixteenth and seventeenth centuries Buenos Aires was not the major contact point for receiving European goods; Lima and Potosí were. Around 1600, the mules of Tucumán began to trod regularly on the roads to Potosí and Lima.

Although mules were first shipped from Córdoba to Peru as early as 1600, donkeys were also available in Tucumán. In general, donkeys were smaller than mules. These offspring of male and female donkeys were used for draft purposes on farms, in commercial transportation, and as sires in mule production. The average size donkey is capable of carrying eighty to one hundred kilos over thirty-five to forty km a day. They required less feed and less care than horses, but they were not as desirable as the mule. The mule was (and is) courageous, hard of hide, sure of fooot, sound of constitution, and what was more important for the trade between Tucumán and Peru, able to resist changes in climate and withstand thirst and hunger.[2] Less frequently bred but present on ranches of Tucumán was the hinny, the hybred of a female donkey and a male horse. Hinnies (also called *machos*) are more horse-like in appearance than the mule, have great stamina, are long-lived, and are also used for riding.

Mules were bred for three purposes: for draft, pack work, and for riding. There is no record of the height of Tucumán's mules but it can be assumed that the tallest were used for riding. The mule is not best suited for the plow, and slow agricultural work is best done by oxen, but teams of mules are efficient wagon animals. Mules of ordinary size (thirteen to fourteen and one half hands), from about 3/4 years of age, can carry 150 kg over thirty-five to fifty km a day. And they work well until they are eighteen or twenty years of age. Their small hooves make them sure-footed, an invaluable asset in mountainous terrain.

One of the most important qualities of the mule, and one which certainly was a major factor in the continued existence of the mule trade between Tucumán and Peru, was the mule's ability to recover quickly after strenuous effort. After a day's work of ten to twelve hours, one night's rest seems to be sufficient to restore strength completely and begin another day's labor—quite different from a horse. The mule's advantage is not only in its disproportionate strength in the muscular development of hindquarters, but also its general muscular development is even of more practical value.[3] The mule was physically capable of making the arduous trek from Tucumán into the Andes, and then continuing to work in the mines or on haciendas.

Although the mule trade to Peru started around 1600, recent research puts the starting date of a significant trade a half-century later.[4] Between 1657 and 1698, over 73,000 mules were shipped from Salta, and from all indications the annual average was maintained throughout the eighteenth century. Toledo's figures show that in 1660, twenty-one mules left Salta for Potosí, and only eight years later 1,376 mules without cargo were shipped. Either the trade made a remarkable advance in less than a decade or the 1655–1660 records are incomplete and might well have been a bridge indicating a gradual increase of the mule trade. From this period on, the annual average was anywhere from 2,000 to 7,000 mules. Shipping costs were partly determined by destination. Salta to La Paz cost ten *reales* a head; Salta to Oruro and Oruro to Cuzco were each seven *reales,* and Salta to Potosí was about eight *reales.* These prices remained fairly steady in the seventeenth and eighteenth centuries.

A necessary concomitant of the trade was the mule wintering and fattening business in Salta and environs. After the long trek from Santa Fe, Buenos Aires, or Córdoba, mules pastured for almost a year before leaving for Peru. That mine of useful and sometimes useless information, Concolorcorvo, wrote in the eighteenth century that:

> the major business of this city (Salta) and its environs consists in providing facilities for wintering mules. The pasture owners profit as do also the traders. Those who prepare the mules for departure for Peru grow wealthy from the Great Fair that takes place in February and March—the greatest assemblage of mules in the whole world.[5]

By the middle of the eighteenth century, the Salta Fair attracted as many as 60,000 mules during February and March—the rainy season, but a good time for departure for Peru. Most of the mules had come from the pampas around Buenos Aires, Santa Fe, and Corrientes. The grazing lands of these areas were considered much more beneficial for breeding and raising young mules than the areas around Tucumán, which were considered better for strengthening and feeding a two-year-old mule. Mules born with the districts of Tucumán and Salta, called *criollas,* were considered weaker and thus inferior to those from places like Buenos Aires or Chile. Herds of six hundred to seven hundred mules made the trip with about twelve men in the drive. Shipping charges from Buenos Aires to Córdoba were about four reales a head. After a year or so in pasture, a second drive was made from Córdoba to Salta at the end of April or in early May in order to arrive in early June. Herd size was 1,300 to 1,400 head. About twenty men and seventy horses accompanied each herd to Salta. Horses were used to keep the herd together and make sure that herds did not mingle. For feed and keeping in Salta, eight reales per head were paid to the owner of the pasturage. But great care had to be taken that the owner did not list the best mules as stolen or dead, when they were in fact removed and sold by the pasture owner, apparently a common occurrence.

The major wintering pasturage for Jesuit herds was found in and near the broad and fertile Valley of Lerma, in places called Sillita and Escoyape. Further away were the Calchaquí Valley, Candelaria, Guachipas and Tafi near San Miguel de Tucumán. Wintering sometimes also involved taming and gelding two-year-old mules. This was an additional expense for the owner.

In April or May when the mules were taken from their pastures and brought to Salta for sale and shipment, owners hired transporters to bring the mules to a specific place. Others sold mules to agents from Peru, and still others sold outright to middlemen who contracted further sales. The shipper ordinarily assumed all costs and risks and sometimes was required to supply an advance to the transporter for expenses he would encounter on the way. During the heyday of the trade, agents from Peru took up residence in Salta during February and March to insure good mule purchases at competitive prices. Shippers were paid at the destination. Prices fluctuated, of course, over the years in Salta and in Peru. Factors of a mule's age, condition, and market requirements were taken into consideration. Selling outright in Salta took away the risk of loss or damage on route but also eliminated the possibility of acquiring a higher price at the destination. As we shall see below, the Jesuits of Paraguay established a "listening post" in Potosí whose function was to inform Tucumán's Jesuits of the local business climate and the right moment to ship the most advantageous goods.

Jesuit Mules

The mule-breeding and raising enterprise of the College of Córdoba was shared by the ranches of Altagracia and Candelaria. In Altagracia was located the breeding operation, the *cria de mulas,* while the 2,800 square km of rolling hills of Candelaria provided the pasturage *(potrero)* for raising mules up to three years of age and selling time. Each year mules were transferred from Altagracia to Candelaria. Table 2 shows the number of mules transferred.

The significant drop in mules transferred (produced) in the 1740s accounts for the Jesuit provincial's concern mentioned at the beginning of this chapter. In 1747 and presumably for several years previously, there were 3,300 mares in Altagracia bred with 200 male donkeys. Apparently not enough mares produced foals, so Querini suggested that their number be increased to 6,000.

Table 2. MULES TRANSFERRED FROM ALTAGRACIA TO CANDELARIA

Year	Mules Transferred	Year	Mules Transferred
1696	1250	1741	600
1697	1300	1743	591
1698	1280	1744	461
1699	1322	1756	823
1700	1250	1757	801
1701	1272	1758	985
1719	606	1759	1189
1725	1149	1761	1194
1726	1121	1762	1173
1729	1157	1764	1636
1733	1255	1767	1138
1739	724		

SOURCE: "Entrada y saca de mulas de esta estancia desde marzo de 1718," APA.

Altagracia had not always been solely a mule breeding ranch. Extensive pasturage was only acquired in the 1650s when the college obtained the estate of Achala. Up to the early 1700s an equally important focus was its textile mill which produced cloth for sale and for the growing college slave population.[6] The ranch had four major ranges or locations where breeding took place: San Antonio, San Ignacio, Achala, and San Miguel.[7] In the 1740s, 3,305 mares used for producing mules and 168 mares for producing horses were divided amount these ranges. The mares used for producing mules were bred to the 200 male donkeys. Foals would be kept in Altagracia for a year after birth, then transferred to Candelaria. In 1747 Altagracia had 370 mules a year old or below. To produce donkeys, females were bred to males on Altagracia. Five hundred to six hundred of the former were kept on the ranch. An outline of cattle holdings on Altagracia throughout the eighteenth century is given in table 3.

The sharp increase in mules produced in (and transferred from) Altagracia to Candelaria in the 1760s was no doubt due to the increased number of mares used for producing mules as shown in table 3. The threefold increase in mules produced was almost exactly proportionate to the rise in the number of brood mares in Altagracia over the same period. However, other factors might have been partly responsible for the increase.

53

Table 3. Cattle on Altagracia

Year	Mares	Male Donkeys	Horses	Cattle
1718	6,299	125	949	4,363
1719	5,749	?	1040	9,000
1723	7,000	300	1500	2,500
1724	6,449	253	1511	3,000
1747	3,305	200	?	?
1760	8,000	600	1975	13,500

SOURCE: LCC

An eighteenth-century report on breeding mules in Altagracia pointed out several difficulties. Mares that produced mules had a much shorter life span than those that did not and it was therefore necessary to replenish frequently the herds. Fillies were often trampled by the males and some were slaughtered outright in order to insure that the mare was physically capable of producing a mule the following year, as well as to permit her to nurse only donkeys.[8] Sometimes the cold, lack of water, or sudden storms wiped out entire herds of newly-born mules in a year. In 1796 such a storm annihilated whole herds along the Río Tercero and Río Quarto in five or six days of blustery torrents. More damaging than the climate were the mountain lions and the continuous rustling that went on in the mountain ranges. Rustling both mules and cattle was considered the major problem around Altagracia and Candelaria. As a report put it: "Many cattle and mules are killed by mountain lions, some die upon being castrated or shod, but the highest toll is taken by rustlers and thieves who continually ply their trade."[9] This was probably one of the reasons why the three Jesuit ranches of Altagracia, Candelaria, and Santa Catalina retained so many slaves. Guarding cattle was a major activity.

Added to these problems were the low reproductive rates of the mares themselves. It seems that only 10 to 20 percent of the mares produced mules annually and roughly the same percentage produced colts. The pasturage of San Antonio in Altagracia was set aside solely for colts and fillies. In 1734 the provincial, Jaime Aguilar, ordered after his visit to Altagracia "that 1,500 to 2,000 mares for producing colts and fillies be put into San Antonio in order to strengthen the herd of horses. In this way it will not deteriorate as happened in past years."[10]

The transfer of mules from the *cria* of Altagracia to the pasturage of Candelaria took place when the mules were about a year old. In the eighteenth century Candelaria had seven ranges or grazing areas called *puestos*. Only one was called the *potrero* and it was used almost exclusively for grazing mules. Candelaria's lands were extensive, enough for

14,193 head of cattle, 6,034 mules and horses, and 6,000 sheep. These animals were divided among the following ranges:[11]

Santa Sabina
14,193 cattle
808 mares

San Luís

418 mares for mules

Minas
413 horses
312 mares

San Guillermo
790 mares
379 horses and mares

203 mules

San Ignacio
791 mares
145 horses and mares

33 donkeys 2 yrs.
old and up
21 nursing donkeys
53 mules

Potrero
194 mares
297 horses and mares

546 mules for market
19 mules (mansas)

Candelaria
376 mares
50 mules criollas
186 horses

From the above division, it is clear that Candelaria was not only a passive repository of mules, but also an active producer of livestock. Horses were apparently bred on Minas and San Guillermo, and cows and steers grazed on the pastures of Santa Sabina. Caring for these animals was a work force of several hundred. The stable work force on Altagracia and Candelaria was composed of black slaves, complemented by *conchabados* and *peones.* Overseeing the estancia was a majordomo who directed the foremen, *capatas,* in charge of each puesto. The number of slaves on each estate is given in table 4.

Table 4. SLAVES ON CANDELARIA AND ALTAGRACIA

Year	Candelaria	Altagracia
1718	87	187
1721	75	150
1723	76	150
1736	112	
1748	98	
1756	124	
1760	170	250
1762	170	
1765	192	
1767	201	275

SOURCE: LCC; LC

More will be said below in Chapter 5 about labor costs and general expenditures. Suffice it to point out here that the labor costs on Candelaria included salaries for majordomos, conchabados, foremen and peones, as well as their food rations and clothing. The original capital expenditures for slaves was large, and continual upkeep and housing was considerable. In the 1760s about 20,000 pesos annually was spent for labor on Candelaria, not including slave purchases.[12]

The total slave population working in the College of Córdoba and on its ranches and farms fluctuated between 700 and 1,000 in the eighteenth century. Around 45 percent of these worked on the ranches of Altagracia and Candelaria. The rest were divided among the different enterprises that functioned within the college compound and the farm of Jesús María.

The number of slaves was even higher on the ranch of Santa Catalina. Mixed farming and ranching characterized this estate and a strong emphasis was placed on raising mules for sale in Salta. Cattle holdings and stable labor force are given in table 5.

Table 5. CATTLE HOLDINGS AND SLAVES ON SANTA CATALINA

Year	Slaves	Mares	Donkeys m.	Mules
1718	366	4,755	309	
1724	279	4,200	316	3,527
1735	355	5,752	250	1,874
1746	304	4,000		2,400
1748	317	7,000		400

SOURCE: LOPP

Three other institutions that had extensive mule breeding enterprises were the Colleges of Buenos Aires (ranch of Areco), the College of Asunción (ranch of Paraquari), and the College of Santa Fe (ranch of Santo Tome). Of these three, the massive farm and ranch of Areco (with 42,500 head of cattle, 9,500 brood mares, and 4,700 mules in 1767) had the largest enterprise, followed by Asunción and Santa Fe.[13] The mules of these colleges, as well as those of Córdoba and Santa Catalina, were either sold or prepared for shipment in the wintering grounds of Salta.

Salta and Mule Distribution

In the seventeenth century and in the early years of the eighteenth, it seems to have been more common for Jesuit colleges to drive their herds of mules and cattle directly to Peru, avoiding the expense of

56

wintering in Salta. The gathering point for the animals coming north-west from Buenos Aires and Santa Fe was Córdoba and Salta and from here they would push on to Jujuy, Yavi, and Potosí. The Jesuit brother, Francisco de Sépulveda, wrote from Potosí in 1669 after having driven 2,000 mules to Oruro and Chuquiabo, that he had sold almost 1,000 of the mules owned by the province in the Cuzco area and he foresaw lit-tle difficulty in selling the rest.[14] The cows and steers were already on their way, having started out in September with expected arrival in Ju-juy in February where they would rest and winter. Probably these cat-tle were from the Buenos Aires ranch of Areco. Every two years the ranch would ship about 20,000 head to Peru for sale, with most going to the mining region around Potosí.

In the 1680s a Jesuit "listening post" was established in Salta whose main tasks were to provide the Jesuit colleges and province with key data on the best available prices for mules and cattle and information on the best time for shipping animals directly to Peru. Diego Al-tamirano, the Jesuit official in Tucumán who established this "listening post" thus explained it:

> The reason for instituting a Procurator's Office in Salta is pri-marily to obtain a good price for the mules and cattle that go from the province and colleges' ranches to Salta either for sale or for wintering before proceeding to Peru. Frequent communication is necessary between Peru and the colleges so one of the major re-sponsibilities of the office will be to advise the colleges when to send them for wintering and when is the best time for sending the animals to Peru. Special care should be taken to learn the appro-priate time to sell mules and goods. If mules or goods cannot be sold in Salta, then send them on to Peru for sale. Each college's ac-count is to be kept separate so no confusion arises. If clothing ma-terial cannot be purchased in Salta, then buy it in Potosí. All business with laypersons should be transacted in cash or goods.[15]

Altamirano went on to caution against lending money and encouraging the procurator to befriend officials and local government officials. The office was to be supported financially by all of the colleges doing busi-ness in Salta. For this reason all significant losses and debts were pro-rated among the colleges.

It was this type of organizational ability and networking that cata-pulted the Jesuits from amateur ranchers to professional businessmen. Such "listening posts" or information centers were common in Eu-rope where trade and commerce were long used to such tactics. In

57

South America, however, it was an innovation that required imagination and an uncommon ability to take a risk.

It is clear from the instructions given above that wintering mules in Salta was often an important part of the distribution process. Mules driven a long distance, say from Santa Fe or Buenos Aires, needed a long period for rest and rehabilitation before beginning another long trek to Peru. But this was not true for mules originating from ranches around Córdoba or in Tucumán. A late seventeenth-century letter from Blas de Silva to the rector of the novitiate (owner of Santa Catalina) suggested that the mules then in Santa Catalina should move on to Salta, not to winter there because of the excessive costs, but either to be sold outright or to regroup for the trip to Peru. Good muleherders should be hired and the best possible price obtained in Potosí.[16]

However, in the eighteenth century most of the Jesuit mule herds sent to Salta wintered there for anywhere between five and twelve months. The herds that belonged to the Jesuit province, as a corporate body distinguished from the colleges, were contracted to individual owners of winter quarters. For example, in 1762 the Jesuit province procurator, Luís Toledo, signed an agreement with José López y Aguirre to winter 2,820 province mules on the latter's pastures. López mortgaged his house, four slaves, and the pasture lands he owned as collateral in the transaction.[17] At this time the cost of wintering was around twelve reales per mule. Table 6 lists the number of Jesuit province mules that wintered in Salta for a little over a decade.

Table 6. PROVINCE MULES WINTERED IN SALTA, 1747–1755

Year	Number	Sold	Injured	Dead	Sale Price
1747	1,324	1,264		60	
1748	1,851	1,800	57	20	7p
1749	1,853	140	4	4	6
1750	2,079	2,000	79	8	8p6
1751	2,138	2,100	38	0	10
1752	1,600	1,503	97	3	11p
1753	1,526	1,492	34	0	11p
1754	1,045	1,009	36	0	11p4
1755	2,076	1,800	276	3	11p
1759	3,048	—	—	—	—
1760	2,974	—	—	—	—

SOURCES: Razón de las mulas que han venido de este oficio de Salta a inbernar . . . 1748–1755. AGBA, Compañía IX, 6/10/4; Cuenta . . . 1759, *Ibid.*, 6/10/5.

The number of mules that wintered in Salta did not increase appreciably in the decades following 1755. Nor do the above figures in table 6 represent all of the province-owned mules. Other winter quarters, such as Tafi in western Tucumán, San Antonio south of Jujuy, San Carlos, and Perico, a little southeast of Jujuy, were also used as wintering quarters. As mentioned above, the ranch of Candelaria was used as and called wintering quarters as well as *potrero,* serving principally the mules of the college of Córdoba.

The number of Jesuit-owned mules involved in the trade (6,000 to 7,000 annually) was dwarfed by the total. In 1727 it was estimated that 50,000 mules were legally transported to Peru, to which number had to be added those shipped surreptitiously. No estimate of this number was made. But the total number was expected to increase the following year. It is evident that the volume traded fluctuated according to Peruvian requirements. Between 1689 and 1700, the shipments lessened considerably because of decreased mine demands that affected not only the mule trade but also the shipments of agricultural produce and cattle on the hoof. In 1689–1690, mules from Buenos Aires were sold for a peso a head, almost 800–900 percent below ordinary price levels. There was also a sharp dip in price from 1710 to 1715, but it is not clear whether the demand in Peru had decreased or a glut in the Salta Fair occurred.

Perhaps because of widespread avoidance of the *sisa* tax, the local government in Salta attempted to bring the mule trade under their strict control. In 1739 the governor and provincial council of Salta issued an order limiting the pricing, sale, and distribution of mules to three deputies appointed by the council. They alone would be responsible for collecting the tax. Also under their jurisdiction would be the import of goods acquired in Peru from mule sales. In other words, the government wished to set up a government-controlled operation, a monopoly if you will, of the purchase, sale, and price fixing. The plan did not get very far. The ecclesiastical *cabildo* of Córdoba, in concert with the representatives of the religious orders of the city, including Dominicans, Franciscans, and Mercedarians, all agreed that the new imposition was unjust, unfair, and unenforceable.[18] It is more than likely that local lay interests voiced similar opposing sentiments. No more was heard of the order so apparently it was allowed to die a quiet death.

In the eighteenth century, I would estimate that the four combined entities of the College of Córdoba (Candelaria and Altagracia), the Jesuit Province of Paraguay (Santa Catalina), the College of Buenos Aires (Areco), and other colleges (Asunción, Santa Fe, and Corrientes), shipped a combined total of approximately 400,000 to 500,000 mules from Salta to Peru, or 12 to 15 percent of the overall total. This represents the single largest ranching enterprise involved in the trade.

Financial transactions at both termini of the trade were substantial and complicated. The price obtained for mules fluctuated enormously and was dependent on a number of factors. Higher prices obtained in Cuzco had to be weighed against the possibility of injury or theft and higher transportation costs. Outright sale in Salta, eliminating messy complications, had to be balanced against higher prices available in Oruro, Potosí, or Cuzco. Size, age, quality, and place of a mule's origin were other factors affecting price. To understand, weigh, and act on these factors required expertise in animal husbandry, sales manage-

Table 7. INCOME FROM SALE OF COLLEGE MULES, 1718–1761

Year	Number	Proceeds (pesos)	Price (pesos)
1718	770+	2,286	8p.4r
1720	1,221	10,989	9
1722	—	3,000	
1724		2,587	
1725		11,480	
1726		1,723	
1727		16,150	
1728		4,092	
1729		7,111	
1730		3,897	
1732		2,527	
1733		800	
1734	703	3,779	
1739		500	
1740		3,500	
1741		6,335	
1742		6,672	
1743		4,945	
1744		4,000	
1747		3,500	
1749		38,730	
1750	1,600	6,480	
1752		20,050	
1753		2,000	
1754		7,000	
1755		10,000	
1756	2,469	11,367	
1757	1,095	10,506	
1758		13,864	
1759	1,200	6,000	
1760	274	2,481	
1761		13,631	
TOTAL		241,982	
AVE.		7,502	

SOURCE: LCC

ment, and finance. For this reason, the Jesuits established listening posts in Potosí and Salta, and at the time of the Salta Fair a committee decided how and when the mules were to be distributed.

The finance records of the College of Córdoba show that between 1718 and 1767, college mules were sold in Salta, Cuzco, and La Paz. Prices varied from three pesos to nine pesos a head. Proceeds were often paid half in silver and half in goods or in locally-made cloth. The college account book listing of income from mules is shown in Table 7.

The income from the mules sold was fairly steady. A two or three year turnaround was expected between the time the mules left Salta and the time the proceeds were deposited in the money chests in Salta or Córdoba. However, the income records do list advances from mule sales, so it may be that some contracts required a down payment on a future sale. Often the price of mules was paid in cloth. A *vara* of locally made cloth, a coarse frieze called *ropa de la tierra,* was equivalent to a peso and passed as currency in Tucumán. A very important ingredient of mule herds going to Peru was well-trained horses who with their cowboys would seek out stray mules and keep them in the long drawn-out herd. In most cases these horses were supplied by the ranch of Candelaria. Usually fifty were required for a drive to Peru. Even so, mules were lost on the way. Some were deliberately rustled by the foremen of other herds who had lost mules, some mules were incapacitated by hoof injuries, others were lost, and some actually died on the trip. The mule report for June, 1749, stated that: "1,563 mules were sent to Salta and of these, 1,400 were sold in La Paz at twenty pesos a pair. The rest were sold in Salta and sixty were lost on the way. Fr. Andrés Parodí paid the wintering expenses of the mules that went to Peru in 1745 from this sum."[19] These losses of mules must be calculated in the overall costs and income from the mule trade.

A rough estimate of costs based on a mule herd of 1,500 head would be as follows:

Drive to Córdoba:	750 pesos	
Labor:	192 pesos	
Drive to Salta:	314	2,568[20]
Wintering in Salta:	1,312 pesos	
Drive to Peru:	1,500 p	
Labor: foreman—	500	4,560
hands—	2,560	
Total:	7,128	

Not included in these basic costs are the rental or usage of horses and mules for the drives to Córdoba and to Salta as well as incidental expenses. If the herd were sold in Salta for seven pesos a head (for a total of 10,500 pesos), then almost twenty-five percent would have been spent on expenses. This percentage is fairly close to that calculated for the 1740s.[21] If they were sold in Peru for twenty-five pesos a head, expenses would remain at about twenty percent. So it seems that costs ran anywhere between twenty and thirty percent of the proceeds from sales. More will be said about this in Chapter 6.

When Jesuit mules were sold in Salta, contracts were drawn up that today tell us a good deal about the details and dynamics of the trade. The one given below, drawn up in 1756, is a typical sales contract between a Jesuit official in Salta and a local buyer:

> Those present, buyer and seller, state the following. I, Pedro de Echezarraga, Father Procurator of this college, do sell to and agree with Don Gabriel de Torres, citizen of this city, to sell him in February or March of the following year 1757, 400 mules that I have wintering. All of them are four years old, fat, capable of journeying to Peru, free of any sickness and they are now in one of the corrals of Salta. The price of these mules will be twelve pesos six *reales* per head. At the transfer of the mules, Torres is to pay me 3,000 pesos in silver, and the rest (2,865 pesos) in silver within five or six months from the time of transfer. The said Don Gabriel agrees to send this money to the college by means of his *capatas* as soon as possible and not in time payments. I, Gabriel de Torres, agree to all these conditions as certain. And both of us oblige ourselves with all legal formalities to their fulfillment. We sign this in Salta, October 5, 1756. Pedro de Echezarraga. Gabriel de Torres.[22]

A note on the margin of the contract states that Echezarraga was the business manager of the College of Salta. Torres was a middleman who would purchase herds of various sizes and organize their sale in Peru. Torres had to have a sizeable amount of working capital to pay 3,000 pesos down in silver and the rest in six months. Apparently, he did not have to wait for the return of the proceeds from Peru. All of the transactions may well have been completed in Salta with agents from Peru. Anticipated transactions such as those in this contract and the frequency of advance payments listed in the College of Córdoba account book indicate that the transactions were not primitive buying and selling activity that took place during February and March of each year, but were rather sophisticated "futures" dealings that involved considerable sums of money and were predicated on a thorough knowledge of the market.

A list of middlemen with whom the Jesuit office in Salta primarily dealt appeared on a balance statement of 1746. Listed on the left were those who made payments for mules sold, and on the right were the ultimate recipients. The transaction was organized by the Province Office in Salta.

Received from		*Paid to*	
Basibilbaso	23,706 pesos	Colegio Máximo	18,249
Zamalloa	1,038	Finca	21,976
Ganza	15,000	Province	23,551
Enriquez	15,000	Office of Salta	3,428
Frias	850	College of Tucumán	758
TOTAL:	55,594[a]		67,962

SOURCE: AGBA, Compañía, IX, 6/10/1, doc. 371.
[a] not including 12,000 listed for the bishop

For all intents and purposes, the names listed under "Received from" were middlemen involved in handling mule sales for the Jesuit office in Salta. Not enough of these balance sheets have been found to enable us to determine how often the same middlemen were used. However, it is more than likely that once confidence was established, the same agent was used as regularly as possible. But just as the Jesuit office used regular middlemen, it seems that certain lay owners used the Jesuit office in Salta and Córdoba to sell their livestock. For example, Don Gregorio Carriño Cegada of La Rioja gave power of attorney to Andrés Parodi of Salta to sell 800 mules of his in Peru in 1745.[23] Apparently, they were to go with the Jesuit herds directly to Cuzco. How widespread this type of service was is unknown but it is likely that close associates of the Jesuits profited from the experience, connections, and network that the Society had constructed over its century-long involvement in the mule trade. Carriño Cegada, mentioned above, was the Maestro de Campo in La Rioja who might have been eligible for a favor from the Jesuits. Apparently, in the late seventeenth century too many of these favors were extended to lay ranchers. In 1673 Cristobal Gómez, the provincial, issued a strict order prohibiting cattle or other goods belonging to laymen from being shipped to Peru along with Jesuit cattle and merchandise. No specific reason was given, only that "it was troublesome," which could have meant anything from customs problems to being shortchanged. However, mules and cattle could be shipped with the Jesuit college herds as long as they bore distinct brands and were officially declared to the inland customs office as not owned by the Jesuits.[24] Judging from future repeated admonitions to avoid selling and shipping cattle and valuables belonging to friends and relatives, the 1673 order had little effect.

The vicissitudes of acting as middleman in the sale of Jesuit-owned mules were numerous. There was pressure from other Jesuit college rectors who wanted their mules sold immediately for the highest possible price. Such a situation occurred in 1743 (and on other occasions), when the rector of the College of Santiago del Estero, Bruno Morales, sent 200 mules to Salta for sale. Morales was in need of immediate cash and wanted seven to eight pesos a head for the mules. Andrés Parodi, the procurator, had to tell Morales that the mules arrived in Salta too late in the year for a trip to Peru; the most he could get was five pesos for each, and because the mules were recently worked, they had to remain four or five months in Salta. No one would take them to Peru.[25]

More serious was the loss of over 400 mules in 1733. Fernando Redo, a middleman used by the Jesuits in Salta, set out for Peru with 1,430 mules. Redo, who was transporting the mules himself, died on the way. Only 1,030 mules arrived (in Jujuy or Peru).[26] The rest, it was reported, either died or were left exhausted by the side of the road. Such situations as this made the Jesuit procurator, Simon Baylina, "hope to God that I will soon finish this mule business that has given me so many grey hairs."[27]

In 1766 toward the end of the Jesuit presence in Tucumán (and in Latin America), the mule trade was experiencing one of its periodic dips, to be followed shortly by a recovery. Not only could mules not be sold in and around Córdoba, but Huancavelica mine was reported to have had an excess of 6,000 mules that could not be sold. It was also reported that much less money was circulating in Córdoba because people had invested in agricultural land that proved to be nonproductive.[28] However, this depression did not last long and by 1768 the trade was back to its normal, if not even higher, volume.

After the expulsion of the Jesuits in 1767, the ranches of Candelaria, Altagracia, and Santa Catalina were operated or leased by the government's *Temporalidades* office until sold or disposed of. During the hiatus in ownership, herds diminished considerably. Candelaria's dropped from 2,583 head (in 1767) to 389 in 1771, and Santa Catalina's from 4,798 to 3,037. But each of these ranches, under different ownership, continued shipping mules from Salta to Peru. Nor does it appear that any significant drop occurred in the overall number of mules shipped, even though Jesuit enterprises accounted for about 20 percent of the trade before 1767. The trade was a major economic enterprise well into the nineteenth century whose investors and shippers were quite eager to and capable of picking up the slack caused by those who withdrew from the trade. *Concolorcorvo* wrote accurately when he said that the mule trade was the most stable economic enterprise in Tucumán.[29]

In a very real sense, the region of northwestern Argentina had become an economic satellite of Charcas and Upper Peru. The mule trade dipped alarmingly in the closing decade of the seventeenth century because silver production in Potosí had declined.[30] A ripple effect took place in the entire Upper Peru region and in mercury production of the Huancavelica mine. However, almost simultaneously with the Potosí dip, Oruro began producing amounts of quality silver ore, and although it never equalled Potosí's output, its spin-off development impacted both on the region and on the mule trade with Tucumán.[31] Oruro, La Paz, Potosí, and the Peru coast formed the major markets for Tucumán's mules.

Although mules were a crucial and the most valuable sale item of Tucumán, they were by no means the region's only product. Local consumers required foods, mostly European, such as wheat, flour, wine, maize, and cattle by-products. Production of these items and their distribution occupied much of the rural world's time and activity.

CHAPTER 4

Works and Days:
The Functioning Farm

When Walter Larden revisited his brother's estate in Argentina in 1908 after an absence of several decades, he credited him with transforming a wasteland into a prosperous ranch.[1] He was correct, for it was the heyday of agricultural development in the pampas. New strains of cattle were imported, new kinds of farm machinery were being used, and foreign immigration discharged boatloads of European farmers eager to plow the soil.[2] Indeed, a startling transformation of the land took place between 1850 and 1920.

Less startling but no less significant was the agrarian transformation that took place in the seventeenth and eighteenth centuries. Spanish conquistadors and explorers found no mines of silver or gold, so agriculture, trade, and commerce became the major economic activities of colonial Tucumán and the Río de la Plata. As mentioned in Chapter I, large units of land were distributed in Tucumán in the sixteenth and seventeenth centuries, in actuality more suitable for ranching than farming. Scattered throughout the northern pampas by the 1700s were hundreds of ranch and farm units that easily responded to the increasing food demands from the rising populations of local rural villages and the larger towns. Córdoba's population jumped from 3,000 in 1600 to 5,000 in 1650 to 8,000 in 1700. San Miguel de Tucumán's population rose from 2,000 in 1600 to 4,000 in 1650 to 7,000 in 1750. Rural villages became towns with offices, stores, schools, shops, warehouses, and markets.[3] Colonial Tucumán, landlocked as it was, never had to produce large quantities of food for an external market, but an increasing population required an increasing agro-pastoral production. The major economic focus of the northern pampas was the export of mules and cattle to Peru, but to support this there was needed an agricultural infrastructure. Therefore, farming was a significant, albeit minor, component of Paraguay's economic life. Other estate enterprises, such as textile production and carriage making, viticulture, hide preparation, and a wide variety of other activities, created a unique dynamic peculiar to the large estate of colonial Tucumán.

Production

The only modern hint that the Jesús María estate once had a thriving viticulture enterprise of 48,000 vines is in the large estate warehouse, where there still could be seen the huge vats used for storing wine in the eighteenth century. In the seventeenth and principally in the eighteenth century, Jesús María produced a regular supply of wine, and also some brandy, which was sent to the College of Córdoba both for consumption and distribution. The areas around Mendoza and La Rioja took major advantage of the introduction of grapes from Peru or Chile in the sixteenth century in order to develop vineyards. Both became major domestic suppliers of wine and remain so to this day. However, other districts near Buenos Aires and Córdoba, of which Jesús María was one, also produced wine.

Between 1695 and 1729, the 20,000 vines of Jesús María produced about seventy-six *botijas* or large vats of wine annually.[4] Between 1725 and 1733, almost 30,000 more vines were planted thereby doubling production. Between 1733 and 1760, the annual average was 208 *botijas*. Apparently, the estate administrator thought that the vineyard should be producing much more. In 1736, production of 600 *botijas* was estimated, a figure that had never before been reached by the estate. However, keeping in mind that the vineyard sold and used wine on the estate, and that listed in table 8 are the number of *botijas* shipped from the estate to the college, it may well have been possible for actual production to have reached close to 500 *botijas* in certain years, and a goal of 600 *botijas* might not have been implausible.

The waning moon in July was the signal for vineyard activity. The vines were then pruned, the ground weeded and irrigated.[5] All the stubble was gathered in little heaps and burned on chilly nights in the vineyard to keep the frost off vines and plants. By February the vineyard was ready for harvesting. Grapes were brought into the pressing room and the juice fermented into wine. Five huge vats (*cubas*) and four smaller ones were used to store the wine, which when the fermentation process was completed, was transferred to earthenware jars

Table 8. WINE *(BOTIJAS)* SHIPPED FROM JESÚS MARÍA TO COLLEGE

Year	Vines	Botijas		Slaves
1695	20,000	59		70
1696		100		
1697		87		
1698		91		
1699		73		
1700		18		
1701[a]		87		
1721		110		
1723		105		84
1724		44	(41)	
1727		41		
1728		65	(65)	
1729		113	(103)	
1733	48,000	145		
1736		193		
1740		204	(142)	
1741		180		
1744		232		
1746		173		
1747		157[b]	(200)	
1748		396	(382)	114
1750		112	(129)	
1751		140		
1758		200		
1760		368	(227)	201

[a] combines 12-month periods of 1695 and 1701
[b] estate administrator notes that although one-half of the vines were damaged by frost, total wine production was 250 *botijas*
SOURCES: "Libro de cuentas corrientes de las estancias y haciendas," AGBA, Compañía IX, 6–9–4, fols. 884–904; in parenthesis are figures sometimes significantly different, in LCC.

called *botijas* for shipment to Córdoba. The price of wine remained steady through the eighteenth century at ten pesos per *botija*. Sometimes the wine was shipped in barrels which were slightly larger, about 1.6 *botijas*. Further distillation changed the wine into aguardiente, or brandy, that was valued at twenty pesos a *botija*. Very little aguardiente was produced, no more than five or six *botijas* a year, certainly nothing approaching the quantities produced on the Jesuit vineyards of coastal Peru. The production of the Jesuit college vineyards of La Rioja and Mendoza was considerably less because they had fewer vines. La Rioja's vineyard of Rodrigón, just east of the city, was only about 400m by 160m and the vineyard of Nonagasta only 147m by 100m with 1,750 vines.[6] But each produced a healthy 250 to 300 *botijas* annually, which does not say too much for Jesús María's efficiency. As on Jesús

María, the stable work force in the vineyards of La Rioja and Mendoza was composed of black slaves. Suffice it to point out here that in 1710 when the vineyard of the College of La Rioja first started operating, there were ninety-three slaves working in the college and its two estates.[7] Thirty years later the number jumped to 171, but by 1753 it had decreased to 150. Purchases raised the number to 164 in the following year but of these, only about sixty worked on the vineyard.[8] College income between 1750 and 1754 averaged about 4,925 pesos a year, most of which was realized from wine sales.

For the College of Córdoba, wine production constituted an important dimension of estate production. Not only did it provide a beverage for meals, but also an essential ingredient for religious ritual, and also a convenient medium of exchange. In 1741 Fr. Antonio Machoni, the provincial superior, ordered that a *cuba* of wine should be kept and sold, the income from which was to be used for buying male slaves "in order that there be enough workers for vineyard labor and also to balance the large number of widows the estate possesses."[9] At the time, Jesús María had fifty-five unmarried female slaves. However, the instructions left by provincials after inspection visits give one pause about the quality of vineyard administration. Many of these instructions, such as repairing the *cubas*, cleaning the vineyard, or reseaming the vats "lest the wine sour again" were of so basic a nature that one wonders whether the admonitions were simply reminders to experts or actual advice about the winemaking process.[10]

Wheat, corn, flour, and salt were the four other major products of Jesús María. Between 1695 and 1701, an average of 385 *fanegas* of flour and 148 *fanegas* of corn was sold or otherwise made available to the college. Flour sold at six pesos a *fanega* and corn at three. Wheat was valued at four pesos a *fanega*. Income from estate products is given in table 9.

Table 9. INCOME FROM JESÚS MARÍA PRODUCTS (PESOS)

Year	Wine	Wheat	Flour	Corn	Salt	Other	Total	Expenses
1695	590	95	1,367	466	—	—	2,681[a]	1,792
1696	900	330	2,550	453	97	36	4,516	2,061
1697	770	145	1,985	192	144	—	3,236	2,383
1698	810	544	1,985	300	120	24	3,783	1,992
1699	630	80	2,215	630	112	12	3,679	2,439
1700	180	124	1,075	306	—	—	1,693	3,869
1701	60	48	155	126	—	—	701	1,372
Total	3,940	1,366	11,332	2,473	473	72	19,977	15,908

[a]includes income from wine production

SOURCE: "Libro de cuentas corrientas de las estancias y haciendas...," AGBA, Compañía IX, 6–9–4, fols. 884–904.

Through the eighteenth century, flour and corn production continued at just about the same levels as given in table 9, with a dip in corn after 1736. Killer epidemics afflicting the labor force, locusts that decimated fields, or crop blights could have been responsible for the dip as they had been on other occasions.[11]

Textile Mills

Clothing materials and textiles in general were expensive and scarce in colonial Tucumán. Early on within the college of Córdoba's compound a small textile mill was operated, geared almost exclusively to weaving woolens for hundreds of college dependants. In 1629 the Jesuit rector of the college, Cristobal de la Torre, requested permission from the Jesuit superior general in Rome to start a larger mill enterprise.[12] He agreed, only if the present college mill was inadequate to meet demand. Apparently it did not start, for shortly thereafter the ranch of Altagracia became the site of another textile enterprise.

By 1681, 10,000 sheep were supplying wool to the weavers of Altagracia. More than enough cloth was produced for college use and by at least 1710 the mill of Altagracia produced a surplus of clothing material that was sold. Production and income at the turn of the century is given in table 10.

Table 10. ALTAGRACIA TEXTILE PRODUCTION (IN *VARAS* AND *PESOS*)

Year	Grogram		Shawls		Sackcloth		Baize		Total pesos
1695	1,033	(1,946)	87	(630)	424	(475)	643	(643)	(3,694)
1696	3,642	(5,003)	143	(1,072)	590	(642)	222	(222)	(6,939)
1697	3,682	(4,921)	238	(1,760)	165	(185)	801	(801)	(7,667)
1698	3,940	(5,421)	47	(376)	274	(302)	594	(594)	(6,693)
1699	3,949	(5,425)	192	(1,536)	766	(806)	790	(790)	(8,557)
1700	4,618	(6,200)	101	(742)	888	(963)	617	(617)	(8,522)
TOTAL:	20,864	(28,916)	808	(6,116)	3,107	(3,373)	3,667	(3,667)	7,012 = Avg.

SOURCE: Libro de cuentas corrientes de las estancias y haciendas. . . , AGBA, Compañía IX 6–9–4, fols. 884–904.

Grogram production accounted for seventy-two percent of the textiles made and sixty-nine percent of income realized from sales. The total income of Altagracia during these years, including sales of mules and farm products, amounted to 62,479 pesos, of which sixty-seven percent came from textile production. During the same period expenditures were 23,728 pesos, leaving a profit of 20,407 pesos.

During the eighteenth century, textile production in Altagracia decreased sharply, to a third of the level achieved in the last quinquennial of the seventeenth century, until in the early 1730s the mill on the college compound became the major textile producer.

Table 11. VALUES OF TEXTILE PRODUCTION, 1720–1762*

Year	Total production value (pesos)	Major production item
1720	2,595	grogram (1,680)
1723	725	grogram (274)
1725	1,089	grogram (810)
1727	545	grogram (312)
1728	323	grogram (212)
1730	348	cambulo (133)
1731		
1735	582	grogram (109)
1737	2,579	fine woolens (1,500)
1740	4,449	fine woolens (2,488)
1743	2,539	fine woolens (1,420)
1745	2,292	fine woolens (944)
1748	2,221[a]	fine woolens (632)
1751	655	serge (231)
1752	2,961[b]	fine woolens (1,484)
1755	1,144	fine woolens (552)
1756	3,031[c]	fine woolens (1,056)
1758	2,264	grogram (926)
1759	2,856	fine woolens (1,036)
1760	2,700	fine woolens[b] (720)
1761	2,081	grogram (845)
1762	2,550	baize[c] (700)

SOURCE: LCC
[a]grogram production this year was 698 varas with a value of 960 pesos
[b]almost same amount of woolens, serge, grogram, and baize was produced this year
[c]almost equal value amount of baize, grogram, serge, and fine woolens was produced this year
*1720–1730 Altagracia production; 1735–1762 College of Córdoba production

Serge and fine woolens were major additions to the eighteenth-century production line in the College of Córdoba. Grogram was still produced in quantity but, as table 11 indicates, the fine woolen *paño* became the major item in the 1730s. These commanded a higher price, four pesos a *vara,* but had been in less demand. The prices of Altagracia and college-produced textiles, per vara, were as follows:

grogram *(cordellate)*	—	8 reales
serge *(estameña)*	—	10 reales
fine woolen *(paños)*	—	4 pesos
baize *(bayeta)*	—	6 reales
shawls *(fresada)*	—	6-8 pesos each

The shift from the inexpensive grogram and baize to the more expensive woolens illustrates a change that had taken place in management thinking. The coarsely woven grogram and baize fabrics were mainly used for clothing slaves and workers of the college (the college possessed 460 slaves in 1710 and 758 by 1740). Altagracia continued to produce most of the grogram and baize but these fabrics were also produced in the mill of the college compound and in a modest weaving enterprise set up in Candelaria. The College of Córdoba therefore concentrated on the more expensive woolens destined for sale on the local or provincial market. In June of 1748, the 360 *varas* of baize woven in the college was marked in the college income ledger as: for the workers. This may have been their salary, since cloth was a common medium of exchange, or as clothing for estate employees.

By the middle of the eighteenth century the two textile milling enterprises, on Altagracia and in the college, had two quite distinct roles. The three new looms set up in Altagracia producing mainly grogram, baize, with some serge and coarse woolen cloth, functioned mainly to clothe the estate workers. On the other hand, the college mill had five looms in service, for fine woolens, shawls, serge, and baize, supplying an outside market. Income from sales amounted to about 3,000 pesos a year, and it could have been more, wrote the business manager, "if there were more spinners in the mill."[13]

Several other colleges had textile mills on their estates supplying clothing material. Buenos Aires, Santa Catalina, and others maintained modest-sized mills. None were as large as nor produced as much as Córdoba's, for none were geared to an external market.

Herds and Hides

The cattle introduced by Spanish colonists in the sixteenth century multiplied rapidly in the Río de la Plata's pampas, in Tucumán, and in Entre Ríos. In these regions water was available, droughts infrequent, and grasses plentiful. These cattle were a hardy breed, light to medium in weight, inefficient beef producers, with low milk-producing capacity, used primarily as work animals in the Iberian peninsula.[14] On the northern and southern pampas they flourished. In the seventeenth century cattle hunts were organized to replace depleted herds or to increase old ones. Hunts were usually authorized for the months of January to July (summer and autumn), when cattle gathered in great numbers at rivers and calves were old enough to survive. Hides could be well dried and transported by ship with no danger of moth infestation.[15] For the right to hunt cattle, local town councils claimed one hide out of ten as a tax. Apparently, the indiscriminate hunting and slaughter of cattle soon took its toll. In 1614 the governor of Tucumán, Luís de Quiñones Osorio, forbid the slaughter of cattle for three years.[16] No one could ship hides or tallow to Buenos Aires or to Peru. Quiñones cited shortage of cattle as the reason for the prohibition.

Some of the major Jesuit colleges in the Río de la Plata and Tucumán had substantial herds of cattle. But, as table 12 shows, some did not.

Table 12. COLLEGE CATTLE HERDS

College	1710	1720	1740	1753	1760
Córdoba	2,000	—	11,500	20,000	30,000
Buenos Aires	12,000	—	10,000	20,000	
Asunción	17,000	14,554	12,400	26,000	
Sta. Catalina	—	7,200	9,000	—	
Tucumán	1,000	2,000	6,000	4,000	
Corrientes	350	8,000	7,000	1,000	
Santiago del Estero	800	800	3,600	2,500	
Santa Fe	—	4,000	4,400	—	
La Rioja	—	—	1,600	1,400	
Salta	700	2,800	300	5,500	
Tarifa	800	930	1,500	4,400	

SOURCE: Catalogus Rerum Provinciae Paraquariae, ARSI, Paraq. 6, 5

A wide variety of reasons explains the disparity in herd size; not that each college, of course, should have had the same number of cattle. Córdoba, Buenos Aires, Asunción, and Santa Catalina supported the largest number of Jesuits (an average of 122 in the eighteenth century) and combined educational activities. Their cattle, agricultural, and slave holdings reflect this preponderance. Some ranches would have preferred larger herds. For example, in 1720 the economic report on Salta's ranches noted that poor administration of cattle was responsible for decreased income, and in the same year the administration of Tucumán's ranches was rated as poor. Ten years earlier Santiago del Estero's ranches were said to be poorly run and producing little. These comments appeared in the triennial economic reports, so they must have underlined the extreme or notorious cases of mismanagement and neglect of ranches and herds. Some colleges, such as La Rioja, Tarifa, and Santiago del Estero in drier areas, did not have the extensive grazing lands that cattle needed. So even the mongrel-colored creole cow was hard-put to survive the disease, ticks, and ravages of wild dogs, mountain lions, and scarcity of grassland and water.

Colleges raised cattle for sale, for beef consumption, and for slaughter. Prices, of course, varied according to time and place. In 1613, cattle in Santiago del Estero sold for thirteen *reales* a head, in 1640 for nine *reales*.[17] Around Córdoba the price was six *reales* in 1711, rising to a peso in 1722 and to two pesos between 1729 and 1734. Thereafter, the price dropped to one peso where it remained until at least 1767. Each year the College of Buenos Aires sold around 2,000 head of cattle to the city slaughter house from the ranch of Areco.[18] Earlier in its history the college ranches were engaged in substantial cattle sales to Peru, but it seems that this lessened considerably and was completely discontinued in the eighteenth century. Local sales would have produced modest but significant incomes.

Jesuit ranches also provided meat for consumption. The brother *estanciero* of Altagracia was instructed to send "good meat" to the college every two weeks.[19] Both workers on the estates and in the colleges received set portions of meat per month. Jesuit students and faculty also were allotted portions of meat. The quantity used for college consumption rose steadily from fifty-four head in 1711 to 140 head in the 1760s. The available supply of cattle rose over this period, but the demand rose as well. In 1710 there were fifty-six Jesuits in the college; in 1753 there were 103. The college slave population fluctuated in the eighteenth century, but it did show a considerable increase—from 460 in 1710 to 961 in 1760. The number in the college *rancherías* of Santa Ana and Calera in 1760 was 340.[20] The others worked in Altagracia (250), Candelaria (170), and Jesús María (201).

How much meat an average head of cattle provided in eighteenth century Tucumán is difficult to assess. Cattle were usually slaughtered when they reached about twenty months of age and approximately 270 kg. Only heifers and cows were shipped to the college for slaughter, although the account book recording shipment uses both cow *(vaca)* and the generic word *res,* which could have been either heifer, cow, bull, or steer. I would estimate that the amount of beef carved from the carcass was no more than fifty to one hundred kg. This, very roughly, amounts to 4,050 kg per month. Divided among a total of 200 persons, including slaves, hired hands, Jesuits and students, this equals about one-half kg each per day. This estimate may not be too far from the reality. Regular supplies of fish and mutton were also stored monthly by the college's kitchen to be used as the main course at dinner supplementing the beef and veal. On days of abstinence from meat during the year and in the Lenten Season, special foods were prescribed, which means of course that regular meatless meals were the exception rather than the rule.[21] The community of the College of Córdoba—faculty, students, workers—was a community of meat-eaters and this in itself must have set them apart as a special "class."

The modern cattle industry has discovered a number of useful cattle by-products in addition to meat and milk products. The blood, bones, hair, sinues and hooves are important sources of products. However, in the eighteenth century only two major by-products of cattle were used: the hides and the tallow, or animal fat. Up to the 1730s, the ranches of the College of Córdoba sent an annual average of forty arrobas (around 500 kg) of tallow to the college for use as candles and for making soap. This was because the herds were smaller and fewer cattle slaughtered. In the 1730s the amount increased considerably, to 191 arrobas in 1738, 236 arrobas in 1748, 262 in 1750 and a high of 361 arrobas in 1755. For the next decade, between 200 and 230 arrobas a year were sent to the colleges from Altagracia and Candelaria. The price of an arroba of tallow fell from eight reales in the 1730s to six in the 1750s and 1760s. Scarcer and more highly priced was the grease or fat, called *grasa,* which was softer than tallow. It was usually measured by its liquid quantity (not by weight), the jar *(botija)* which was subdivided into *pelotas,* twenty-three to a *botija,* and each valued at six pesos. The *botija* was sometimes also called an arroba.

Although we know that hides were preserved when cattle were slaughtered, the college account book does not record income for them until the 1750s. It was probably only then that they were sold commercially, previously having been used mainly for domestic leather production.

Hides, of course, were an important export commodity for the entire Tucumán and Río de la Plata region. In the early seventeenth century, the cimarrón or alzado cattle, which had propagated and spread from Córdoba south through the pampas, were hunted in bands called *vaquerías,* and skinned. Between 1700 and 1725, an estimated 75,000 hides a year were exported from the port of Buenos Aires.[22] In the next quarter fewer were exported. But many hides were of course illegally shipped and never recorded. Jesuit ranches sent thousands of these hides each year to Buenos Aires where they were sold in order to purchase supplies needed by a particular college or its estates. In 1700, for example, the College of Buenos Aires sold 500 cueros de toro, for which it received black cloth, ponchos, tobacco, wax, six dozen drinking glasses, and six dozen wine glasses.[23] The colleges whose estates were heavily involved in ranching, the Colleges of Córdoba, Buenos Aires, Corrientes, and Santa Fe, sent the most hides to Buenos Aires. As far as I can determine, each sent anywhere from 300 to 600 hides a year to Buenos Aires for sale. The principal kinds of hides were steer hides (cuero de toro, cueros de novillos), and cowhides (cueros de vacas). Price depended upon size and quality, but in the eighteenth century the usual price was one to three pesos per hide.

In 1754 a decree of the governor of Tucumán forbade the transport of hides from Córdoba, but the Jesuits argued that the papal bulls and concessions allowing tax-free sales of the produce of their haciendas destined for the upkeep of the colleges freed them from the prohibition. Their argument was accepted, so in 1759 the college loaded seven wagons with 840 hides and shipped them to Buenos Aires. The money obtained from this sale purchased 1,200 lbs. (twelve quintals) of iron, sugar, two sacks of tobacco, rice, and cloth.[24] As in previous years, hides sent to Buenos Aires continued to be a steady source of income until the end of the Jesuit presence in Córdoba.

Rentals and Other Land Uses

Although cattle, raised for meat and by-products and requiring extensive grazing lands, and agriculture were the major foci of college estates, enough land remained unused to permit rentals. The exact nature and specifics of legal obligations that bound owner and renter are hazy. But some college land was rented outright, for a specific period of time and for a specific quantity of rent.[25] The College of Buenos Aires worked out an arrangement with a number of its workers whereby they would pay a portion of seed wheat each year to the college. In 1767 at least thirty-seven farmers owed the college a total of 162 *fanegas* of wheat but most of these debts were two years in arrears, and some, six.[26] The rented lands were in the Pago de Magdalena near the Areco ranch. Each year a collector, who himself was allowed to keep a third of the wheat collected, visited each of the farms and carted sacks of wheat and seed back to the college procurator's warehouse in Buenos Aires. The College of Salta also rented lands for four years at forty pesos a year to several individuals, and Corrientes had seven renters on its property in 1767.[27]

The scattered references and occasional rental contract are more intriguing than enlightening. Were the estate laborers that worked college land more tenant farmers than college laborers? How much land did they work? Judging from the amount of wheat owed the College of Buenos Aires, the amount of land was considerable, assuming it was only a portion of the harvest. Between 1750 and 1767, the College of Buenos Aires listed thirty-seven *sujetos* or permanent workers. In 1758, 150 to 200 *fanegas* of wheat were collected from rented lands; in 1761 over 550 *fanegas* were collected.[28] Either more land was put out to rent or the harvest had increased. Did the rental of estate land arise as a means to counter the severe shortage of farm workers; or did it arise because it was an efficient form of procuring wheat for the college, or because it was a traditional emolument for workers on large estates, as it was on the lands of Quito's textile mills? It seems clear that in the case of Salta, and possibly Corrientes and Catamarca, it was a mechanism to put unused land to use for a profit. Where land was plentiful, as on the northern and southern "frontiers," rental land was available. And one might ask why would anyone have to rent, given the abundant spaces available. Only in the more densely populated and used areas were rentals feasible or necessary.

The most productive and diverse agro-pastoral enterprises outside of Córdoba were owned by the College of Buenos Aires. A complex of farms and ranches with secondary enterprises formed the complex that supported the major Jesuit educational center in the Río de la Plata. A summary of its activities in the eighteenth century gives us a clue to the internal dynamism of the large estate near the La Plata estuary.

In 1608–1609 the Jesuits were established in Buenos Aires, and by 1617 a small college was functioning in the city plaza.[29] In 1614 the college acquired vineyards and farmland for its support and by 1619 a large cattle ranch had been obtained, "which will be the major income-producer of this college.[30] The college's growth, just as the city's, was slow. By the last decade of the seventeenth century, only ten Jesuits were in the college, which was supported mainly on income realized from cattle and mule sales. The financial report for 1710 stated that the college with 185 slaves on its holdings had "debts and no means of paying them off." But the general economic upsurge of Buenos Aires at the end of the seventeenth century and continuing through the eighteenth was reflected in the college's financial state. One indication of this is the increase in estate slaves, most of whom were purchased. In 1720 the college owned 129; in 1740, 192; in 1744, 250; and in 1753, 347 black slaves were working on the college enterprises.[31] By this time the ranches and farms had developed into major enterprises.

Areco was the major cattle ranch. 6,000 head of cattle purchased between 1755 and 1758 were added to the 2,000 head left over from the "old herd." There were six breeding ranches for mares which in 1761 numbered 8,500, including fillies and mares. There were 225 male mule producers, and over 1,000 horses two years of age were kept in Areco. One thousand others were not yet branded. Seventy oxen were kept on Areco for hauling carts and for plowing the ten to twelve *fanegadas* of wheat land. A columned portico surrounded the main house

77

and chapel; the building housing the 110 slaves had a limestone foundation.

Conchas was called an *estanzuela,* or small estate. On it were 500 mares and horses as well as a herd of swine that provided slabs of bacon and pork for the college community.

The Chacarita was also the location of a brickmaking factory and wheat fields. In 1758 the factory was just starting to function and it could not furnish enough adobe bricks for a granary which was being constructed. By 1761 it was producing 200,000 adobe bricks a year as well as several thousand roof tiles. The Chacarita was also the site of the college's wheat fields. A mill ground the wheat into flour. Two hundred oxen were available to plow the land that produced forty-five to sixty *fanegas* of wheat annually. Over 1,000 *fanegas* were in the storehouse for sale in addition to what was needed for the year 1761. By this year a bell tower, granary, and cemetery were completed. Riding horses and 300 sheep were also on the property. Three looms produced ponchos and shawls for workers and some ponchos were put up for sale. The Chacarita had 116 slaves in 1761, 44 men and 75 women.

Calera was a limestone deposit that supplied lime for the mortar and plaster used in college building construction. Operations at this deposit began a little after 1758, and three years later 600 fanegas of lime were in storage. Nineteen slaves worked on the deposit. Five hundred head of cattle, 3,000 sheep, 50 oxen, and 150 horses and mules were also kept on Calera's lands.

The kilns of Carcaburo supplied bricks for construction and repair work. Although in 1758 it was classified as almost totally useless, by 1761 the kilns of Carcaburo were producing 70–80,000 bricks a year. Ten slaves and six peones constituted the permanent work force.

This complex of enterprises which supported the College of Buenos Aires was not physically contiguous. The ranch of Areco and the farmlands of Conchas were sixty-five to eighty km distant from each other. Light industry in the form of lime production and brick kilns were also separated. Unlike the factory-like complex at Córdoba, these enterprises were scattered, a result of initial site availability and purchase patterns. However, their production and activities were coordinated by a central college office, thus giving them a sense of harmony and meaning.

The economic activities that supported the college were a microcosm of the types of enterprises found in other Jesuit colleges. Farm, ranch and associated enterprises, brickmaking, lime production, and a modest weaving enterprise, were the basic activities found on college properties.

What was produced on these enterprises was destined for either domestic consumption, that is, within the college community, or for commercial sale, the proceeds from which were purchased other necessary items. The colleges with extensive enterprises such as Córdoba and Buenos Aires, or to a lesser degree Asunción, were never completely self-sufficient. Basics such as food, clothing, and building materials were mainly produced on college-owned enterprises but even then fairly large quantities of foodstuffs were purchased, such as butter, vegetables, and beverages, as well as luxury items such as tobacco, for slaves and workers. The two major estate complexes located in Córdoba and Buenos Aires came closest to self-sufficiency. Córdoba almost completely supplied its own community of students, Jesuits, and workers with the following:

Foods	Clothing	Building Materials
meats	baize	lime
wine	grogram	bricks
flour	serge	plaster
vegetables	sackcloth	
fruit	blankets	
butter	shawls	
eggs	woolens	
poultry		
pork		
greens		
cooking fats		
corn		

That which was not used by the community, in the larger sense, was sold for a profit. However, this was not an arbitrary proportion each year. The colleges knew how much they needed in a particular year, how much a harvest or the supply would be, and therefore how much income they could expect. Only when natural disasters struck, such as blight, killer epidemics, floods, or Indian raids on ranches and farms, was the calculation thrown awry. For example, the administration of the College of Buenos Aires knew that each year 8,425 pesos were needed for expenses in addition to regular food and clothing supplies from college enterprises. More will be said about this in Chapter 6. Suffice it to indicate here that necessary maintenance expenses above and beyond food, clothing, and building supplies had to be acquired from sales of enterprise products in order to keep the institution functioning. Sales of estate products were completed both locally, therefore quite simply, and at a distance, which at times became complicated and quite involved.

79

Product Distribution

In 1615 Governor Diego Marín wrote that the city of Córdoba produced abundant supplies of wheat, corn, cattle, and sheep. Fields and pasturage were extensive. But, he continued, these products had few or no sales outlets. Santiago del Estero, the closest major settlement, produced more than it needed and prices there were low. Flour cost no more than eight reales a *fanega* and corn a little less. Córdoba's cattle could be sold in Potosí at a profit, but the enormous distance to the market over rough, mountainous roads and trails made the trip hardly worth-while. Marín thought that Brazil was a potential outlet but official trading would have opened the door to Spanish America even further for unwanted Portuguese businessmen. Marín really did not suggest any viable markets for Tucumán's products.[32]

Governor Marín's remarks illustrated a problem that plagued Tucumán throughout its colonial existence: it was landlocked. The city, therefore, focused its activity to the northwest, on the rich mining communities of Alto Peru. The Jesuit colleges of Paraguay and the Río de la Plata participated in this general commercial trend, but they also maintained lively, if less lucrative, commercial relationships within and outside of Paraguay.

There were definite axes in the colonial period on which traveled the bulk of goods originating on Jesuit estates. On the Córdoba-Salta-Peru axis moved the mules and cattle. Between Córdoba and Buenos Aires moved cattle and mules shipped north to Peru and hides collected in Córdoba and sent to the port of Buenos Aires. From Missiones, Corrientes, Santa Fe and Asunción, mules, *yerba mate,* tobacco, sugar, and textiles were shipped to Córdoba to be either transhipped to Peru or to Chile. Hides and yerba from these four points were sent south to Buenos Aires for transhipment either to Chile or to Europe. From the La Rioja–Mendoza regions, wines were transported to Córdoba and Buenos Aires. The principal transportation mechanisms were muletrains and ox-drawn wagons. All college estates had some form of wagon repair shops, but Córdoba and Santiago del Estero became widely known for the magnitude of their wagon-construction and repair operations.

The key financial and distribution points of the trade network were the various regional business offices which coordinated the purchases and sales.[33] These regional offices were in reality central purchasing and distribution points for missions and for colleges that maintained widespread commercial operations. In Córdoba, the Paraguay Reductions (Missiones), Santa Fe, Potosí, Buenos Aires, and Salta were located regional business offices that acted as broker, trader, supplier, and warehouse. The College of Córdoba, which throughout its Jesuit existence acted as hub of this trade, also maintained direct commercial relations with some of the tea-producing towns of the Jesuit reductions. Córdoba often stored, shipped, and financed the sale of mission tea, and to a lesser extent tobacco, in Chile and Peru. Sturdy canvas from the looms of the Guaraní reductions also found a ready outlet in Córdoba.

The mechanisms of long-distance trading were enormously faciliated by other Jesuit business offices located in key foci. The office in Potosí was a listening post set up to inform Córdoba of prices and the business climate in Peru. Mendoza was a key jumping-off point before crossing the Andes for Santiago de Chile. The Jesuit college there was a major gathering and distribution point for goods crossing the Andes in either direction. Lima and Buenos Aires were major port cities and economic poles. Each of these points played key roles in an integrated system of trade.

The major routes were either wagon trails or rivers. Muletrains were often used north of Santiago del Estero, usually because of the denser underbrush and trees as well as the hillier terrain. Wagons were used on the flatter lands. These were no doubt the same kind described by Concolocorvo in the eighteenth century: two high, heavy, wheels, on the axle of which rests the box of the cart. The sides were covered with woven reeds topped by an arched roof of willow wood. The wagons normally carried a load of 1,700 kg pulled by four oxen. The wagon attendant sat under a forward roof on a large box in which he carried his belongings. Water, firewood, parts, and grease were part of essential baggage. The carts made in Mendoza were wider than those from Tucumán and could carry an additional 200 kg. This was because the trails around Mendoza were wider whereas the one leading north from Córdoba encountered two thick forests "which made the road narrow. Those from Mendoza cross the pampas experiencing no damage to their bodies."[34] *Yerba mate* and hides were transported by barge down the Paraná or Uruguay Rivers to Santa Fe or Buenos Aires, or overland from present day Missiones to Asunción.

The transporting was done either by Jesuit brothers or by professional merchants who hired waggoners or muleteers. River transport was done by Indians directed and accompanied by Jesuit missionaries. Transportation costs varied. One longstanding debt of the College of Córdoba was partly for shipping: "the business office for Missiones in Santa Fe is owed 2,100 pesos which P. Julio de Casas spent in shipping wagon loads of *yerba de palos,* some pelotas and jars of grease to this

College and to Salta."[35] Usually the College of Córdoba account book listed shipping costs as follows: "80 pesos for transporting 177 arrobas of tobacco delivered to the College."[36] This probably meant two wagons making the journey from Santa Fe.

The infrastructure for Jesuit trading activity was minimal but adequate. On roads and trails, at least from the eighteenth century on, were placed waystations every fifty km or so for everyone's use. Warehouses were located in key foci, usually within college compounds, but on site market sales were left to laypersons.

Only Indian raids were capable of damaging the infrastructure, interrupting the flow of goods along the trade routes. This was true during several periods of the seventeenth and eighteenth centuries. In 1701–1702 Indian raids forced the town of Santiago del Estero to change its site. The Mocobies, Abipones, and Guaycurus raided farms and ranches in the vicinity, and what was more serious, attacked merchants and herds going and coming from Peru on the Royal Road. The northern towns of Santa Cruz and Tarija were actually under seige.[37] In 1714 the Mocobies were again attacking the trade routes to Potosí and Peru;[38] a few years later the College of Santiago del Estero lost much of its cattle to Indian raids and was forced to sell its mules at a ridiculously low price. The rector of the college grew so concerned that he wrote that he did not know how he could keep the college open.[39] The Indians were getting closer and closer and the majordomos of Jesús María and Caroya were advised to put a wall around their slave quarters if Indians got too close.[40] Between 1745 and 1755 continual fighting engulfed the pampas from Santa Fe to Mendoza. Farms and ranches were burned, captives taken; Spanish reprisals were fruitless and a full scale Indian-Spanish War erupted.[41] In 1753 the Pampas and Serrano Indians were raiding haciendas and roads 150 miles from Buenos Aires, and the Marqués de Ensenada wrote: "Indian attacks are almost continuous, not only on the frontier but in settled regions."[42] Only the Indians and an occasional killer epidemic were capable of putting a halt, if only temporarily, to the flow of goods that were produced on colonial farms and ranches and transported on colonial roads.

Colonial Role of Ranches and Farms

The function and role of the farm and ranch in colonial Argentina contrasted sharply with the role these landed institutions played in coastal Peru or Interandine Quito. In general terms, the Argentine establishments were more directly oriented toward an export market. This is not to say that smaller farms did not supply food to regional towns and markets. What it meant is that the general focus, the collective character of the larger Jesuit agro-pastoral enterprises outside of Buenos Aires, used most of its energy to produce goods that were sold far from their places of origin. This, of course, was also true of the large textile mills operated by the Jesuits in Interandine Quito. The bulk of their incomes was derived from sales of textiles in Lima. But farms and ranches associated with the mills operated primarily for the local, regional economy, and sometimes exclusively to supply food for Indian textile workers. The Jesuit cattle ranches of coastal Peru, like Ambar north of Lima, supplied their Jesuit slave communities with meat, and the food grown was used for the same purpose. The commercial products, sugar and wine, were by and large sold locally for a profit.

The agro-pastoral enterprise in Tucumán also played a political role in forming an occupied zone that stretched over and up to the reductions of Paraguay. This formed a barrier to Portuguese expansion from Brazil and severely limited the amount of land available to the original indigenous population of the area. Epidemic diseases, Spanish military reprisals, and flight had reduced the Indian population of Tucumán and surrounding regions. A Jesuit who resided in the area for forty years, Bartolomé Jiménez, wrote to the Council of the Indies in 1717 that in the 1640s the Indian population of Tucumán had been more than 40,000. In 1717 it was down to 700 or 800. In Santiago del Estero the decline went from 80,000 to around 2,000, and so on.[43] Jimenez' figures represented an estimate that was probably based more on feeling and a sense of loss than on actual population counts. However, he did say that the original population lists *(matrículas)* were the sources of his statement. If his population estimates were accurate, then the decline rivaled, if not surpassed, that of central Mexico in the sixteenth and seventeenth centuries.[44] In support of Jiménez's figures, recent research has shown that population estimates for early colonial Argentina must be revised upwards, thus making the eighteenth-century decline in native population even sharper.[45] This of course meant that as more Indians abandoned or were driven from the land, Spaniards could claim it. Even though the Spanish population was small to begin with, its ranching enterprises required vast amounts of land, unlike farming, whose cultivated land was limited by the amount of produce able to be absorbed by a market or by the amount of available labor. Size of the market for cattle products also determined ranch and herd size but much less rigidly.

The institutional farm and ranch as examined in this chapter fulfilled a dual function. It supplied the owner college with essential goods, such as wine, wheat, and cloth, while at the same time supporting it financially with income derived from sales of mules, beef cattle, or farm products. Economic and social relationships extended from the college to the farm or ranch with its laborers and land lessees, and even further to local villages with their artisans and suppliers who furnished the large estate with goods it did not produce. The economic organization of this complex or set of relationships was intricate, at times disordered, but effective. It is precisely here that the agrarian structures of the rural world of colonial Tucumán began to take shape. The rural textile mills required a corps of workers to tend and raise the sheep, skilled labor to shear, to operate looms, to dye wool; enterprises needed resourceful administrators to oversee activities and energetic distributors to market the product. Contractual and informal relationships between lessee and owner, supplier and producer or purchaser, between owner and distributor, and between laborer and employer, all of these relationships created layers of rural liaisons and associations that formed the fabric of rural society. The foremost of these relationships or linkages was the one that bound laborer to employer. Circumstances of time and place made native labor scarce and hired labor expensive. Thus, the black slave became the permanent, stable worker on the large farm or ranch of colonial Tucumán.

CHAPTER 5

Labor: Salaried and Slave

Personal Service

That Jesuit enterprises throughout Latin America could produce anything at all was due to the successful organization of labor forces in each major region. Coastal Peru relied on the black slave. Interandine Quito depended on the Indian *gañán*. Tucumán and Paraguay depended on the black slave and a variation of the Andean *gañán*, called in Tucumán the *conchabado*, because he "entered into an agreement," *(se conchabó)* to work on an estate for a specific period of time. He differed from the *peón* in that the latter was hired for a day or two or a relatively short period of time.[1] The *conchabado* stayed on for months or years. These three labor categories evolved out of the bitter disputes over personal service that occupied Tucumán in the late sixteenth and early seventeenth centuries. The dispute between crown and colonists over the right to exploit native labor was as bitter in Tucumán as it had been in Peru. It might not be too cynical to assert that only the lack of mines of precious metals in the region pushed the conscience of the crown to abolish personal service of any kind in Tucumán.

In the years immediately following the foundation of the string of towns from Salta to Córdoba, from roughly 1573 to 1600, the Indians of Tucumán were forced to work either as domestic help in towns or as farm labor on estates. The inability of the Indian to pay tribute to the encomendero either in specie or in kind was the justification for this *servicio personal.* The Indians sowed and worked on farms, took care of the cattle, or wove clothes, blankets, bedcovers, and cotton goods which were shipped by the encomendero to Peru for sale. The Indian had virtually become the slave of the Spaniards. They were transferred by owners from one town to another, made to work exhausting hours in small sweatshops and were separated from wives and families for long periods, to say nothing of the brutal punishment they received at the hands of their masters or foremen, called *peruleros*. Governor Pedro Mercado de Peñalosa was shocked at the condition of the Indians he found on what was apparently the first official inspection tour of Tucumán, begun in October 1568.[2] He reported that the arbitrary dispersal of such great numbers of male Indians to estates and to the city of Córdoba, and the poor treatment given them, sharply reduced the male and female Indian population. He ordered the inspection because he himself did not know how many Indians were actually working in Córdoba. He was surprised to find that at least 426 male Indians, most of whom had wives and children, had simply been taken from the countryside and forced to work in the city. It is not known to what use Mercado's report was put. He himself made no dramatic adjustment of the situation, as the Bishop of Tucumán reminded Philip II two years later. More than likely it added to a growing dossier on Tucumán that the Council of the Indies in Madrid was compiling.

The "personal service" controversy in Tucumán and the Río de la Plata was brought to an end by Francisco de Alfaro. In 1610 the Audiencia of La Plata commissioned Alfaro to inspect the audiencia district with a view to improving the lot of the Indian. As Alfaro uncovered serious abuses and exploitation of Indians, he sent Spaniards to prison and even to the galleys.[3] In 1611 he composed a set of regulations called *Ordenanzas* that protected Christian Indians and those living in towns. They could only work voluntarily for a salary. However, the five pesos annual tribute could be commuted to thirty days of labor for their encomendero. In 1618 Philip II promulgated Alfaro's regulations under force of law.

Spanish settlers were incensed over the government's action. They traced all the economic and social ills of Tucumán back to Alfaro's regulations. That Indians fled to the mountains, revolted, refused to sow wheat or corn, that famine struck, and even the "plague of Egypt" that ravaged the region in the 1630s were all laid at Alfaro's doorstep.[4] Even black slaves were unavailable to pick up the slack. In 1633 the city of Córdoba complained that its fields were unattended because farmers could not purchase slaves. "They were all being bought up in Buenos Aires and they remained in the Río de la Plata or in Asunción."[5] And slaves would not have been needed if Alfaro had not pushed through his *ordenanzas*!

But the law and its implementation were two quite different matters. Personal service was still being practiced in 1633, and it is evident from even superficial examination of the Escribanía documents in the provincial archives of Córdoba that *Indios de Servicio* remained very much a fixture in Tucumán well into the eighteenth century. Even the terminology used in documentation hinted that little change had taken place: a *"merced de Indios"* was commonly used for *encomienda de Indios*. A Jesuit, Juan Romero, writing from Córdoba in 1620 for some guidance and advice from his brother Jesuits in Peru, stated that encomenderos continued to lock the Indians in the textile mills at night and lashed them frequently. The encomienda manager, called a *poblero,* received a quota of work to be finished by the Indians—so many varas of material, so many bedsheets, etc., so it was common to keep the Indians weaving late into the night.[6]

Nor were some Jesuits totally without blemish in mistreating Indians. The provincial superior, Francisco Vásquez Trujillo, wrote a set of guidelines around 1620 for the Jesuit estates in his province. He stated quite explicitly that lay brothers on farms and ranches had been guilty of punishing Indians with their own hands and of calling them insulting names. He went on to say that if any priest or brother did this in the future, the guilty party would be whipped in the dining room in full view of the Jesuit community.[7] In 1646 the superior general, Vicente Carrafa, wrote that it was reported that black slaves were harshly punished on Jesuit estates, and in 1707 Miguel Angel Tamburini wrote to Blas de Silva warning him about excessive punishment of blacks, especially by blows, and cutting Indians' hair "because it did not look nice to Europeans." In 1722 Miguel Angel Tamburini again protested that some missionaries were accused of putting reduction Indians in cells so small and with so little food that some died. He pleaded, "By the blood of Jesus Christ I command you to remove from his post any missionary guilty of these excesses."[8]

In 1696 the Jesuit superior general in Rome, Thirso Gonzalez, had leveled another criticism. He told the provincial that he had received repeated complaints that the Jesuits of the province were quick to condemn Indian labor only when the Indians were not working for them. The fathers lived in spacious and comfortable dwellings in the reductions and colleges while the Indians around them lived in hovels.[9] These complaints might have originated with disgruntled encomenderos who ran afoul of the missionaries or from the traders of Asunción and Santa Fe who bitterly resented the Jesuit economic operations in the reductions and along the Paraná River, but they had more than a grain of truth to them. Gonzalez ordered the provincial, Lauro Nuñez, to visit the houses of Indians when he made his triennial visitation of the Jesuit houses in the province. Were they as inadequate as reported?

On the other hand, it would be absurd to think that Jesuits spent all their time whipping Indians or lounging in their well-appointed dwellings. The hundreds of visitation reports that I have seen indicate that the provincials, missionaries, and colleges in general were very careful about the quality of life of the people who worked on their estates. There are examples of deep concern and even friendship. When Fr. Carlos Aguirre wrote to the former chaplain of Jesús María, Sebastián Garrán, in 1754, he concluded his chatty letter with: "Both Alexander the barber and Juancho the Indian gardener have died. Perote married a girl from Caroza. I think her name is Esperanza. Such is the news about your old parishioners."[10] Hardly the news that whippers or loungers would be interested in!

Conchabados and Peones

The organization of labor in colonial Tucumán was influenced, if not dictated by, population shifts on the one hand and by the newly introduced economic order on the other. The Indian population decline and limitations in personal service diminished the pool of available Indian workers.[11] The gradual rise of the Spanish rural population and the rising number of farming and ranching units increased the demand for laborers. Farms and ranches demanded a steady work force buttressed at harvest, branding, and drive-to-market periods by even more workers.

Traditional Iberian attitudes towards manual work excluded any possibility of Spanish immigrants providing labor. Several non-Spanish Jesuits caustically censured this attitude when they confronted it. Michael Hare wrote in the early eighteenth century: "In this part of the New World (Río de la Plata) anyone who comes from Spain, that is, anyone who is white, is considered a noble, even though he differs from everyone else only in language and clothes. Their food and homes are like all the others, that is, like beggars. But still they remain proud. They despise all kinds of manual work and anyone who does it is looked down upon as a slave, while on the contrary, he who does nothing and knows nothing is looked up to as a noble, a gentleman."[12] His colleague, Josef Claussner, said much the same in 1719, and in 1729 the Italian, Cayetano Catteneo, went so far as to say that if it were not for the black slave, the Spaniard in Buenos Aires would not survive: "Even the poorest Spaniard coming from Europe refuses to work for a fellow Spaniard."[13] As in other parts of Latin America, the Spaniards looked outside of their own numbers for a labor supply.

The new rural economic organization composed of farms and ranches that supplied both regional and distant markets demanded a steady supply of laborers. Once the personal service controversy officially ended in 1611, and forced labor was theoretically changed into voluntary paid labor, an almost immediate scarcity of Indians developed which was echoed throughout the seventeenth century. As mentioned above, killer epidemics and flight were the major causes of the diminished native population around Córdoba, but the reduction was also felt around Buenos Aires. In the late seventeenth century the city council of Buenos Aires wrote to the governor of the Río de la Plata, Agustín de Robles, complaining that the inhabitants of the city had no Indians or slaves to collect the wheat harvest. In an astounding statement, the city council revealed that in the past, harvests had been left to rot because no Indians or blacks were available; no one even imagined the possibility of Spanish citizens doing the work. In such years the price of wheat skyrocketed from two *reales* to four pesos per *fanega*. In 1692 soldiers volunteered to harvest wheat, receiving one peso a day to do so. But this was not enough. The council asked the governor for permission to purchase ten black slaves and to impress during the December harvest time Indians that came to Buenos Aires from the Jesuit reductions to trade or sell tea.[14] The increasing demand for labor and the decreasing supply of laborers never balanced out. The battle between Indian and Spanish settler that flared so frequently was not over scarce resources, either land or water. Rather the Spaniard had alienated the Indian in early colonial days to an extreme degree, and further incursions into Indian-held land in the late seventeenth and eighteenth centuries assured continued enmity and warfare.

The few Indians that freely made themselves available for labor on Spanish enterprises fell into two distinct groups, conchabados and *peones*. Within the former, which was characterized by long-term paid labor, there sometimes occurred arrangements similar to those associated almost exclusively with the Andean region. For example, the *mita* was a system of paid labor organization used in the La Rioja–Catamarca region of the mountainous west. Each year the *caciques* of the town of Vichigasta would supply the Jesuit estate of Nonagasta with a fixed number of workers. At the beginning of the year a specific number of Indians would be assigned for each month of the year. Each worker was assigned a salary whose amount depended on the type of work performed. As each worker finished his appointed term, he was paid, and this was indicated on the master list. Apparently, salaries went directly to the Indian worker, and not by way of the caciques. It was the caciques' responsibility to free-up his Indians for estate labor, and although nowhere indicated, it seems safe to assume that he was rewarded in some way for this service.[15] How widespread this system was is unknown but it well could have been extensively used in the region whose cultural affiliation with the Andes peoples is evident.

There is also some scattered evidence that resettlement of Indians took place occasionally on a fairly large scale. In 1682 Cacique Francisco Balquia persuaded the Protector of the Indians to prosecute Gil Gregorio Balzan, an encomendero near Córdoba, for attempting to move Indians from their towns of Malfin and Aldogala.[16] This directly contradicted a decree of the governor, Fernando de Mendoza. In 1713 the Indians of the town of Guamacha were resettled in another town. Domingo Irusta was given a grant of land and Indians in encomienda. He alleged that unless they were moved to the town of Caisacate (Córdoba), they could not receive lessons in christian doctrine. They were ordered to move and of course lost their lands in the process.[17] Admittedly, these scattered references do not prove that a resettlement program existed, either to provide labor gangs for specific areas or to hasten land dispossession. But the fact that displacements did occur, and with enough frequency to warrant a decree forbidding them, points to another possible factor in population change, and a possible mechanism for assuring a regional labor supply because of a scarcity of laborers.

The major form of paid labor used in colonial Tucumán was the conchabado, a contracted salaried worker. The conchabado was the generic category into which fit several other categories of workers, all of whom were salaried. "Se conchabó como _____ ," or "he signed on as a _____ ," was the frequent phrase to indicate how the worker was formally contracted. Workers came to estates as individuals or in groups. Sometimes they came recommended by other estate owners, as Melchor Coceres did. He carried the following note from the Jesuit administrator of Rincón de la Luna (Santa Fe), Fernando Alles, to Francisco Valdes of Córdoba:

> The bearer of this note is Melchor Coceres who wishes to sign on for the cattle roundup. He needs some clothes and things that Your Reverence can supply. He is a ranchhand experienced in roundups and he came to Misiones with Bro. Antonio Lugas. He is trustworthy, a good hand, and you can furnish him what he requests. Rincón, March 4, 1767. Fernando Alles.[18]

If Coceres was hired, he probably lost his job the following month when the Jesuits were expelled from all of the king's domains.

Indian workers also signed on in groups, not as part of a mita as mentioned above, but as independent workers who were part of an encomienda owned by a Spaniard. In 1690 the Jesuit estate of San Ignacio belonging to the College of Santiago del Estero enrolled eleven Indians from Collagasta and neighboring villages. Their group contract stated explicitly that they were signing of their own free will, but of course this meant little. The estate administrator could have worked out an arrangement with their encomendero whereby they "volunteered" themselves for work. In any case, the group contract stated that the estate "needed to contract some Indians who had come looking for work on the estate or even outside of it. . . . The Indians presented themselves and signed a contract in the following manner: Juan Miala of the encomienda of Sergeant Major Francisco Ledesma signed on for a period of one year at a salary of forty pesos, plus food and medicines in case of illness."[19] Another signed for thirty-five pesos, the rest for thirty pesos a year. Probably because they came to the estate as a group, a separate contract was written out for them which they and the estate's representative signed. Individual conchabados did not sign contracts but their names were entered into a master list kept by the majordomo. Each time the worker was paid or drew goods on his account, it was registered on the list.

Conchabados were often hired for specific tasks such as: *domador* (horse tamer), *chacarero* (field hand), *portero* (gate keeper), or as an all-around hand, *"para todo."* Skilled laborers, such as brickmakers, masons, or carpenters were also contracted, but at much much higher salaries than the general hand or *peón*. The *capatas,* or foreman, was also considered a conchabado, often having risen from the ranks after showing leadership qualities. The majordomos were hired on but they were not listed as or called conchabados. They were at the top of the skilled-labor ranks, more administrator than worker. All paid labor was called *gente libre* as distinguished from slaves, or unpaid labor. Various names, e.g., *peón,* mozo, serviente, or jornalero indicated the same unspecified lower-rank work category commanding the lowest salary. Schematically the labor pyramid is shown in Figure 4.

The relationship among administrators, slaves, and paid labor was based on a curious blend of subservience and fear. In the late eighteenth century Manuel Rodríguez wrote that extremely close ties existed among peones.[20] Peones spoke a variation of Indian Quechua, although they were urged to speak Spanish. They never told tales about each other. Rodríguez, who owned a part of the Altagracia ranch, would allow peones to care for cattle only if there was a non-Indian foreman with them. He considered them untrustworthy. Rodríguez went on to say that they showed some loyalty to their former Jesuit employers, but the Jesuits always put a black foreman over them; Indian conchabados were regularly made foremen of slaves.[21]

There was considerable bitterness between black slave and Indian conchabado and one suspects that such feelings were tolerated, if not encouraged, by Spanish owners.

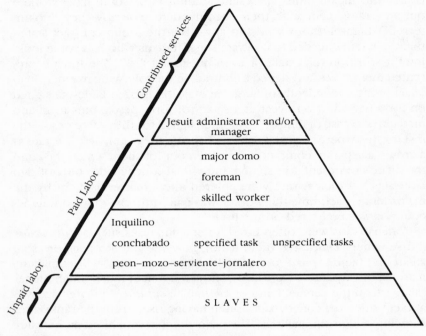

Figure 4. Employment categories on Jesuit Estates

How much of a ranch or farm's labor force was made up of salaried labor, that is, conchabados, depended on the size or affluence of the enterprise. In the 1750s and 1760s the large establishments of the College of Buenos Aires employed at least seventy-five conchabados at one time. The following list of workers that has survived from 1762 reveals a number of agrarian relationships on Areco ranch.

Division of Workers on Areco Ranch

Range of Areco and house	Peones assigned to construction
1. Foreman—Lucho	1. Luis del Baxo
2. Juan de Dios	2. Manuel
3. Salvador, called Chava	3. Joseph Boticario
4. Juancho Mata	4. Joseph Criollo
5. Ignacio Fuentecilla	5. Antonio
6. Jacinto	6. Pedro Antonio
7. Patrico	7. Francisco Pachico

Range of Areco and house
8. Anastasio
9. Agustin, Grande
10. Mariano
11. Bonifacio
12. Manuel
13. Nango
14. Ubaldo
15. Agnatinato de Mata
16. Froncoso
The 16 peones are assigned to farmwork.

Peones assigned to construction
8. Three old men to accompany carts: Marcos, Perico, Estanislado
9. Two boys to carry clay to brickmakers
10. Two sacristans, Luchito and Juan Agustín
11. Six young boys of 3, 4, and 5 years
12. Another sick older boy
13. Francisco, cook

Range of Cañada
1. Foreman—Joseph
2. Pedro
3. Romualdo
4. Antonio
5. Joseph Antonio
6. Isidro
7. Santos
8. Pedro Pascual, young boy

Range of las Palmas
1. Foreman—Basilio
2. Sebastián
3. Juan
4. Fernando, the younger

Range of Bagual de Arriba
1. Foreman—Francisco
2. Valerio
3. Mathias
4. Hermenegildo
5. Ramoncito

Range of Bagual de Abajo
1. Foreman—Ignacio
2. Santiago
3. Miguel
4. Sebastián
5. Fernando grande

Range of Rincón
1. Foreman
2. Eusebio
3. Juan
4. Narciso
5. Joseph Antonio
6. Pedro Vidal
7. Francisquito

There are thirty-four married women; there are eight single women of marriageable age, and six others are very young. There are five babies and two children. The ranch of Areco has 122 black slaves. December 30, 1762.[22]

One of the first things that should be noted about the above list is the number of employees hired for the one ranch of Areco. The college owned other enterprises, as mentioned on page 00, but none employed as large a group of workers. Areco was the main ranch of the college's holdings, with 8,000 head of cattle and 700 mules when the above list was made. If, as one owner indicated, black slaves were not permitted around horses or cattle for fear of injury, hired Indian hands were probably the largest single group on ranches. Nevertheless, 122 black slaves worked on Areco and it is difficult to imagine them not working around livestock.

The range of ages is extremely broad—from children three and four years old to old men who trudged alongside carts loaded with clay, straw, or other materials. Each worked according to his physical capacity. It is not unlikely that the children drew half salaries as they did on the ranches of Interandine Quito; certainly the five- to ten-year-olds did. The very young probably assisted their fathers in their work, learned early on the rudiments of life on the range, and so were kept from under their mothers' feet at home. The conchabados who worked on the ranges usually came to the farmstead or *casco* of the ranch on the weekends which they spent with their families. The sixteen assigned to farmwork on Areco lived on the ranch in bunk houses called *rancherías* or in individual family dwellings. Of the total seventy-five listed, half worked on the farm or in construction. Four to six were at each range.

Family groups, or at least related males, are evident in the list. It can be assumed that some or all of the wives and mothers were among the thirty-four married women. This would probably mean that most of the male workers were married and supported families by their work on the estate. In all, there were fifty-five women and nonworking children, and thus a total of 130 supported by salaried ranch work. Joined with 122 black slaves, the work force on the one ranch becomes a formidable 250.

The salaries of these workers were not indicated but in another place it is mentioned that the ranch paid 200 pesos a year for conchabados. This raises the extremely complex but crucial issue of debt peonage. Two hundred pesos among seventy workers would mean that each received about three pesos a year. The statement was made in the context of how much silver was spent each year for conchabados, so goods in kind might have made up the remaining portions of salaries. How large were the salaries? Were workers kept in debt to retain them on the ranch or farm? What was the buying power of the salary? Did workers use their salaries and advances to some degree as a measure of bargaining power, threatening to move to another estate?[23] Did estate owners refuse to pay workers their due (what was their due?) or did they have little or no cash to do so? How far outside of the monetary economy was the rural worker, dependent as he was on the estate owner for so many of his material needs? Adequate answers to these questions are not now readily available, but the data that is available for the conchabado in Tucumán and in the Río de la Plata to allow us to glimpse the mutual obligations that bound worker to employer and to approach the stark reality of the rural worker's lot.

The conchabados on the estate of San Ignacio de los Ejercicios had annual salaries that ranged from 150 pesos for foremen to fifty pesos for horsebreakers, and thirty for farm and ranch hands.[24] Of the 118 workers who signed on between 1736 and 1748, 77 percent had advances in excess of salary after the first full year of work. Almost 95 percent of the other 23 percent received advances that came within twenty pesos of their total salaries. Ten percent of the workers fled after accumulating debts to the ranch of no more than twenty to thirty pesos or in two cases owing the ranch four and eleven months of service. Two workers were dismissed, one because his master was still alive (apparently the worker was black), and another because he put his own brand on four horses.

The records of San Ignacio's conchabados show that in most cases the advances drawn on salaries increased over the years. For example, Andrés Romo started working in 1742 for an annual salary of sixty pesos. By the end of 1743 he had drawn 143 pesos, 120 in 1744, 142 in 1745, and 102 in 1747. His debt rolled over into the following year and he was caught in a continual state of arrears. The same was true of Miguel Perulero, who began working in 1729 as foreman with a respectable annual salary of eighty pesos. His debts increased yearly even though his salary was raised in 1741 to eighty-five pesos and in 1747 to ninety. Miguel was married with a family. However, a notation in the workers' account book states that after 1747, he had no estate debts. And this was true of at least five peones who accumulated debts but then paid them. Nevertheless, the reverse was more often the case. The worker signed on again owing the ranch money, and then fell into more and sometimes deeper debt.

The salaries of some workers are recorded on a monthly basis, others by the year. For example, the carpenter Joseph Javier was to receive eight pesos a month but by the end of his first year of service had drawn 137 pesos, or forty-one pesos over his salary. Salaries per month usually meant work was to last less than a year and in many cases it did. This was especially true of skilled workers hired for a specific task.

The records of San Ignacio also indicate considerable fluidity in the work force, but at the same time an element of stability as well. Numerous workers left for brief periods of time and then returned to the estate. One horse breaker, Francisco, the son of Pascual, signed on in 1737 for forty pesos a year. When signed on again in 1738, his salary was increased to fifty pesos, but on April 30 he ran away with a horse. He returned on May 16, presumably with the horse, and he began working again. Francisco and others on the estate might have found it easy to obtain employment elsewhere, presumably on other ranches; or their comings and goings might have been dictated by personal circumstances unrelated to other sources of employment. On the other hand, numerous fathers and sons are listed on the ranch's roster. This points to a "way of life" type of employment, in which skills were handed down from father to son and the estate played the patriarchal role of provider and protector. This is reinforced by the number of old folk recorded on the rosters of other ranches. The estate provided what the modern social service organization is supposed to provide—a sense of usefulness and security in the declining years. We see here not simply the seeds of the typical nineteenth-century hacendado who guaranteed security in an uncertain world but a fully-developed sense of the obligations of the large estate toward its workers.[25] They were truly *familiari* in the medieval European sense and as such shared in the benefits of extended family members.

On the other hand, the goods acquired and because of which the workers fell into debt were substantially different in Tucumán from those, say, in Interandine Quito. In Quito, a more total dependence on the estates is suggested since the worker relied on the rural institution for food, clothing, and sometimes shelter. In Tucumán, the workers fell into debt not for food or clothing but for luxury items, if such they could be called. Tea, *yerba mate,* knives, soap, and cloth to be used as a medium of exchange, were the principal items purchased by or advanced to workers. A typical monthly account of a laborer follows:[26]

Barrera. Barrera signed as field hand on October 1, 1722, and he makes forty-five pesos a year. He withdrew:

1 lb. of yerba and 1 lb. of soap	5 reales
½ lb. of yerba	1½ r
1 lb. of yerba	3 r
1 lb. of yerba	—
1 knife	1 pesos
1 libra of yerba	3 r
1 libra of yerba	3 r
18 reales paid to Severino	2 p. 2 r
2 pesos to Jacinto	2 p.
3 varas, ½, ¾ of canvas	5 p. 6 r
9 varas of baize	7 p. 4 r
8 varas of girdle hemp	2 p.
3 varas of coarse material	3 p.
5 varas of canvas	7 p. 4 r
3½ varas of grogram	5 p. 2 r
7 varas of girdle hemp	— (2)
1 lib. of dye	7 r
2 lb. of alum	5 r

1 lb. of soap and 1 lb. of yerba	4 r
4 varas of girdle hemp	4 r
1 lb. of yerba; another of soap	5 r
1 lb. of soap	2 r

Toward the end of the year, Barrera had received the equivalent in goods of about forty-two pesos, close to his stated salary. But of these forty-two pesos, at least thirty were in contemporary legal tender, cloth. The rest was mainly in tea and soap. Payments such as these were closer to the capitalist concept of "wages" than were payments in food and in other essentials more common to the Andean highlands.

Other employment data confirm this.[27] On one Jesuit estate in 1724–1725, the principal advances to workers were in knives, *yerba mate,* soap, shirts, belts, and cloth. On this estate, only 50 percent of the workers received advances in excess of salary after one year and almost all signed for another year's work. The annual salary scale was almost the same as on San Ignacio mentioned above, and this might be important because of its proximity to Buenos Aires. Horsebreakers received anywhere from thirty-four to fifty-six pesos depending on experience; field hands received forty-five pesos a year; general laborers received forty and foremen, sixty.

There was a sharp salary difference between rural and urban wages for peones. When the Jesuit retreat house was constructed in Buenos Aires in 1753, at least thirty-nine peones worked each at an average salary of seven pesos a month. Some skilled laborers, i.e., bricklayers and carpenters, and brickmakers, received a peso a day, and the foreman or supervisor received one peso, two *reales* per day.[28] Black slaves were leased from their owners for five *reales* a day. Each category of workers, skilled, unskilled, or foremen, labored for different periods of time throughout the year at a total salary cost of 3,028 pesos (1,196 for skilled laborers, 534 for *peones,* and 1,298 pesos for oven workers or brickmakers). Such relatively high salaries were largely due to a shortage of skilled and unskilled urban laborers. The countryside had more *peones foresteros* or "wandering journeymen" as they were called, and it might have been that these laborers were generously paid. The Jesuit Provincial Congregation of 1700 (or 1705) noted that there had been excess and extravagance in Jesuit construction prior to 1700. So when starting the building of the church attached to the College of Buenos Aires, an "Instruction of What must be Observed" specified that no *peon* was to work on civil or church holidays; they were to receive a little yerba and tobacco as well as twelve varas of baize and some canvas once a year, free of charge; the Jesuit procurator was to pay the conchabados their daily wages promptly; and supposing the wheat harvest were good, workers would receive bread and the accustomed ration.[29]

Apparently, bread, rations, and cloth were considered part of the urban laborer's total income from work. However, as noted above, this might have been an excessive reaction on the part of the Jesuits. Several years later, Manuel García, the Jesuit procurator of Buenos Aires, reminded a rector of a college that a wage of three or four *reales* a day for *peones* was an excessive wage. Even five pesos a month in goods was a little too much, but acceptable for a skilled worker. Six or seven pesos a month was the salary given only to the most skilled brickmaker. García advised his correspondent, Jerónimo Rejon, to dismiss anyone who would not sign on for five pesos in goods, the "ordinary salary," unless the *peon* had "some special skill which was needed by the estate."[30]

Lower food prices in the rural areas might have been responsible for the lower wages. One can easily calculate the buying power of a wage of forty to sixty pesos a year from the following list of basic commodity costs in the middle of the eighteenth century:

flour. . .twenty-five lbs. for four to six pesos
corn. . .twenty-five lbs. for three pesos
wheat. . .twenty-five lbs. for three pesos
cow. . .one peso per head
lamb. . .four reales per head
1 shirt. . .nine reales
baize. . .one m for four reales

In addition, the rural conchabado often had use (but not ownership) of plots of estate land on which he could grow crops for family consumption or for sale.[31] This was an important salary supplement, which when combined with a daily ration of bread and a weekly ration of meat helped to improve the quality of the laborer's diet.[32] Judging from the numerous references to rancherías constructed on estates to house the conchabados, it seems that in many cases housing was provided by the estate, reducing further the strain on the annual or monthly salary.

The scattered and spotty data for conchabados prevents the formulations of generalizations about the existence or nonexistence of conscious encouragement of debt in order to hold the worker in a form of bondage. From the partial labor records of San Ignacio and other data from Tucumán, one can conclude that some workers were bound to the estate by debt but whether through their own fault or unwillingly is not clear. Wages appear to have been appropriate to the cost of food and clothing items. But there is no proof that workers used their salaries and advances as a measure of bargaining power. Mobility, away from and back to the ranch, was present but whether the worker had originally left for work on another ranch is unknown. Nor is there evidence that employers refused to pay workers their due. What was their due? What wage criteria were used for rural labor? I am persuaded that what was loosely called the subsistence theory was the major criteria of wage determination. The wage was not determined by the nature of the labor but by the status of the laborer. What the worker needed to live appropriate to his state in life was the chief factor. As the laborer became more skilfull or professional, remuneration increased.

Due primarily to the Spanish colonists' inability to harness a sufficient Indian labor force, the conchabado or paid laborer became a key ingredient in ranch and farm production. However, on the largest of private and institutional holdings, conchabados did not constitute the stable nuclear work force. This was composed of black slave labor imported at first from Africa via Brazil. As Jesuit rural enterprises developed in the seventeenth and eighteenth centuries, investment in slave labor increased proportionately. By 1767, the year of the expulsion of Jesuits from the Spanish domains, the Society was the largest institutional slaveowner in the Tucumán and Río de la Plata regions, and probably in all of Latin America.

Slaves

On July 21, 1628, a long wagon train of thirty ox-drawn, hide-covered carts, packed with crates of oil, cloth, wax and ten boxes of books slowly made its noisy way through the city gates of Córdoba. Its human cargo was also of consequence: thirty-eight Jesuits to augment the college community, and twelve black slaves, some with the brand

⊓ on their right arm, and some with ♂
on their right breast.[33] The declared owner of goods and wagons was the Jesuit College of Córdoba.

By 1628 the use and sale of black slaves in rural and urban Tucumán had become widespread. From about 1588, Córdoba had become the distribution center of blacks brought legally and clandestinely from Brazil through the port of Buenos Aires. In Córdoba they were resold and shipped north to Potosí and Alto Peru, east to Asunción and Santa Fe, and west to Chile.[34] Between 1588 and 1610, it is estimated that

561 blacks valued at 149,195 pesos were sold in Córdoba. The average price for a slave was 262 pesos, but one hispanicized black from Angola, a skilled blacksmith, was sold for the high price of 627 pesos. Also 500 pesos were paid for one Pedro and 420 for Anton, both skilled tile makers.

The chronic shortage of Indian labor and the restrictions on using Indians imposed on settlers after Alfaro's inspection and investigation in 1611–1612 stimulated the import of black slaves, and all had a ready market. Independent agents brought slaves to Buenos Aires up to 1702, the year that the French took over the slave trade, only to be supplanted by the English South Sea Company in 1715. Between 1715 and 1726 the British company received in return for its slaves 218,242 hides, 1,081 quintals of animal fat, and 289 arrobas of *yerba mate*.[35] The company even maintained its own cattle ranch close to the port of Buenos Aires. The English company was active up to 1738 when their contract was revoked, but it was restored ten years later. By 1752 the trade had fallen into other hands. The company officially supplied 4,800 slaves a year to America but many of the contract years went by with unfilled quotas, and the number of slaves who were shipped into Buenos Aires undetected is anyone's guess. Torre Revello calculated that 22,892 slaves were brought into Buenos Aires between 1597 and 1680, and 8,600 slaves were brought by the South Sea Company to Buenos Aires between 1713 and 1738.[36] This seems low, since the period 1710–1750 was one of increased agricultural activity and developing rural enterprises.

The Jesuits in Tucumán, like their breathren in Mexico, Peru, and Brazil, participated actively in slave purchases. And many of their slaves were purchased from the English Company. Nor did they question the legitimacy of the institution of slavery. They accepted it as a fact of their environment. Contemporary views on the organic nature of society gave each strata or class a preordained role which was not to be upset by rebellion or even questioned. The two sixteenth-century Brazilian Jesuits who did speak out publicly against the evils of the institution were summarily sent packing back to Portugal, and the argument that slaves were necessary for maintaining missions and residences won the day. Besides the argument from the point of view of the organic nature of society, there was a very pragmatic reason for supporting slavery—the bureaucratic instinct for survival.[37] This motive or rationale became so ingrained in the Jesuit collective mind that in 1677 the Jesuit rector of the College of Mendoza was shocked to receive a command ordering him to sell the college slaves. "This was impossible," he remonstrated, "and also against canon law because slaves when attached to haciendas, are equivalent to landed property *(bienes raizes),* and so rectors cannot sell them unless to get rid of a troublemaker or to buy another better."[38]

The regular source of slaves for Jesuit estates in the eighteenth century was the slave market of Buenos Aires. Between 1715 and 1740, Jesuit officials purchased at least ninety-five slaves from the English Company for 200 to 250 pesos each.[39] In 1724 a letter of credit was drawn up by the Jesuit rector, Guillermo Herrán, payable to the Governors and Directors of the Royal Asiento Company in London for 12,000 pesos, a sum that could purchase fifty to sixty slaves in the Buenos Aires market.[40] Private slavers and other slaveholders, as well as illegals clandestinely shipped from Brazil, were additional sources. Colleges sometimes had funds on deposit in Buenos Aires which they used for slave purchases but what happened more frequently was that proceeds from the sale of several thousand head of college cattle were used to buy slaves.[41] From the available data it seems that the Jesuit establishments were careful to maintain a proportion between male and female. When the provincial, Jaime Aguilar, visited the ranch of San Ignacio in 1734, he suggested that the estate use 2,000 pesos it had on deposit in Buenos Aires to buy slaves, making sure that there were twelve more women than men. That same year he wrote to the College of Córdoba that: "The college and its ranches have many young female slaves that cannot marry unless males are purchased and so I order that this be done, although no more than twenty males should be purchased and distributed where there is the greater need."[42] In 1745 the provincial, Bernard Nusdorfer, told much the same to the College of Corrientes, only this time, females were lacking: "Buy female slaves so that the males can have wives. Do not give males permission to marry a freed woman."[43] The stress laid on providing either female or male partners did not arise primarily from an eagerness to have slaves "breed" but rather from a moral conviction. According to contemporary Spanish beliefs, extramarital sexual relations, encouraged by not having wives, would bring down the vengeful wrath of God in the form of earthquakes and epidemics. Unfortunately, there is little data available on the rate of slave reproduction; and there is no indication that slave "breeding" ever took place on Jesuit haciendas.[44]

Purchase was the chief mode of building up the large slave populations found on Jesuit enterprises of the eighteenth century. It seems that a spurt in slave buying occurred in the late seventeenth century and a gradual increase took place throughout the eighteenth. The three largest slaveholding colleges in the eighteenth century, Córdoba, Asunción, and Buenos Aires, began with modest slave populations in the seventeenth century. In 1648 Buenos Aires had only nine slaves in its already extensive farm, and six on Conchas.[45] A century later, the college's estates had at least 350 slaves. Increases in slave populations are shown in table 13.

Table 13. SLAVES ON MAJOR JESUIT COLLEGE FARMS AND RANCHES

	College										
Year	Córdoba	Sta. Catalina	Buenos Aires	Corrientes	Santiago del Estero	La Rioja	Salta	Santa Fe	Tucumán	Asunción	Total
1710	460	—	185	40	80	93	57	90	17	239	
1720	325	244	129	62	88	89	57	65	19	284	1362
1740	758	—	192	95	150	—	70	109	42	400	
1744	522	—	250	—	195	171	71	100	48	430	
1753	400	—	347	60	158	150	81	—	64	570	2150
1763	961	—	—	—	—	—	—	—	—	—	
1767	1043	244	381	37	326	262	(80)	(100)	121	(570)	3164

SOURCES: LCC; ARSI, Paraq. 6.

Not included in table 13 are the Colleges of Mendoza, Jujuy, or Catamarca which had modest slave populations. As is clear from the table, the overall number doubled in the eighteenth century, as much a reflection of regional as of Jesuit enterprise development. Another reason for the increase might have been the widely-held notion that in order to be free from the taint of "business," all manufacturing had to be performed by the estate's slaves rather than by hired personnel.[46] Apparently, contemporary Spanish moralists considered the slave to be part of the wider farm *familiari* in the medieval sense of a household under one roof. Hence, as the market for estate products increased, more slaves were needed.

Some of the sharpest dips in the figures occurred because of deaths due to killer epidemics. In 1718, for example, a radius of hundreds of miles around Córdoba was affected by an epidemic and the college haciendas lost at least 325 slaves. A traveler in 1719 wrote that the farms and fields were deserted.[47] The same occurred in 1744 when a killer epidemic lowered the college hacienda slave population from 758 to 522.[48]

The distribution of Jesuit slaves shows three major clusters: Córdoba, Buenos Aires, and Asunción, reflecting in fact the three major economic areas of the period. This distribution coincides with general slave distribution throughout the region. Most farms and ranches in the eighteenth century were clustered around these three major cities, so it is not surprising that Jesuit establishments were represented as well. Since slave purchase was a large capital expense, only the wealthiest of enterprises could afford them. Thirty for a household was considered a large number, so the thousands possessed collectively by the Jesuit establishments must have been a number unmatched by private or other institutional farmers and ranchers. Although at least 25,000 blacks entered Buenos Aires between 1742 and 1810 and an equally significantly large number entered during the previous half-century, many were sent on to Chile and through Córdoba to Peru.[49] However, enough remained to make a considerable impact on rural life and labor and on the city of Buenos Aires itself.[50] The 1778 census of Buenos Aires indicates that blacks composed 30 percent of the urban population.

The occupational profile for black males employed on urban and rural enterprises differed. On farms and ranches blacks were engaged in the entire range of occupations, up to estanciero and foreman. After visiting the estate of Santa Catalina in 1714, the provincial ordered the college superior to send blacks as soon as possible to the Reductions of Paraguay "to learn well how to play musical instruments, carpentry, iron working and other trades useful to the College of Córdoba."[51] At Santa Catalina the infirmarian and cooks were black slaves. Apparently, employment for the rural black female was more difficult to secure. In 1718 the College of Santa Fe had numerous female slaves of all ages who were, to use a current phrase, underemployed. The total slave population at this time was about sixty-five, and so about twenty-five females were present. The provincial decided that in order to provide more income for the college's increasing costs and to counteract "the laziness evidenced by black females," two looms for weaving cottons would be provided for the women.[52] Indians from the reductions of Paraguay would set up the entire apparatus and teach the blacks how to use them. Women slaves also performed light farmwork and housework. Females regularly spun yarn on the estates of the College of Corrientes.

The occupations of male slaves attached to the College of Belén in Buenos Aires were curiously broken down as follows according to the civil status of the slave.[53]

Married	*Bachelors*
mason (3)	*estanciero*
miller (2)	tailor and barber
oven worker (3)	mason (2)
estanciero	cook
waggoner	tile maker
cook	gardener (2)
	carpenter
	sacristan

Based on the scattered data of blacks on Jesuit enterprises, it can be said in general that a good attempt was made to teach them useful skills. This was of greater long-term benefit to enterprises because hiring skilled labor was costly. Better to train a slave who would be able to work for a longer period at far less long-term expense.

Food, clothing, and shelter were provided by the slave's owners. On Jesuit estates, weekly rations of meat, tobacco, and yerba were provided by the college's ranches. The account book for Córdoba combines expenses for slaves and paid labor but it is clear that soap, tobacco, and yerba were given to both. To supplement weekly food supplies, slaves were allowed to grow crops on plots of land given them for the purpose. The slaves of the College of Asunción (there were ninety-five in 1740) worked their plots on Saturdays and the college supplied oxen and farming implements for the vegetables, potatoes, and manioc raised. The provincial, Antonio Machoni, referred to the practice of slaves working their own plots on Saturdays as "a long-standing tradition of the college," thus casting some doubt on its existence elsewhere. Machoni wrote that the food raised by slaves themselves provided them with an adequate diet.[54] A meat ration was also furnished but not increased because the college still had too few cows. In 1745, at least, slaves on Santa Fe's estates did not cultivate their own plots. At the time of his visit, the provincial, Bernard Nusdorfer, ordered the college administration not to stop slaughtering two head of cattle (each week) for the slaves "because they have nothing else from the farm."[55]

Special food was provided when a slave became sick, usually the only remedy available on rural farms and ranches far from the city. But in 1714 apparently the slaves of the College of Santa Fe did not even receive this. They complained to the provincial, Luís de la Roca, that they did not receive the customary meat and bread when they fell ill. In his visitation "Memorial" left at his departure, de la Roca ordered that this practice be restored.[56] It is interesting to note that the slaves, at least those of this college, had the courage to bring complaints to the visiting provincial superior who had authority over the local farm or ranch administrator. The slaves knew which button to press.

Clothing slaves was an expensive proposition. One of the frequent remarks by provincials at the time of visiting estates was to improve the clothing of slaves.[57] Estate practice varied. On the ranches of Buenos Aires, slaves received new clothing each May. Some received leather britches and jackets, women ordinarily long gown-like dresses made of coarse material called *ropa de la tierra*. [58] However, material was also distributed to individuals at different times of the year, apparently in exceptional cases. The larger enterprises such as Buenos Aires, Asunción, and Córdoba had their own textile mills that helped clothe slaves. Others did not. The College of Santiago del Estero, for example, used the proceeds from its tannery and carpenter shops to pay for clothing and food for its 150 slaves in 1739. The finished leather and wood products were brought to Buenos Aires "or to some other town" for sale.[59]

Shelter for slaves took the form either of individual huts, *ranchos,* for slave families, or larger buildings called rancherías or *galpón* that provided dormitory-like living arrangements. When Nusdorfer visited the ranch of San Miguel, owned by the College of Santa Fe, he wrote: "Have the blacks construct their *ranchos* close to the *galpón* so the latter can be used as a chapel. And build *ranchos* for the resident priest and Bro. Estanciero separate from the slaves with some kind of cloister." On the other hand, the long list of precepts left by José de Aguirre in 1721 for the hacienda of Jesús María enjoined the rector "to finish the ranchería of the slaves so they can live in some comfort."[60] If one can judge from the sketches of Juan Kronfuss, and even more from the slave structures that remain on Santa Catalina and Candelaria, these buildings were solid constructions built for endurance. Santa Catalina's edifice looks more like a cell block than living quarters—strikingly similar to the slave quarters still preserved on the hacienda of Villa near Lima, Peru. Indeed, Santa Catalina's may well have served as the hacienda jail since there is space for less than fifty slaves, far fewer than the 200 to 300 the ranch possessed in the eighteenth century. If so, the original huts and flimsy slave barracks must have long since disappeared.

The doors of the slave quarters were locked at the time when the bell was rung at night bidding the college personnel to retire. The key was given to a faithful old black "who knew enough to report what happened during the night in order to avoid scandals in the ranchería."[61] But judging even from the scraps of information we have about slave life in rural Tucumán, neither slave nor master always slept comfortably.

Theft and flight were the most common crimes mentioned in Jesuit documents. In 1736 the provincial ordered the College of Córdoba to sell "all bad slaves" even if this meant removing twenty or thirty from each estate.[62] Families were not to be divided. The guilty were to be sold with wife and children. Those slaves who attempted flight from the ranches of Buenos Aires in 1745 were also to be sold with wives and children. Because of the scandal they caused in Buenos Aires and because it was thought that they might induce others to do the same, they were sold.[63] Other *bozales,* slaves born in Africa, were purchased to take their places.

Being put up for sale was probably the most extreme punishment that was inflicted on Jesuit-owned slaves. Encountering a much crueler master was always a distinct possibility. However, it is difficult to imagine more inhumane punishments than those outlined by the Jesuit provincial, Joseph de la Barreda, in 1687.[64] Hacienda officials and others in charge of slaves had been guilty of the most severe viciousness bordering on sadism. Under pain of mortal sin, the direst threat in the Catholic book of intimidations, no slave was to be hung by his wrists so his feet did not touch the ground. For ordinary misdemeanors a slave was to receive twenty-five lashes, seventy for serious offenses. If fifty or more were to be administered, an interval of two or three days would occur. "If the depravity of the slave required that he be kept in a cellar or cell, he should spend no more than eight days there." They were not to be starved but given food, water, and bread. The whip used in giving lashes was not to be of knotted leather so that only a few strokes produced blood or even ripped off pieces of flesh. Suffice it to say that it caused some pain. And never was there to be administered the beastly punishment of dropping melted candle wax on a victim's skin.

The catalogue of punishments says as much about the master-slave relationship in Tucumán as it does about mitigating the harshest of the punishments used by slaveowners. The relationship was based on fear, the fear of physical violence. The Jesuit provincial did not forbid the use of physical violence on Jesuit-owned slaves. Slaves could be hung up, but their feet had to touch the ground. Twenty-five to seventy lashes were allowed. Slaves were punished in the solitary confinement of cellars and cells, but for fewer than eight days. And the instruments of punishment were moderated. Rather than risk killing incorrigible slaves, wrote the provincial, they should be sold. He was concerned lest "by our own cruelty we disregard the laws of charity which we ourselves preach."[65] Physical punishment itself was not at issue. It was its misuse that concerned the Jesuit superior.

However, there are indications that slaves on Jesuit enterprises enjoyed a modicum of unrestricted movement. Slaves from the ranches of the College of Buenos Aires were allowed to enter the city, visit drinking emporia called *pulperías,* and earn enough money to purchase their freedom. One slave, Juan Prado, redeemed his six-year-old son from his owner, Hilario Molina, for seventy pesos, the sum paid by working for Molina nine months at eight pesos a month.[66] Gabriel Jacinto, son of Catalina (an Indian) and Andrés (a black slave), was freed by royal order on May 22, 1697. And there are other examples of manumission and references to freed blacks, some engaged in criminal activity. Freedom, however, brought with it another type of bondage. Rejected because of caste and color, thwarted by ingrained prejudice, most freed blacks chose life on the fringes of society, becoming marginal types outside the mainstream of colonial life.[67]

Labor Costs

Several economic and demographic factors affected the use of slave and conchabado labor. Comparative cost was one; another was the simple availability of Indian laborers. During the eighteenth century, slaves in the Buenos Aires area could be purchased for around 250 to 300 pesos each, and for slightly higher if they possessed a marketable skill. The owner then had to provide food, clothing, and shelter. Judging from the cost of maintaining black slaves on the College of Córdoba farms, ten to fifteen pesos per year were spent on each slave's food and clothing. More specifically, fifty cows per year were slaughtered for a slave population of 130 around the year 1715. Clothing for female slaves cost about 550 pesos per year for about eighty slaves, or roughly six pesos each. It was around the same for men. This comes very roughly to ten to fifteen pesos each year.[68] However, there were additional expenses for slaves, namely for tobacco, soap, and *yerba mate,* whose yearly costs are impossible to determine. The account book that records these items ascribes them to both slaves and conchabados with no way of telling how much was used by each. The cost of a slave bunkhouse with room for 100 to 150 was about 1,500 pesos. Individual huts could be assembled for fifty pesos or less. Thus, the total cost of a slave laborer over a ten-year period, initial price and maintenance included, was around 700 to 800 pesos.

On the other hand, the Indian salaried laborer's minimum cost over a ten-year period was 400 pesos, with the more skilled workers costing 600 to 1,000 pesos. Thus, on the basis of comparable cost, the slave was not preferable. Why then were they purchased especially by large-scale ranchers and farmers? The major factors were the reliability and stability of the slave laborer. The slave owner knew that he would have a certain number of workers for the next roundup or harvest. He was not that certain about conchabados who contracted on a yearly basis. Thus, he could project production and profits more easily than the rancher, who depended solely on hired labor which was scarce to being with. Besides, the Jesuit colleges may have had an additional reason for slave purchasing since goods made by unpaid (family) farm

107

labor could be sold for a profit; whereas sale of goods produced by paid labor smacked of buying and selling, prohibited to ecclesiastics by canon law (see Appendix A, numbers 9 and 11).

The Jesuit estates owned by the College of Córdoba invested heavily in slave labor (see table 13). By 1767 the capital value of the slave population was about 250,000 pesos. The gradual increase in number was due to a conscious decision to rely on slave and not salaried labor. It seems that the salaried labor was used to supplement slave labor with work in the lime pit and factory, and ranch and farmwork at high activity times of the year. Costs of slaves and conchabados in specific years on the College of Córdoba complex are given in table 14.

Table 14. Labor Costs of the College of Córdoba

Year	Conchabados	Slaves/Conchabados	Total
1711	453	942	1395
1712	838	1417	2255
1713	973	662	1635
1714	592	782	1374
1715	937	711	1648
1716	556	530	1086

SOURCE: LCC

As indicated above, it is impossible to determine the proportion of each under the category Slave/Conchabados in the college account book. Therefore, college disbursements to conchabados as given in table 15 must be revised upwards, and what is said below about labor costs must be understood as approximations.

It should be kept in mind that the costs listed in tables 14 and 15 were only for the college compound and the closely associated lime pit and orchards. They do not include the major establishments of Jesús María, Altagracia, and Candelaria. Nor, of course, was the ranch of Santa Catalina included. But each of these enterprises had relatively high slave populations, so general conclusions might hold for them as well.

In listing labor costs, the college account book gives five worker categories: slaves, conchabados, *gente de servicio, peones,* and young Indians and blacks not under contract *(indios y negritos que no tienen conchavo).* In practice, *peones, gente de servicio,* and conchabados were more or less the same, that is, paid laborers. However, it seems that the term *peones* was used when only one or two days of unskilled labor was involved, or to designate those driving mules from Córdoba

Table 15. THE COLLEGE OF CORDOBA DISBURSEMENTS TO CONCHABADOS

Year	Sum (pesos)	Year	Sum
1711	453	1736	600
1712	838	1737	510
1713	973	1739	450
1714	592	1740	450
1715	937	1741	500
1716	556	1745	465
1721	894	1746-1747	1,187
1723	1,000a	1748	585
1724	400	1748	425c
1725	410b	1749	650d
1726	800	1750	221
1727	700	1759	238
1729	998	1760	500
1730	856	1760	656e
1731	669	1761	578
1732-1733	1,372	1762	650

SOURCE: LCC
ᵃfor conchabados, lime, and bricks
ᵇ400 to conchabados, 10p to peones
ᶜcost of 18 peones and foreman on mule drive to Salta
ᵈcost of 18 peones and foreman on mule drive to Salta
ᵉcost of clothing workers in 1760

to Salta. However, the term "worker, hired by the day" *(conchabado, por días)* is also very frequent, as is the term *"conchavo de 18 peones para la tropa").* In the latter case, *conchabar* and *peón* are used interchangeably. There is also the curious term: *conchabados de la ranchería* that seems to say that hired workers lived in a bunkhouse on the college property. This could well have been true since there does not seem to have been more than ten to twenty salaried workers employed at one time. *Gente de servicio* was a general category embracing anyone who worked in a nonadministrative or managerial capacity. This usually meant paid laborers, foremen, and skilled laborers, but sometimes slaves were included. Those in the category "young Indians and blacks who are not under contract" were given clothing materials several times a year. Included in this category were probably children of freed black and Indian conchabados. Costs for them reached 150 to 200 pesos a year.

It seems, then, that given the total labor costs in tables 14 and 15, to which must be added the additional expenditures for *peones,* children of conchabados, constructions for shelter, and miscellaneous items, 2,000 pesos per year for labor costs does not seem exhorbitant. This means that roughly 10 percent of total college expenses went for labor. Since the income and expense figures upon which this percentage is based were calculated from farm and ranch products of all college properties, it is clear that total labor costs that included all college ranches and farms would be considerably higher, perhaps 30 to 35 percent of all expenses. When one adds the original cost of slaves, it becomes evident that the single largest expense of the agro-pastoral enterprises was for labor.

Criticism and Rationale

The results of the personal service controversy of the early 1600s severely limited the availability of Indian laborers. Because black slaves were not cheap, contention arose among Spaniards for the right to use and exploit the native labor that was available. One suspects that this Spanish rivalry over the spoils of conquest lay behind some of the criticism directed against Jesuit enterprises in Asunción and Santa Fe in the seventeenth century. Spanish farmers resented what they perceived to be unlimited labor resources available in the Jesuit reductions of Paraguay. Many of these complaints found their way to Rome and the Jesuit superior general. They came back to Paraguay and Tucumán in the form of admonitory letters cautioning the Jesuits about their role vis-á-vis Indian labor.

In 1696 Tirso Gonzalez wrote that: "the Jesuits were quick to exempt Indians from work when the labor was for someone else but it is another matter when the labor is for them. It has been repeatedly brought to my attention that the Jesuits in colleges and in the reductions live in spacious, comfortable dwellings and the Indians live closeby in hovels."[69] A few years before, Gonzalez had reproved the Jesuits of Asunción for conscripting fifty or sixty reduction Indians to work on the church and paying them four varas of cotton cloth a month. The College of Buenos Aires had "impressed" the Indians who came down annually to sell yerba, making them work on the church tower to the detriment of their own fields. In 1696 Gonzalez, writing again from Rome, roundly forbid the use of Indians for construction work in colleges whether they received a salary or not.[70] Needless to say, this order was totally ignored. The scarcity of labor was too great as the few above examples eloquently testify. In 1707 another superior general, Miguel Angel Tamborini, repeated the same criticism, forbidding the colleges to use Indians for personal service, and above all taking Indians against their will out of their native towns to work elsewhere.

Perhaps worst of all, and more embarrassing, was the repeated censure of Jesuit treatment of their slaves and Indian workers. In the early 1630s Francisco Vásquez Trujillo, provincial of the Jesuits in Paraguay, wrote of "the very great excesses exhibited by lay brothers on haciendas in punishing workers with their own hands, verbally castigating them; and I am even told that they abused female slaves . . ." Vasquez went on to forbid this and to order that any father or brother guilty of punishing female slaves by his own hand should be whipped in public in the dining room before the assembled Jesuit community.[71] Similar orders were issued in 1637 and 1644. In 1707 and 1722, excessive punishments to Indian workers were the subject of letters from Rome—excessive number of stripes, cutting an Indian's hair because it did not look nice to Europeans, putting Indians in tiny ranch jails and stocks with so little food that some died and others came out permanently afflicted. In 1722 Tamburini concluded his grotesque litany to the provincial with: "By the blood of Jesus Christ, I command that if this is true, withdraw immediately those responsible . . ."[72] Perhaps not without some justification was the Indian Cacique Serrano warned by other Indians not to live in a Jesuit town "because he would become a slave of the fathers and would no longer be allowed to see Spaniards."[73] The Jesuit superior flatly denied this claim that Indians were forced to work; they did so freely and those that did work contracted as conchabados. They were also allowed complete contact with Spaniards "except when it came to liquor."[74]

On the other hand, it seems that workers on the estates of the College of Santa Fe were treated far less oppressively, almost to the point of managerial irresponsibility. The provincial, José de Aguirre, had to insist that a certain rigor be applied to correct the continued misconduct of the workers. "The workers," he thought, "had come to recognize the ease with which they had been treated."[75] There must have been some variation from estate to estate in the way workers were treated, but one does get the sense that the harsher period was during the seventeenth century. Perhaps the declining number of available Indian workers helped to mitigate the treatment given them.

As mentioned above, Jesuits in Tucumán and the Río de la Plata in the eighteenth century did not bother themselves with the question of the justice of the institution of slavery. It was a given, but perhaps it should not have been. The two Jesuit authors who most influenced Jesuit acceptance of the institution were Luís de Molina and Alonso de

Sandoval. Molina's carefully-worded conclusions about the slave trade and slavery would allow the institution to continue as long as slaves were acquired by just title. But deep in Molina's thirty-fifth disputation, conveniently overlooked by many of his contemporaries, was the remarkable conclusion that most blacks were "kidnapped" from Africa.[76] Nevertheless, Alonso de Sandoval—the predecessor of the Saint of the Slaves, Pedro Claver, and author of the monumental treatise on blacks, *De Instauranda Aethiopum Salute*—thought that all blacks were slaves of their kings in Africa, were victims of God's punishment, and were brought to America by traders in good faith. By invoking an almost divine origin of slavery, the punishment of God, Sandoval was echoing Augustine who not only thought that the institution of slavery could be good for a man, but that it was God's punishment upon mankind for the sin of Adam.[77]

Sandoval waged a heroic and relentless battle to improve the physical condition of the black slave, but he was silent on the structural injustice of the institution itself. It seems not to have occurred to Sandoval that the institution of slavery itself was evil and corruptive of persons, nor did there seem to have been any contradiction for him between the gospel of Christ and the brutality of slavery.[78] Sandoval, like Aristotle, seemed to say that God had created "slaves by nature," who by some quirk of fortune were destined to serve the white man. God had originally created all men equal, but over time the blacks, like George Orwell's farm animals, became less equal. The task of the priest, wrote Sandoval, was to bring about the "spiritual freedom of their souls," with the body remaining enslaved. "To baptize him, hear his confession, and give him the last rites," are the major and only obligation of the priest to slaves.[79] Sandoval apparently espoused the old notion that the good man is never really a slave, only the bad who is in bondage to his own lusts—a wonderfully comforting idea for slaveowners but of greater assistance in the endurance of liberty than of slavery.[80]

One must conclude that Sandoval and his Jesuit brethren saw slaves as integral parts of society, required for the smooth function of the economic order. Given the dynamic role of the Jesuits in seventeenth-century educational organization and their relentless struggle for Indian rights, one would have expected a growing uneasiness with the institution of slavery. It might have existed but no record of it has survived. Apparently, the perceived need to open and maintain colleges with the sole support from agro-pastoral enterprises that depended on slave labor persuaded the Jesuits of slavery's legitimacy. It is an excellent example of social reality becoming appropriate and thus moral, and a possible instance of bureaucratic self preservation brought to its most alarming extreme.

Labor, whether salaried or slave, was expensive. The *peón* and conchabado had to be paid from farm earnings and it is not at all clear how much rural enterprises grossed annually. If indeed the large ranch or farm spent 20 to 30 percent of its income on labor, as did the Jesuit estates, then we have a good indication why most ranches and farms in the northern pampas were modest in size and operation. Labor costs acted as a leveling mechanism within Spanish rural society. Laymen could and did hire workers and purchase slaves, but nowhere near the massive scale of the religious institution. The organization and utilization of human resources was just one dimension of estate operation. It was closely linked to the economic performance of the total enterprise complex. The flow of cash, credit, goods, and receivables between and among college, estate, and local supportive enterprises demonstrates the complexity of the rural economic organization.

CHAPTER 6

Finance

In 1620, still the early years of the Jesuit presence in Tucumán, the province financial report stated quite laconically that once the college was out of debt, its two haciendas, Jesús María and Caroya, could easily support sixty subjects, for they provided 2,500 pesos annually.[1] Almost 150 years later the college's landholdings, cattle investments, associated farms, and over 1,000 black slaves constituted the most expansive and economically powerful agro-pastoral combine in the region. The size of the holdings of the Jesuit Colleges of Santa Fe, Buenos Aires, and Asunción followed close behind. The college holdings (to say nothing of the Paraguay reductions) required careful financial management, coordination, and sometimes cooperation. A major factor in this activity was a standardized information system upon which decisions were made. The accounting system had to be reasonably precise and accurate in order to insure that sound economic decisions were made.

Accounting Methods

The Jesuit rules of 1553–1554 provided for a business manager for each college and house. He was called a *procurador,* a Latin derivative meaning one who provides or cares for another, a steward or a manager of business affairs. The Jesuit procurador had to "provide the college with all temporal goods, to receive income, money and goods that came to the college." All of these revenues and proceeds were to be recorded in ledgers.[2]

The accounting methods used by Jesuit colleges and enterprises in Tucumán followed roughly the same procedures employed in Peru and Quito. Each ranch or farm attached to a college kept its own journal and ledger; these were usually called *Libros de Estancias*. The transactions on the ranch or farm (or in a textile mill) were recorded as they occurred, in a work book, and they were transferred monthly into the general ledger or estate book. In the estate book were listed revenues, mainly in the form of values of farm products, merchandise, and services produced, and expenses, principally in the form of receipts for supplies and foods from the college. Every four or five years, the provincial superior would visit the farm or ranch, examine the account books and bring them up to date. Revenue would be balanced with expenses for the period since the last visit and the result recorded and initialled by provincial and business manager. At the same time an inventory of estate assets, cash, and collectables was made, all of which could be compared with the inventory and summary account made at the time of the next visit.

An unusual feature of these estate books is the nature of their entries. They are intelligible only when one realizes that the ranch or farm existed solely for the maintenance of the college. Instead of thinking in terms of *revenue* and *expenditure,* one should rather think of "goods sent to the college" and "supplies acquired from the college." That is, the ranch of Candelaria could show an enormous disproportion of cost over revenue, yet be fulfilling its role perfectly and profitably within the Córdoba complex of ranches, farms, and college. For example, the Candelaria estate book recorded the following estate products sent to the college for which no revenue was received and so was put on the *"Datta"* or expense side:

May 1755

120 head of cattle at 2 pesos a head sent to college	240 pesos
20 arrobas of tallow at 10 reales an arroba	24
11 arrobas of animal fat at 2 pesos an arroba	22
692 sheep for the college	346
9 arrobas of tallow sent to the college at 10 reales an arroba	12
1 bolt of coarse woolen material	20
Total	664

Each of the above items was assigned a value according to current prices, but the estate did not receive this price. The college did when or if the goods were sold on the open market. Some of them were; on the other hand, the ranch or estate consumed much of its own produce and also had goods sent to them from the college warehouse, called the *almacén*. The following entry illustrates how supplying the college was recorded.[3]

August 1718

28 head of cattle for meat rations and one fanega of flour for the house	64 pesos
1 jar of wine for the house	10
1 bale of yerba mate and an arroba of tobacco for the workers	12
1 leather jacket for the majordomo	3
6 varas of baize for the majordomo	6
Total	95

The goods listed above, along with other supplies of knives, tools, cloth, candles, construction materials, and whatever could not be made on the estate were sent from the college or purchased elsewhere. Goods thus received were placed under "expenses" as they should have been but often the category under which they were recorded was "Recibo." To say the least this was ambiguous because *recibo* was ordinarily used to describe revenue or cash earnings for products or merchandise sold. As the following statement, made at the time of the inspection of the books, shows, *recibo* was etymologically correct but misleading in an accounting report.

I, Fr. Jaime Aguilar, visiting this ranch of Candelaria on June 24, 1736, find that since the last visit, May 15, 1734, this ranch has given the college 10,804 pesos, and the ranch has received from the college 3,467 pesos. The deficit of the ranch is 7,336 pesos all of which is evident from the *Libro del Hermano Procurador,* here consulted to the satisfaction of both parties.

Recibo   3,467
Datta   10,804[4]

What was received from the college, listed as *recibo,* did not form part of the total annual expenses. Candelaria, with a black slave force of 192 in 1765, plus administrators and occasional laborers, supported well over 200 people.[5] Cattle for meat, clothing material for workers and salaries cost about 20,862 pesos yearly. At least 700 head were consumed annually for meat, thirty *fanegas* of wheat, and bolts of cloth, besides tobacco and *yerba mate.* More will be said below about income from Candelaria. Suffice it to point out here that the estate books must be used with caution when assessing the profitability of an enterprise.

Just as each ranch enterprise kept its own books, so too the owner institution maintained a general ledger in which was incorporated all financial statements, debits, credits, and transactions with its associated enterprises and others outside. The general ledger of the College of Córdoba, upon which is based a great deal of what is said in this book, is a testimonial to accounting procedures in vogue in the seventeenth and eighteenth centuries. It is at once simple in its complexity because the ledger recorded complex commercial transactions with local merchants, with the college's own enterprises, and with distant markets. The ledger is titled: *Libro de cuentas de este Collegio de Córdoba de la Compañía de Jesús, Provincia del Paraguay desde 1 de mayo de 1711. Primera parte del recibo, segunda parte del gasto.*[6] The first 123 folio pages record the income (*entradas*), the remaining the expenditures (*gasto*). Between 1711 and 1720 income was listed by the month with no reference to source. One can presume that before 1711 it was the same. After 1720 income was listed by enterprise. This structuring of categories was probably part of a general improvement in bookkeeping procedures, urged by the Jesuit superior general in 1716 and demanded by the local provincial superior in 1720. In 1716 the superior in Rome, Miguel Angel Tamborini, criticized the local provincial for not following traditional procedures in signing account books and in 1720 the provincial, Joseph de Aguirre, noted in the general ledger of the College of Córdoba that the account book had too many errors and was characterized by "widespread confusion."[7] Entries were listed with no source, debts were not listed as paid when they became so, revenues were duplicated, no income was recorded from houses owned by the college in Potosí, and to top it all, the college accountant listed 14,000 pesos in debts as "uncollectable." "Why?" the provincial wanted to know. All of this was labeled "sloppy bookkeeping."

After 1720 revenues were entered by sources, the bulk coming from the college's farms and ranches. Expenditures were also recorded by the enterprise to which they were sent or by appropriate college departments. What did not fit structured categories was put into the equivalent of a miscellaneous category. The following expenses are for November 1728 and are here given as a typical monthly expense list.

November (1728)[8]

Clothes Room	93	varas of trowser cloth; 5 arrobas of *coperas;* 4 arrobas of soap	120
	25	varas of black linen; 6 ounces of silk; 8 varas of woolen	46

	2	varas of baize; 6 leather jackets; 2 lbs. of thread; 2 varas of linen	13
	2	varas of *cambulo*; 7 varas of linen; 3 of woolen	12
Pantry	81	cattle; 119 sheep; 5 cheeses	324
	6	jars of wine; 6 lbs. sugar; 13 pesos worth of eggs; 8 sheep	76
	12½	arrobas of figs; 8 pesos chickens; 5 arrobas of raisins; 4 fanegas corn	60
	3	fanegas peppers; 1½ fanegas salt; 1 fanega barley; 1 fanega wheat	28
	12	pesos biscuit; 12 lbs. sugar; 6 oz. pepper	15
		Ream of paper for Bro. Librarian; 30 pesos 2 reales wood	34
	7	arrobas yerba; 3 lbs. snuff; 3 arrobas sugar to friar	32
	5	varas of baize; 5 varas linen; ¾ vara of cloth for a slave	13
	40	varas of cloth for slaves; and 8 arrobas of yerba, 1½ arrobas of tobacco as rations	54
	6	lbs. of snuff; 4 arrobas of tallow for lamps	28
Sacristy	1	arroba of wax at 10 reales	31
Jesús María	7½	arrobas of yerba; 1 arroba tobacco; 2 fanegas lime; 18 hoes	41
	2	arrobas yerba; ½ arroba tobacco; 2 lbs. snuff	9
Altagracia		tobacco; wine; 38 arrobas wool; pair wooden wheels	82
	54	pesos in *mares*; paper	54
Candelaria	89	varas cloth; 1½ arrobas sugar; 12 knives; 3 lbs. snuff	102
	8	arrobas yerba; 2 arrobas tobacco; 2 varas cloth	36
	4	pair_____; paper	

20	fanegas flour; 10 head of	
	cattle in Calera	160
Luís de la Roca		Manuel Gonzalez

It is clear that the college acted as a broker or supply center for its farms and ranches. Goods from Jesús María were stored in the warehouse and transhipped to other destinations. Mission products, such as yerba and tobacco, were purchased by the college and redistributed, and items were purchased from (or exchanged with) other regions and sent to the college's ranches or farms. The general ledger recorded all of these transactions and informed the college business manager of the monthly financial state. There is evidence that a general budget figure was fixed at the beginning of the year and periodic assessments were made measuring expenditures against anticipated income.

These assessments took place when the books were closed, not at the end of a fiscal year, but every three years or so at the time of the inspection of account books by the provincial superior and college business manager. A summary inventory of college goods was also made, with debts and receivables noted. The assessment in 1736 was as follows:

I, Fr. Jaime Aguilar, inspecting the books of the Procuradoría of the College of Córdoba on April 30, 1736, find that since the last inspection on December 1, 1734, the expenditure has been 34,964 pesos, 1½ reales, and the income has been 27,872 pesos, 7½ reales. Expenditures exceed income by 7,091 pesos, 2 reales.

Gasto	34,964 pesos 1½ reales
Entrada	27,872 pesos 7½ reales
Alcance	7,091 pesos 2 reales expenditures exceed income

State of the College
The college has 200 slaves, 240 oxen, 240 sheep and goats in Calera, 2 wagons, 4 new carts. In the wintering grounds of Salta the college has 1,500 mules; and in the grazing lands of Candelaria about 1,500 mules.

Debts
The college owes:
to Monastery of Nuns of Santa Catalina of Córdoba
    4,475 pesos with an annual interest of 5 percent   4,475

to office of Missions of Santa Fe	4,500
to Domingo Basavilbasso	1,800
to office of Missions of Buenos Aires	2,000
to the Cathedral Chapter (tithes?)	406
	13,181

Owed to the college:

office of the province for food sent to the novitiate up to end of April of this year	4,400
by Superior of Missions 495 arrobas of yerba as payment for clothes material sent from college mill at 4 pesos	1,980
Inventory and receivables	3,411
	9,791

(signed)   Jaime Aguilar[9]

These periodic inspections were essential for the smooth functioning of the college, for the financial well-being of the enterprises, and for pinpointing weaknesses in the income supply. They hold the majordomos and administrators accountable and permitted the provincial to make rational economic decisions based on first-hand knowledge.

Another important mechanism of accountability was the periodic *entrega,* or handing over of the goods in the college storehouse from a business manager to his successor. This was also a rendering of accounts, of a sort, a "discharge" of office in the medieval accounting sense. With the goods in the storehouse went the cash on hand, in silver, kept in the locked safe or *caja.* Receivables were also listed. Every single item in the storehouse was listed in the general ledger at the time of the *entrega,* along with its current value. Cloth, thread, tools, paper, nonperishable foods, tobacco, yerba, and snuff, were only part of the catalogue of items.[10] Such a list enabled the incoming business manager to know exactly what cash and goods, outstanding debts, and receivables were on hand.

Every three years the college would send to the provincial superior's office a summary of the economic state of the college and its estates. This information was combined with similar information from other colleges to form the *Catalogus Tertius* or economic report of the province. The accounting methods reveal an economic style, an attitude toward the enterprises that furnished the base upon which was constructed the local educational institution. They reveal something about the business of agriculture.

120

Revenue and Expenses: Córdoba

Through the seventeenth century the income of the College of Córdoba kept pace with increasing expenses. The economic reports of the 1620s stated that when the farm and ranch provided the cows, livestock, wheat, corn, and wine, supplies exceeded needs. In 1623 no income was recorded, only food supplies valued at 1,500 pesos for regular college consumption. The college owed nothing, not even for the fifty slaves it possessed. By 1651 the college's economic activities had so developed that the 250 slaves it had were deemed "insufficient for the work to be done."[11] The annual income was 14,000 pesos. A clear indicator of even further development throughout the century was the increase of the slave population. It grew from 300 in 1686 to 455 in 1692 to 460 in 1710. As we will see below, the number of slaves working on just Córdoba college estates in 1767, the year of the expulsion of the Jesuits from Latin America, exceeded 1,000.

Although the finances of the Province of Paraguay dropped slightly between 1689 and 1700 due to a combination of poor crops in Tucumán and a drop in the mine production of Peru, the major province market, they recovered and picked up momentum in the eighteenth century.[12] From around 1720 on, a great deal of monumental Jesuit construction took place, especially in Córdoba and Buenos Aires. This was the result of successful and increased economic activity.

The major income producers for the College of Córdoba were mules, livestock, dairy products, textiles, and the yerba trade. Less income was provided by real estate in Potosí, while much if not most of the farm products were consumed by the college inmates. Clothing, kitchen, construction, salaries for workers, estate subsidies and general miscellaneous items constituted the major expenses. By the late 1660s these income producers accounted for an annual income of about 20,000 pesos. The college had no debts to speak of and a handsome sum of 32,678 pesos on hand. However, due to a number of factors, within two decades this healthy financial situation was reversed. In 1686 a debt of 12,000 pesos was current; the following year a cattle epidemic depleted stocks; and in 1697 epidemic disease reduced the sheep flock from 18,000 to 5,000; so by the end of the century the financial affairs were considered only fair. Córdoba "no es tan sobrado," said the annual report; "not quite on top of things," we would say today.[13]

While the annual college income jumped from 9,000 pesos in 1644 to 14,000 in 1660 and to about 20,000 in 1700, expenses kept abreast throughout most of the eighteenth century as table 16 shows.

Table 16. THE COLLEGE OF CÓRDOBA'S INCOME AND EXPENSES, 1711–1760

Years	Income	Expenses
1711–1713	48,817	48,817
1713–1718	124,149	122,043
1718–1719	26,582	25,353
1718–1720	45,303	44,959
1720–1721	51,347	43,801
1721–1723	41,235	38,015
1723–1724	40,246	36,507
1724–1726	64,601	56,204
1726–1728	61,052	51,862
1728–1731	73,339	54,562
1731–1734	70,690	81,170
1734–1736	27,872	34,964
1736–1740	59,370	77,651
1740–1742	45,118	43,297
1742–1743	20,846	22,132
1742–1745	78,413	79,754
1745–1748	68,915	63,617
1748–1750	105,662	96,631
1750–1754	100,488	96,844
1754–1760	155,520	140,192
TOTAL	1,315,565	1,258,375

SOURCE: LCC

The average annual income between 1711 and 1731 was 28,833 pesos while expenses were 26,106 pesos. Between 1731 and 1760 income dropped to 25,479 pesos annually while expenses remained near the prior twenty-year average, at 25,388 pesos. As mentioned above, the single largest income producer was the annual sale of mules which accounted for anywhere between 20 to 50 percent of the yearly income. Textiles from the mills in Altagracia and in the college compound were used mainly to clothe workers. Cattle was used both as an income producer and for college consumption. Dairy and cattle products such as tallow and animal fats were frequently sold in order to generate income needed for purchase of items not produced on the farms or ranches, such as fish, tools, and other types of manufactured goods. The general storehouse was stocked with estate goods that were frequently used for salary payments or sold monthly for silver. The monthly selling of some storehouse items was called the *permuta*. For example, in March 1719 the *permuta* took place. Goods were sold in order that a large quantity of wheat could be purchased for college consumption.

Excluding the income from mules, monthly revenues were made up chiefly from lesser-valued items. Cattle shipped from Altagracia or Candelaria to the college (fifty to seventy-five head a month) was put into the credit side of the ledger.[14] Renting workers to other ranches or farms was done occasionally, for a modest sum. *Yerba mate* from the reductions of Paraguay was also a healthy income producer for the College of Córdoba. More will be said about this below because it belongs more properly under the heading of trade with Chile, Lima, and Potosí. Suffice it to say that income from yerba sales varied. In March 1736, 6,637 pesos was collected from Chile; in August, 1723, 1,210 pesos was received for yerba sold to Don Pedro Bustamente; and in March, 1746, 4,000 pesos were realized from sales in Chile. Frequently listed under general miscellaneous income was the category *"li-mosnas"* or alms, usually in the form of yerba or cloth from the Paraguay missions or Santa Fe. Such alms from other Jesuit institutions appear regularly in the Córdoba account book. It seems unlikely that the largest of educational institutions having the most productive complex of ranches and farms would go hat in hand begging for alms from less financially stable houses. Apparently that is what they did. The only justification for this that comes to mind is that the alms was an unofficial tax levied on other houses to defray the expenses in educating young Jesuit seminarians. Since they were later to be assigned to the different province houses and works, it would have been considered appropriate that these houses contribute toward their philosophy and theology studies. Indeed, it seems that in the eighteenth century (at least in the 1720s), the rector superior of the College considered it a major role to seek alms personally from other Jesuit houses. In 1732 during a particularly difficult financial period, the Jesuit superior general in Rome, Francis Retz, was not surprised that the college had debts totaling over 1,000 pesos. He thought they should be higher, given the poor quality of administrators assigned to the college's ranches and farms. And he added: "If the rector spends all of his time collecting alms from the mission reductions, then surely what can prudently be expected but the decline and total ruin of the college."[15] But if he did spend as much time as alleged, the minimal results do not seem to have justified the effort.

Although not a specific item generating income, the "cash on hand and current assets" item, called the *alcance,* was an important factor in each accounting period. The assets were often turned into cash or carried over into the next fiscal period. Debts were often measured against the *alcance* which steadily increased until it was no longer referred to as the *alcance* but merged with inventory and receivables around 1740. This *alcance* is not to be confused with the college community miscellaneous fund, kept in the safe mentioned above. One is tempted to use the term "petty cash" fund, only it was not so petty. In

1760 over 9,000 pesos in silver was in the fund and from it was period-ically drawn cash to pay for black slaves. Other major expenses were sometimes paid from this source.

However, most expenses and expenditures incurred by the college were listed in the general ledger. They were chiefly for salaries and supplies for workers, food and supplies for college inmates, construc-tion, and support of the college ranches and farms. With a few excep-tions, each expense item was relatively small, but goods were often purchased monthly in quantity (e.g., twenty-four *fanegas* of flour at six pesos a *fanega*), and these might be called fixed monthly costs that were substantial. Chief among the fixed, major annual costs was 900–1,500 pesos for shipping the mules to Salta. Sixteen *peones* cost 640 pesos a trip, and 260 pesos were needed for just the foreman and his assistant. Such a premium was put on honest muleteers. Wintering costs, of course, were extra. Paid conchabado labor, examined in Chapter 5, was 800–900 pesos annually, and at least forty to sixty pesos a month were spent on supplies of soap and cloth for black slaves and paid laborers. These were the highest expense items. Among the least expensive items were the guitar strings purchased for a peso or two needed "for the music." Apparently the strings for the church or ranch musicians were broken or replaced fairly regularly, for they appear frequently in the general ledger: "cuerdas para la música."

It was only in 1717 that categories were initiated in the general ledger indicating how expenses were divided. The kitchen (*cocina*) in-corporated food expenditures; the clothes room (*ropería*), different kinds of cloth and clothing material; the church (*iglesia*) needed regu-lar supplies of wax, church ornaments, and oil; construction (*obra*) was periodic but costly, requiring lime, tools, and workers' supplies; farms and ranches (*estancias*) needed regular supplies of a variety of items; and all else went into a miscellaneous (*general*) line item. The line item under kitchen included only food items, either purchased from other estates or on the general market. Flour for bread and beef cattle were considered staples. Irregularly purchased were figs, fish, wine, and vegetables (4,000 onions were bought in 1717 for eighty pesos). After 1730 general expenses were listed with kitchen items. So paper and library supplies, salaries and clothes for workers, and even shovels and tools were listed. The clothes room required regular sup-plies of soap, and of course, materials for repair and making of cloth-ing. Construction was in one sense an irregular line item, but the Calera that supplied lime for bricks and the ovens for firing were in continual operation for maintenance, and repair was constant. The large college estates of Altagracia, Jesús María, and Candelaria were also considered major expense items. The average monthly expenses of the college in the eighteenth century were around 1,500 pesos with extremes ranging from 1,000 to 6,368 (in 1717). During most months, however, it hovered between 1,500 and 2,000, and a good part of this regularly went to the maintenance of the three large ranch/farm/mill complexes.

To take the year 1749 as an example (a typical year in the sense that general community and college expenses as well as estate and clothes room expenses were average), expenditures were divided among general college and community expenses, sacristy, clothes room, and estates. The proportion of expenditures is shown in Figure 5.

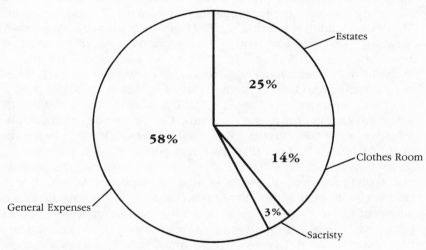

Figure 5. College expenditures in 1749

Included in the general expenses were the monthly supply of beef cattle and flour; also 4,925 pesos in *censos* (mortgage) payments and 1,204 pesos in debt payments. Wages for conchabados, kitchen supplies, mule purchases, and tithes were also listed. The clothes room spent over 1,000 pesos for flour and corn, presumably for workers. The estates column included 800 pesos for *censos* and 150 pesos for conchabado's wages. I include this only to point out that by 1749 each college division had its own set of priorities to fulfill, whether wages, food, clothes, or general supplies. And there is not too much difference in amounts expended by these categories from 1725 to 1760. The absolute sums increase slightly after 1750 but the proportion remained just about the same. The only exception was the category of "estates," whose expenditures decreased slightly, but apparently some of these were shifted to other categories.

At the turn of the century, 1695–1700, the college enterprises of Altagracia and Jesús María accounted for about 14,000 pesos of the annual income.[16] This came mainly from cloth produced in the mill of Altagracia; cattle, mules, and sheep sold from Candelaria, (then considered a range of Altagracia); and wine and farm products raised on Jesús María. The college for its part supplied the estates with around 7,000 pesos a year in the form of supplies and silver coin which were destined for the salaries and maintenance of administrators, paid workers, and slaves. To specify this even further, between 1715 and 1765, the ranch of Candelaria accounted for an average of about 4,600 pesos of the yearly college income; requiring in return 1,213 pesos monthly. This was in addition to what the farm or ranch supplied for its own personnel. Between 1695 and 1701, for example, Altagracia used an annual average of 1,587 sheep, 4,750 lbs. of corn, and 1,500 lbs. of wheat from its own ranch and farm to feed the estate personnel. During the same period, Jesús María fed its administrators, hired hands, and slaves with ten jars of wine, 3,750 lbs. of corn, and 1,500 lbs. of wheat grown and prepared on its lands. The total value of goods consumed over the period 1696–1701 was 9,037 pesos. It might be appropriate to point out here that over this period the listed excess of revenue over expenses was 41,160 pesos, and this did not include over 9,000 pesos in farm products used to support personnel. It was calculated that each of the sixty Jesuits (faculty and students) needed a budget of 120 pesos per year; this was a fixed annual expense of 7,200 pesos. But the categories of Sacristy, Construction, Missions, and Lawsuits required 21,500 pesos, which meant that 23,240 pesos were needed to cover the expenses of this six-year period. These data were gathered by the Jesuit business office in Córdoba to convince the diocesan tithe officials of the inadequacy of the college's income, so they must be taken with a grain of salt. Missions and lawsuits were not fixed or recurring expenses, and construction was periodic. No breakdown of these expenses was given. However, they are of great value in helping us assess the proportion of revenue accruing from the different enterprises and the cost of supplies that had to be furnished from outside the ranch or farm.

A further note: with the exception of a "petty cash" fund kept on estates, no money actually passed between estates and colleges. That is to say, when the general ledger indicates that Jesús María sent ten jars of wine to the college worth eight pesos each, the farm did not receive eighty pesos from the college. In fact, the ledger would show a revenue for the college, while the estate book would indicate that so much wine was sent to the college—not quite an expense, but neither was it listed as a revenue.

An examination of table 16 shows how closely revenue matched expenses in the eighteenth century. It appears that little "profit" was-made. But this impression might be the result of using only a sophisticated workbook as a guide. The *Libro de Cuentas* was not intended to be a full financial report. Transactions were emphasized, not the value of current assets, cash, and receivables that would soon be turned into cash. One gets only fleeting glimpses of this from laconic mention of the *alcance*, or the receivables listed with inventory. In the college treasurer's office was the safe in which the cash on hand was stored. This was the foundation or bulk of estate "profit," or built-up excess of revenues over expenses. Capital goods in the form of livestock, buildings, slaves, and receivables comprised the rest of college wealth. As we shall see below, the college made European investments, but these were minimal. The bulk of Córdoba's assets were derived from and remained in Latin America.

Revenue and Expenses: The Province and Other Colleges

The Jesuit Province of Paraguay, as a corporate body distinct from its individual houses and colleges, maintained its own sources of income because its expenses were separate. Its chief income producer was the massive ranch of Santa Catalina whose farmland, grazing land, and orchards, valued at 36,539 pesos in 1767, stretched for ten to twenty-five km from the nuclear farmstead.[17] From its founding in 1620 the estate developed slowly—the farmstead buildings composed of house, church, and slave quarters, the development of farmlands, and over seventeen *parajes* or pieces of grazing land in the surrounding region. In 1644 the income of Santa Catalina, commonly called the "Province Estate," was 5,000 pesos and from this sum was paid annually 130 pesos for the maintenence of each Jesuit novice then living at the College of Córdoba. The financial report of 1644 explained that: "when there are few novices and the income from Santa Catalina is more than sufficient for their support, the provincial distributes what remains to the reductions and to the colleges, especially Córdoba. In the past three years, the ranch has acquired thirty-two slaves and has purchased neighboring lands."[18] The ranch had 250 slaves in 1697. Besides supporting the growing number of novices, the province ranch paid for the expenses of the provincial office: the inspection visits made to colleges and missions, travel fare of missionaries coming from and going to Europe, and miscellaneous province expenses. By the eighteenth century, the agro-pastoral complex of Santa Catalina reached its peak, as indicated in table 17.

Table 17. INVENTORY OF SANTA CATALINA

Year	Mares	Mules	Horses	Sheep	Cows	Slaves
1718	4,755	—	1,041	14,258	6,487	366
1724	4,200	3,527	1,092	11,000	10,500	279
1734	5,752	1,847	2,037	7,000	2,200	355
1748	7,000	400	2,000	4,000	8,000	317
1767	3,707	4,798	3,778	8,690	6,213	436

SOURCE: LOPP

The major focus of the ranch was the production of mules that were shipped to Salta for sale. Cattle also was a major item. Food and dairy products were raised primarily to feed the slave population and paid workers, all of whom worked for at least a few years in the eighteenth century under Pedro, the slave estanciero or administrator. This ranch provided the bulk of the income of the province as a corporation, totals of which are given in table 18.

Table 18. JESUIT PROVINCE OF PARAGUAY, INCOME AND EXPENSES 1711-1750

Years	Income	Expenses	Debts	Receivables
1711–1713	54,683	43,988	—	—
1713–1715	31,278	29,448	11,115	21,045
1715–1718	68,548	62,815	14,729	47,973
1718–1719	17,419	24,626	18,671	33,609
1719–1720	54,425	47,422	21,984	24,665
1720–1721	61,816	41,034	22,404	26,258
1721–1723	46,338	33,905	12,083	31,474
1723–1724	24,722	20,918	5,068	13,682
1724–1726	25,058	18,700	12,305	18,532
1726–1728	34,533	25,773	11,215	36,359
1728–1734	86,006	100,489	6,930	16,079
1734–1736	32,284	31,491	14,496	24,920
1736–1740	48,446	63,516	18,219	4,952
1740–1742	78,842	58,461	16,259	28,605
1742–1746	232,296	227,062	115,898	14,867
1746–1748	94,025	91,076	179,660	107,670
1748–1750	152,317	123,822	53,296	19,056
TOTALS:	1,146,038	1,044,545		

SOURCE: LOPP

The yearly income average over the years given in table 18 was around 23,000 pesos, with expenses around 20,000. Income was generated from 1,500–3,000 mules of Santa Catalina sold annually in Salta and from an almost equal number of cattle. In the 1740s mortgages or *censos* held by the province accounted for over 21,000 pesos a year, and *yerba* sold in Potosí likewise provided significant sums. The province maintained close investment ties with Europe, mainly by means of the Jesuits returning periodically to Spain and Rome. In 1748 over 50,000 pesos were owed in Europe, and at the same time the mortgage debt was 30,000 pesos. This was a period of heavy province borrowing. Apparently there were several such periods. In 1736 the provincial, Jaime Aguilar, ordered that the houses owned by the province in Potosí be sold and the Jesuit agent in Potosí, Simon Baylina was told to send 4,000 pesos to the provincial's office immediately.[19] The province administrative office was in heavy debt and had no money to pay the expenditures to be incurred by the procurators returning to Europe. It seems that the debts incurred by the province office were less predictable than those of other institutions. Emergency assistance, sudden travel costs, plus the fixed yearly costs of administration tended to be erratic so the treasury tended to be emptied fairly rapidly.

On the other hand, the colleges were able to budget more rationally because much of their income and expenses was recurrent. To take the College of Buenos Aires as an example, their business office stated the projected expenses and projected income in the yearly report. In order to support thirty-two college administrators and faculty and the slave population of 300, the following was needed:[20]

1) For administration and faculty:

Wine, foods, sugar, honey	3,600	pesos
Clothing materials and supplies	800	
Snuff, paper	400	
	4,800	

2) For slaves:

Clothing	1,000
Yerba, tobacco	450
	1,450

3) *Censos* and ranches:

1,025 pesos paid annually in interest	1,025
Subsidy to estates and farms; wagons	1,000
200 pesos for conchabados	200
	2,225
TOTAL:	8,425

129

This total amount was needed in silver coin in order to purchase or pay for these necessities. Not included in this sum was the daily supply of meat, tallow, grease, wheat, flour, fruits, and other dairy products supplied by the college's ranches and farms. The supply of silver for these costs came from the following:[21]

1)	Rents from real estate	5,000
2)	The ranch can supply 1,200 mules at 4 pesos	4,800
3)	1,500 hides	1,500
4)	500 steers at 3 pesos	1,500
5)	Tallow, animal fat	300
6)	Calera can give 1,000 fanegas of lime at 12 reales	1,500
7)	Caraburo can produce 200,000 bricks at 8 pesos per 1,000	1,600
8)	500 fanegas of wheat from renters of our lands at 20 reales per fanega	1,250
9)	Use of flour mills	800
	TOTAL:	18,250

The cost of living varied from region to region, but in general, the cost of maintaining one Jesuit in a college was about 200 pesos a year.[22] The associated expenses of construction and reinvestment in the farms and ranches required, or course, much more money. The major colleges, Córdoba, Buenos Aires, Santa Fe, and Asunción, had yearly incomes that surpassed the simple maintenance costs. As is clear from the above figures, Buenos Aires had a considerable sum available each year for reinvestment in various enterprises. But such sums were not available to all colleges, resulting in some heavy borrowing, as will be discussed at length in the next chapter. Suffice it to point out here that not all colleges were equally endowed with financially adept administrative personnel. Salta, for example, had an especially difficult financial history. A provincial visitor wanted to close the college because of its shaky finances. It seems that one naive rector put the two best college estates in the hands of a lay friend, one José de Arias, and Arias would not give up control. The college's wintering pasturage, a significant income producer, had been ruined and most of the college income was spent on conchabado salaries and other hired laborers.[23] Not much came from the three existing estates to support the twelve Jesuits in residence in 1760.

Outside of the larger colleges mentioned above, the other colleges

throughout Tucumán and Paraguay were modest in size and personnel, as is evident in table 19.

Table 19. SIZE OF JESUIT STAFF IN COLLEGES

Year	Córdoba	Buenos Aires	Santa Fe	Asunción	Corrientes	Santiago del Estero	Tucumán	Rioja	Salta	Tarifa
1660	70	9	5	9	—	—	—	—	—	—
1710	56	12	9	11	7	8	5	8	9	7
1720	84	17	9	13	6	9	6	8	9	10
1740	78	19	13	13	8	10	9	10	13	11
1744	58	23	14	11	8	9	10	11	13	13
1753	103	28	15	18	9	8	10	13	13	15
1763	74	32	15	17	9	8	11	11	12	9

SOURCE: ARSI, Paraq. 6

The first four colleges listed in table 19 accounted for 70 percent of
the total college personnel in the Jesuit province. It is not surprising
then that these four institutions, founded early on, were the largest
and most developed. They had solid economic bases. They were located in towns with wealthier citizens and potential donors. But with
the exception of Cordóba and Buenos Aires, the distribution of personnel was fairly even. The remote town of Tarifa had almost the same
number of Jesuits as the major city of Asunción.

The ranches and farms associated with each of these colleges provided the major source of income, followed close behind by trade in
yerba; this was especially true of Santa Fe and Asunción. Asunción's
large cattle holdings (24,000 in 1753) and farm enterprises (with 600
slaves) made the college a major economic force in the area. From the
estate of San Miguel alone, the College of Santa Fe realized
4,000–5,000 pesos annually. Contrasted with these major enterprises
stand many other modest ranches barely supporting the owner-
college. For example, the ranches of the College of San Miguel de Tucumán had 5,000 head of cattle and 2,200 mules furnishing the college
with 850 pesos a year—hardly sufficient for the maintenance of the ten
resident Jesuits.[24]

But these are all relative figures and terms. The effect of a small ranching enterprise in San Miguel de Tucumán might have been more far reaching and profound than that of a major one in Córdoba or near Buenos Aires where they were one among so many. However, as far as the colleges were concerned, the ranch or farm's purpose was to provide a suitable income; the rate of return had to be appropriate to place and time.

Return and Reinvestment

An annual rate of return can be calculated by dividing the annual profit (income minus expenses) by the total investment (land, buildings, livestock, and slaves). Using this formula for the estates of Córdoba, the resulting average rate of return is below 2 percent. The specifics of the investment would be as follows:[25]

Investment			Profit	
slaves	150,000	pesos	1750–1760	2,108 average
land	10,000			
buildings	8,000		*Rate of Return*	
tools	2,000		1.7–2 percent	
Total:	170,000			

The difficulty with calculating a series of rates over the eighteenth century lies in the fluctuating investment costs. Slave populations were not the same; buildings were added, tools were purchased as needed and size of the cattle herds fluctuated. The above figure is based for the most part on the evaluation of land and property made in 1767 or thereafter. Thus, no account is taken of gradual investment increases. In addition, there are indications that the figures given in the general college ledger must be supplemented by the cash kept in the safe of the college. We know that at one time the cash kept in this safe was upwards of 9,000 pesos. How was this cash-on-hand accumulated? Is it the *"alcance"* referred to at each auditing period, or rolled over profit? It must have been a steadily sufficient sum because from it apparently came money to purchase slaves. The college and its estates had around 1,000 slaves in 1767, yet no indication of purchases was ever made in the expense column of the ledger. Where were slave purchases recorded? Other types of capital investment were. Moreover, if we take the total of income minus expenses for the years 1711–1760, as given in table 16, and divide the result by a total investment figure adjusted downward by 75,000 pesos, the rate of return would still be minimal—less than 1 percent. The inescapable conclusion is that based on the available financial reports and data, the massive farms, estates, and operations of the College of Córdoba just, and barely just, met college and religious community expenses. As an economic unit, the farms, ranches, and mills were quite productive and lucrative. They fulfilled their role as income provider, but little and sometimes no surplus remained at the end of a fiscal year.

Apparently better off, at least as concerns the rate of return, was the College of Buenos Aires. In 1767 the total investment amounted to about 190,000 pesos and the annual "profit" came to around 10,000 pesos for a return of 5.2 percent.[26] As a final example, let us cite the ranches of the College of San Miguel de Tucumán. Five pieces of grazing land, including the range of Tafi, the hacienda of Vipos, and the estate of Lules, cattle, buildings, and the 121 slaves were valued at 112,360 pesos in 1768. Between 1750 and 1754 they were chiefly responsible for the profit of 3,370 pesos enjoyed by the college after expenses were paid: a return of 3 percent. I suspect that many if not most of the estates owned by colleges in the Jesuit province of Paraguay returned no more than 3 to 5 percent.[27] But this is no more than an impression based on calculations of the spotty available data on income returns and estate inventory estimates.

The major reason why the return on the Córdoba investment was low, and really we do not know whether it *was* low until we can compare it with returns from other similar enterprises and business investments, was reinvestment of funds. The general ledger shows that capital expenses in the form of ranch and farm repair and replacement of depleted stock required considerable sums; but not only was upkeep and repair maintained but additional improvements such as bridges, farm constructions, infirmary, pharmacy, new tools, mills, additional vines and livestock, and most expensive of all, more black slave laborers, were continually added to the estates of Córdoba in the eighteenth century. The college church was also the recipient of large sums in the form of elaborate ornaments. For example, in June, 1755, 7,134 pesos were spent on silver ornaments, and between 1750 and 1754, construction of a college kitchen, pantry, clothes room, chapel, and church consumed major sums.[28] But for the most part, the revenue was placed back into the income-producing sector of the college, not into elaborate churches. A mill, large shears for cutting wool, lumber for farmhouses, and those kinds of expenses normal to farmers or ranchers are what appear in the general ledger. This was not an unconscious pattern but a definite policy frequently encouraged and repeated by provincials on their visitation inspections. The "Compañía" section of the Archivo General de la Nación in Buenos Aires is filled with the memoranda or instructions left by provincials for estate administrators. Fix walls, build graneries, replace stock—a continual litany of directives aimed at keeping the sources of income in excellent condition. The financial effect of this was a heavy reinvestment in the estates, thus not permitting them to become run-down.

The purchase of slave labor was a major form of reinvestment. In 1767 the ranches and farms owned by Jesuit colleges in colonial Argentina possessed over 3,400 black slaves. About a third of these worked on the estates of the College of Córdoba. At around 200 pesos each, their total value was about 680,000 pesos, a princely sum in those days and times. The fact that such massive investment in labor took place was testimony to the seriousness of the Jesuit economic enterprise and to the ability of the colleges to either lay hands on the silver required to purchase slaves or to borrow it. Their credit was good, as we shall see in the next chapter.

To be more specific about reinvestment, it would be helpful to look at how the College of Buenos Aires reinvested in its estates and in forms of real estate in the 1750s and early 1760s. In 1758 a granary was built on the large farm of Chacara and roof tiles were put on the chapel and main house. Bell tower and cemetery were also added. A pond was dug for the water wheel and a canal put in to carry water. Each year in Chacara, 200,000 adobe bricks were made as well as thousands of tiles; 200 oxen were stabled on the estate. The timber and bricks were supplied by the limestone pits and brickmaking enterprises of Calera, the Hornos de Carcaburo, and from Chacara itself.

What must surely have been one of the earliest housing projects in Latin America was constructed and operated by the Jesuits of Buenos Aires in conjunction and close cooperation with their other properties. The following description of improvements made in the complex in 1758 conveys a good verbal image of what an eighteenth-century rural house was like.

On the western side of the houses of Carcaburo five medium-sized apartments have been made. Each has a living room, bedroom, small servant's room, patio with a little corridor, kitchen with oven and chimney and its common rooms. The living rooms, corridors, kitchen and common rooms have been repaired and partitions divide bedroom from living room. The patios have new bricks and a 4 vara-high adobe wall surrounds the house. Rooms have been whitewashed and each apartment has a new window with an iron grill facing the street and a smaller one facing the patio. The entrance to the street and to the patio have been repaired. Tiles and the ridge of the roof gables have been replaced. A walkway of bricks five *cuartos* wide has been put down as far as the street and the existing walkway outside the walls has been reinforced with a meter-long strip of mortar. The material used in those five apartments were 60,000 bricks, 4,200 tiles, 1,000 reeds and 50 *palmas* for corridors, rooms, and kitchens. Each one of these apartments produces 6 pesos a month in rent, or 360 pesos a year.[29]

This type of improvement was also made in the fourteen other apartments and two houses owned by the college in Carcaburo. They were all rented each year, producing at least 2,000 pesos. In this particular period the total reinvestment in rehabilitation was over 7,000 pesos, divided as follows:

Lumber	2,531
Salaries for carpenters	800
Iron	1,612
Carbon	665
Cañas, palmas, lime, opening wells, locks purchased	938
8 wagons for hauling materials	596
	7,142

Not included in this list were 250,000 bricks, 10,000 tiles, nor payment to masons or *peones*. These would have added at least 3,000 pesos to the cost. Other houses owned by the college were also periodically repaired and improved. From all of them the college realized 5,000 pesos yearly.

It is impossible to calculate their return since the initial construction cost is unknown. However, the major point here is that the college reinvested in its estates (chiefly by farm constructions and increasing herds), as well as in its real estate, thus adding considerably to the non-human wealth of the institution. The human wealth (over 326 slaves in 1761) constituted the single richest possession of the college.

The tithes which the bishops exacted from Jesuit estates, a flat sum up to 1765 and a percentage on products thereafter, made little dent in the overall finances of the colleges and estates, although a great deal of paper was used to prove both sides of the question: the right to collect and the right to exemption.[30] The exemption from civil taxes was another boon to Jesuit ranches but was also a source of envy and resentment.

The complexity of the financial organization of each set of college estates was often in direct proportion to the size of the rural enterprises, which in turn maintained proportional linkages with other external financial and economic entities. Major expenditures went for college food and clothing supplies, both for residents and workers. And it seems that at least 30 to 40 percent of monthly expenditures were used for college farms and ranches. Unrecorded in available account books are major capital expenditures for slaves and building construction. This omission reduces the accuracy of estimates of reinvestment in the estates. Finance records were kept both to determine accountability and to provide the basis for rational economic decisions. The flow of money along economic levels and transactions agreed upon and completed formed the warp and woof of the economic fabric. The framework or base of these linkages was shaped by credit mechanisms and the infrastructure of colonial trade and commerce.

CHAPTER 7

Credit, Money, and Colonial Trade

When the account books of the College of Córdoba were audited in 1731, the list of debtors included the provincial's office. The debt was thus recorded: "The *oficio* of the province owes more or less 4,000 pesos."[1] This almost casual attitude about a 4,000-pesos debt was not due to the nature of the debtor but more to a generally cavalier approach towards finance. Key administrative personnel cared a great deal about how income was increased and records kept but a similar keenness did not filter through the rank and file and on occasion was not possessed by those who should have had it. The world of business, commerce, trade, money, and markets was still very much a murky if not an openly sinful sphere. Medieval attitudes confusing borrowing and credit was usury were present in sixteenth and seventeenth century America. This was a major factor that prevented the adequate organization of credit.

In order to discuss adequately the exchange and trade that existed among the Jesuit Colleges of Tucumán and Paraguay, and the key colonial business centers of Potosí, Lima, and Santiago de Chile, one should have a clear, and at least accurate, general picture of colonial business. We do not. The state of the money market is unknown. How currency problems affected prices, banking mechanisms, credit, loans, and investments are question marks. The merchant banker of Lima or Buenos Aires acted as lender by allowing purchase on credit, or accounts to overrun. Bills of exchange were often passed as payment for slaves imported in Buenos Aires. But who were the third, or fourth, parties? We know that some religious institutions engaged in activities commonly associated with banking, but no systematic analysis of these questions has ever been attempted for early colonial America.

What is said below about colonial finance is more exploratory than intensive. The credit transactions entered into and the trade network constructed by Jesuit colleges represented a limited type of activity engaged in by one colonial corporate owner. Nevertheless, colleges' activity was diverse, widespread, and financially significant. Because of this, they shed light on the wider financial world of colonial Latin America. The network of economic relationships extended far beyond the immediate estate environs.

Currency and Prices

The finances of each Jesuit institution as well as other private economic enterprises depended in great part on the local and regional pricing mechanism. In the sixteenth century Tucumán had little metal currency so a length of linen was used as money. The value of the cloth, whether linen in Córdoba, or *sayal* or iron in Buenos Aires, was largely determined by the dominant economic elite who controlled trade within the region.[2] These were landowners and the controllers of Indian and slave laborers. At the same time that the city of Córdoba was declaring itself "poor," its individual businessmen were negotiating business transactions involving large sums of money (in silver). In 1618 the home government began to regulate the monetary system and to determine the values of goods used as regional currency.[3] For its silver coins, Córdoba and Buenos Aires was in the early days, as well as through much of the eighteenth century, dependent on Peru. The sale of mules and cattle in Potosí provided silver for trade with Brazil, with foreign interlopers, and with other long-distance American commercial houses and businessmen. When the mule business temporarily declined, as it did between 1670 and 1699, either due to mine failures or Indian raids, metal currency grew even scarcer.

Prices often fluctuated wildly and it fell to town councils to control them. In 1630 the city council of Córdoba grew enraged over the high prices of corn and wheat. The council fathers decreed that 4½ pesos a *fanega* was the limit either could be sold for in the city; four pesos if sold on estates.[4] To send a wagon with freight from Mendoza to Córdoba cost fifty-five pesos in 1650. But the threat of war that was bruited about in 1762 drove prices up by forty percent in Córdoba.[5] Spanish and European manufactured items were the most prized and so subject to fluctuation.[6] Estate products were the most stable, some remaining the same throughout the eighteenth century. Some of the more basic items and prices are given in table 20.

Table 20. PRICES OF AGRO-PASTORAL ITEMS, CÓRDOBA, 1695–1760

Year	Wine (botija)	Sheep	Cattle	Flour (fanega)	Wheat	Corn
1695	10p	6r	4r	5p	3p	2½p
1723	10p	4r	1p	6p		3p
1729	10p		2p	7p		
1736	10p	4r	2½p	6p	2½p	
1741	10p	4r	1p	6p		3p
1748	10p	4r	1p	6p	3p	3p
1758	10p	4r	1p	6p		
1760	10p	4r	1p	6p		3p

SOURCES: LC; "Libro de cuentas corrientes de las estancias y haciendas," AGBA, Compañía IX, 6-9-4.

Steers and cows were ordinarily two pesos each, but oxen were twice that. Horses sold for twelve *reales;* an *arroba* of wool remained steady at a peso, lambs at two *reales,* and an *arroba* of tallow was valued at one peso throughout the eighteenth century.

The inconsistency of natural phenomena affected grain and cattle production and their prices. Too much rain or too little, dust storms, and locusts seem to have been the major natural factors in eighteenth-century Tucumán. A dry spell might aid the wheat harvest but it destroyed grazing land and reduced water availability necessary for cattle. During the devastating dry spell of 1797, the price of wheat rose about 300 percent and corn at about the same proportion. Sugar, wine, and textiles rose anywhere between 25 and 60 percent.[7]

The shift from feast to famine was oftimes abrupt and totally unexpected. In 1796 an economic report from Córdoba recounted the abundant harvests, green pasturage, and gradually lowering prices as a result of plenty. In fact, the writer cautioned that the lowered price of a *fanega* of wheat (eighteen or twenty *reales*) had convinced many farmers not to plant in the future since increased costs would make wheat growing unprofitable.[8] Export without restrictions was the only solution suggested by growers. Within months a destructive dry spell set in.

These natural phenomena and their effects were felt at the end of the eighteenth century. Nevertheless, at least the former were present throughout colonial times even though specific effects differed. Short-term climatic changes directly affected both farmers or dairymen, and consumers.

Prices are meaningful only if series can be compared over long time periods. Nevertheless, knowing prices of items at specific times is helpful, for they not only indicate the values of enterprise products but they provide one reason (often one among several) why agro-pastoral specialization did not occur.

139

Credit Mechanisms

One of the major forms of credit prevalent in the eighteenth century was the *censo*. Originally, the *censo* was a normal form of investment in land. Nobles frequently sold a *censo* on their possessions, an obligation to pay an annual return from fruitful property. The *censo* was considered to be a loan, although it was not clear what exactly was lent or sold.[9] The buyer of the *censo* was in the lender's role; he provided the property or cash lent. The seller was the debtor who bound himself to annual payments at fixed rates. This was an area of credit where profit in finances was acceptable and not considered usurious.

In Latin America, landed property, a ranch, or a farm, was the usual object of a *censo*. Frequently, portions of the value of the piece of property provided an annual return to a designated individual or charitable corporation. When a piece of land was purchased, the new owner assumed payment of the *censos* on the property. The sale document stated that of the total sale price, say 10,000 pesos, 3,000 pesos were to be paid in cash (*de contado*), and 7,000 pesos in *censos*. Frequently, the 7,000 pesos were divided among many holders. As an example, in seventeenth-century Córdoba, Bartolomé de Ubeda bought the estate of Casa Grande in the valley of La Punilla, Córdoba, for 479 pesos in 1682 from Don Manuel de Garay of Córdoba. 339 pesos were paid in cash and 140 pesos were in *censos* payable at 5 percent to the Hospital of St. Eulalia of Córdoba.[10] This meant that each year the hospital received seven pesos from this fund; at first sight not a large amount of money, but if the hospital drew funds this way from other *censos* the final sum could have been significant.

Land *censos,* however, seem to have played far less important a role in financing than they did in Peru, possibly because land in Paraguay was so much more abundant. Mentioned with much more frequency was money borrowed *a censo,* usually at 5 percent interest. It seems that the term, *a censo* was equivalent to "at interest." The principal of the loan was usually listed as the debt. For example, in the list of debts owed by the College of Buenos Aires in 1758 (the total of which was 44,870 pesos), there was: "*a censo* 6,280 pesos," which in 1761 had increased "in principals of *censos,* 9,725 pesos." The general ledger of the College of Córdoba for November, 1746, mentions the interest rate: "4,000 pesos were borrowed this month *a censo* at 5 percent from the Convent of St. Teresa."[11] However, much more often than not, the time-honored Spanish phrase reserved for borrowing was used and this did not include the interest rate, probably because it was universally known. Whether the interest was to be paid in goods (*géneros*) or in silver coin (*plata*) was also frequently stipulated. In June, 1748, the College of Córdoba borrowed 1,000 pesos from Ana Suárez, payable at 5 percent in goods "at current silver prices." When the college borrowed 1,500 pesos from Juan de Carranza in February, 1748, at 5 percent, it had to be returned in *pesos dobles*. Many of the debts incurred by the College of Córdoba in the eighteenth century were payable at 5 percent interest and all of these were described as being *a censo*. In 1761 the College of Buenos Aires paid 1,025 pesos annually as interest on outstanding debts. Twenty-five hundred *pesos dobles* had been borrowed from Don Antonio Cebreros at 7½ percent, the highest interest rate listed in either the Buenos Aires or Córdoba college records.

Not all of the debts of the Colleges of Córdoba or Buenos Aires involved interest payments. Some were for sales of mules or cattle or transactions made on behalf of other Jesuit institutions. However, actual loans, as in 1719 when the college borrowed 1,339 pesos from Domingo Corrales "to buy wheat and other supplies for the college," almost always involved interest payments. The debt record of the College of Córdoba in the eighteenth century was as follows in table 21.

Table 21. DEBTS AND RECEIVABLES OF THE COLLEGE OF CÓRDOBA, 1718-1760

Year	Debt	Receivables
1718	40,837	19,100
1720	47,293	2,009
1723	19,525	2,760
1724	9,337	18,114
1726	16,350	18,326
1728	9,455	23,431
1731	11,219	12,120
1734	13,617	16,937
1736	13,181	9.791
1740	17,700	21,530
1742	11,108	29,458
1745	14,712	26,195
1750	44,079	—
1754	2,400	—
1760	2,037	17,929

SOURCE: LCC

Two peak periods, 1718–1720 and 1750, are evident in table 21. In the former, the largest debts were to General Don Bartolomé de Ugalde for 13,768 pesos and to the province business office for 9,853 pesos. Fernando Garay was owed 4,638 pesos in silver and the Master of Camp, Benitez, was owed 3,500 pesos, likewise in silver. The reason for the 1718–1720 debts seems to have been the cost of increased construction and purchase of cattle. In 1713 lumber from Tucumán used for the construction of the college patio and wagons cost 1,020; 4,000 cows purchased for 1,750 pesos were put on the grazing land of Achala; and mules sent to Salta cost 1,800 pesos.[12] This year, 1713, was the only one prior to 1718 to have exceeded by several thousand pesos the monthly expense average of 1,500 to 2,000 pesos. In the income of July, 1713, were 7,984 pesos, for which no source is given, only the blank statement, "7,984 pesos of which I assume responsibility." This could have been the loan from Ugalde mentioned above. However, as early as 1710 the economic report spoke of "debts for construction of the building," indicating the borrowing anticipated in 1713.[13] By 1721 most of the debt to Ugalde was paid. Between 1720 and 1721 the college sent him 6,642 pesos in silver and 1,289 pesos in cloth. Thereafter, his name does not appear on the list of college creditors. But Matias de Silva, a tea merchant from Paraguay, took his place and appeared with regularity for a decade.

The debts assumed around the other peak period, 1750, were due to replacement and rehabilitation of the labor force after a devastating killer epidemic in 1744 took the lives of over 200 black slaves. Ranch, farm, and textile production was seriously retarded "with great harm resulting to the material life of the college."[14] Money to purchase slaves was borrowed from the Monastery of Santa Catalina of Córdoba and from the Convent of Santa Teresa, likewise of Córdoba. Between 1743 and 1750, the college borrowed around 40,000 pesos at 5 percent, much of it from the two religious institutions mentioned above. However, between 1750 and 1754, the college redeemed 38,026 pesos in debts, of which 25,929 were from the Monastery of Santa Catalina and 12,047 from the Convent of Santa Teresa. In 1753 the college owed only 15,000 pesos and a decade later there were no debts whatsoever.

Between these two peak debt periods ran a fairly steady and level debt accumulation. Between 1724 and 1745 the average annual debt was 13,000 pesos. Rarely is the reason for college borrowing written in the general ledger. On several occasions it is, but hardly with enough frequency to generalize. On one occasion, July, 1719, a note indicates that 1,336 pesos were borrowed to buy wheat and other supplies for the college. In June, 1749, 3,500 pesos were borrowed from Santa Catalina to pay Don Juan de Arguello and others (merchants) for goods bought from them. It also seems that the monthly borrowing in 1747, 1748, and 1749 was primarily for the purchase of slaves. As mentioned above, new construction must also be included as a reason for borrowing. Credit came fairly easily to the College of Córdoba because collateral in the form of goods or silver either on hand, or at some distance awaiting shipment to the college, or owed to the college, was almost always available. Table 21 shows that receivables almost balanced debts and indeed sometimes an annual financial report would explicitly point out that debts for the year were easily covered by receivables. Combined under receivables in table 21 are both cash loans made by the college to individuals and the value of goods in Chile, Potosí, or Buenos Aires awaiting shipment to Córdoba. Payments for mules sold in Peru or Salta were also sometimes listed. A typical list of debtors to the college would be that of 1730, given below.[15]

General Matias de Angeles in silver	3,250 pesos
Simón de Aguinague left 400 pesos in Chile	400
Simón de Aguinague given 127 arrobas of yerba caamini to bring to Chile for sale	414
P. Cura of San Miguel	2,000
Yerba caamini in Potosí	1,110
For remaining mules	1,647
P. Rector Pedro de Arroyo, in silver	400
Don Antonio Boyan de Alfaro, 336 lbs. of wax	336
Don Juan de Molina, 88 p. in silver, 248 in goods	336
Sebastián Maldonado, 20 p. in silver, 103 in goods	123
P. Martín Lopez	167
Caldevilla who lives in Santa Catalina, in silver	136
Doña Petronilla Carranza, in silver	74
To the collegians of Salta, son and nephew of Ibarguren	82
Maestro Castro in La Rioja	90
Bartolome Peredo of Santa Fe whose obligation is held by Don Antonio Marquez	64

There is no indication in the general ledger that some or any of these loans were made at a 5 percent interest rate. One can question whether they were in fact really business or personal loans in the proper sense of the term. From the above list, 34 percent of the total of 10,629 pesos was explicitly in goods, tea, mules, or wax. However, the largest sum, 3,250 pesos, owed by General Matias de Angeles, and other large sums from other years, seem to have been owed by long-distance merchants or traders. In June of 1749, 3,500 pesos were borrowed from the Convent of Santa Catalina to pay Don Juan de Arguello and other merchants to whom the college was in debt for goods it purchased. Therefore, it seems that much of the debt to the college was either from goods purchased or sold, stored shipments of the goods, the equivalent silver owed, or for advanced payments made to long-distance traders who needed business capital. Thus, the college provided a form of credit and acted like a commercial bank would today. On the other hand, most of the smaller debts to the college owed by individuals probably represented people in need of immediate financial help. Mechanisms for consumer credit were rare, so friends, relatives of friends, or benefactors of the college frequently turned to it as a source of financial aid. There is also reference to the college holding money in deposit for an individual. Reluctance to keep substantial sums of money at home and the absence of banks made some turn to monasteries and convents as secure places for depositing money. In 1746 the College of Córdoba borrowed 2,500 pesos from the deposit of one Domingo de Castro, probably at 5 percent interest.[16] Other scattered references to *depositos* make one suspect that they were a fairly common occurrence in the college. Although the inventories made after 1767, at the time of the expulsion of the Jesuits, do not list large quantities of deposits, they might well have been withdrawn before the sequestration of Jesuit property took place.

The debts of the College of Buenos Aires followed the same pattern as those of Córdoba only they were never matched by receivables. Between 1700 and 1740, debts ranged below 10,000 pesos but in 1740 they jumped to a total of 43,000 pesos.[17] Much of this was *censos* principal that in a few years was reduced to 8,000 pesos. But apparently the college did not worry too much even about the larger sum. The financial report for 1740 said, "praeter 43,000 nulla gravatur," or "besides the 43,000 pesos there are no debts"! In 1758 the college debts had increased to 44,870 pesos, of which only 14 percent or 6,280, were *censos* principals; 44 percent were owed to other Jesuit institutions, and 18 percent (8,229 pesos), were a deposit of the silver of Otalora.[18] With the exception of 6,000 owed to the sisters of Carcaburo, the remaining twelve debts were relatively small, ranging from 140 pesos to 852 pesos. Receivables amounted to only 4,091 pesos. By 1761, the total debt remained almost the same, 43,415 pesos, and 44 percent of this was owned to Jesuit institutions (11,343 to provincial's office). *Censos* had increased slightly to 9,725 and the heirs of Carcaburo were still owed 5,893. However, three other substantive loans had been incurred, included in the following list of debts owed to non-Jesuits.

Principales de censos	9,725 pesos
To the heirs of Carcaburo	5,893
To Don Manuel Díaz	3,328
To Don Manuel Escalada	2,600
To Don Juan de Eguía	445
To Don Francisco Campana, 200 steers @ 2 pesos	400
To the child of Pessoa if she enters the convent	500
To Don Manuel de Borda	1,359
Total:	24,250

Added to these debts in a postscript was 2,682 pesos at 7½ percent interest borrowed from Don Antonio Cebreros and 1,000 pesos spent in the litigation of Otalora. Díaz, Escalada, Cebreros, and Borda were local merchants who required immediate payment and in 1761 even the provincial was politely but firmly asking for the 11,343 pesos owed his office for several years.

The size of and reasons for the debts of the Colleges of Córdoba and Buenos Aires provide a clue to the scope of economic activity engaged in by these institutions. The debts of other colleges were much smaller and it is clear that their range of activities was restricted. Table 22 outlines debts of other Jesuit colleges in the Jesuit Paraguay Province.

Table 22. DEBTS OF COLLEGES, ( ) = RECEIVABLES

College	1710	1720	1740	1744	1753	1763
Corrientes	0	1,000(3,000)	8,000	0	6,000	0
Santiago	0	6,121(20,000)	3,500(6,000)	5,500	0	0
Tucumán	0	3,000	1,279(3,139)	2,220*	3,728	
La Rioja	0	0		3,620	2,752	
Salta	?	5,000	5,600	1,097	8,000	
Santa Fe	0	10,000	9,131(8,515)	10,000		9,000
Tarija	0	600	10,263(5,252)	8,000(5,000)	0	
Asunción	0	0	6,000*	0	17,555(35,212)	

SOURCE: ARSI, Paraq. 6
*sufficient receivables to pay debt

With the exception of Santa Fe and Asunción in the middle of the eighteenth century, none of the colleges had significant debts—as much an indication of economic inactivity as of possible capable administration. But even these small debts weighed heavily on smaller institutions. In 1767 Manuel García of Santa Fe wrote to a friend: "the

145

feast of St. Ignatius Loyola is approaching and although I do not feel like doing anything extraordinary with a 9,000-peso debt on the college, it is necessary to do *something*."[19] Santa Fe was not the smallest of the colleges and its livestock tramped the northern pampas on their way to Córdoba and Salta. They, along with livestock and products of other college estates, contributed to the development of a trade network that spanned most of colonial Latin America.

Oficios and the Trade Network

The markets of Jesuit ranch and agro-pastoral production of Tucumán and Paraguay were scattered throughout Latin America. Jesuit tea grown in the Paraguay reductions had ready and brisk sales in Chile and Lima. Cattle and mules from Areco, Santa Fe, and Córdoba were driven to Alto Peru and Potosí via Salta. Hides were exported to Europe through the port of Buenos Aires. Much of the man-made infrastructure for this trade, namely roads, mule trains, or coastal shipping, was shared by Jesuit and lay traders. Some was not. Storage points in key trading centers and qualified and efficient human resources were available to Jesuit colleges that perhaps spelled the difference between ordinary and excellent commercial mechanisms. This was translated into higher financial returns.

Two extremely important commercial mechanisms possessed by Jesuit colleges were the business offices *(oficios)* and storage facilities provided at key commercial centers. The Jesuit business offices provided a wide variety of commercial services: sales to local merchants, credit, exchange, business information, handling and storage facilities in the college warehouse. This was especially important when prices were depressed and nonperishable goods were involved. These offices maintained regular contact with each other and issued periodic reports and statements detailing credits and money owed. Apparently, in the seventeenth century the office of the procurator of missions was one of the first to function. He was given two storage rooms within the compound of the College of Buenos Aires and the rationale was to store all goods sent from the reduction missions and facilitate their sale. In turn, the office was to purchase and send all supplies that individual mission parishes requested. By the middle of the eighteenth century the following had business offices for the same general purposes: Córdoba, Buenos Aires (missions), Santa Fe (missions), Salta, Potosí, and Santiago de Chile. In addition, each of the colleges had a business office (a *procuraduría*) that could be called upon to provide certain commercial services if need arose. The *oficios,* however, were the officially designated commercial offices whose full-time personnel took care of business-related transactions.

An especially active commercial relationship developed between the Office of Santa Fe and the college as well as the Office of Córdoba. Santa Fe was used as a very convenient dispatch point for the products of the reduction missions of Paraguay. From there tea, sugar, hides, tobacco, and cloth were sent overland to Córdoba in exchange for cash or Córdoba's agro-pastoral products which often included sacks of salt and large jars of wine. In 1730 Córdoba sent sixteen sacks of salt and 200 gilt-edged books, in return for which the Office of Buenos Aires shipped sixty-seven arrobas of caamini tea, eighteen arrobas of sugar, sixty arrobas of ordinary tea, twenty arrobas of tobacco, and thirty arrobas of yerba de palos.[20] Besides the transfer of goods Córdoba also received money drafts sent from other colleges to be drawn on certain individuals (lenders?) in Córdoba.[21] While Santa Fe served primarily those missions and colleges close to the Paraná river, the office of Buenos Aires was more convenient for those missions on the Uruguay River. The Office of the Missions in Buenos Aires regularly supplied the College of Corrientes with items ranging from thread and raisins to steel and printing presses.[22] The Office of Missions received tea and mission products, sold them, and purchased items needed by the colleges and parishes. This required a fairly keen understanding of price mechanisms, buying and selling, current credit procedures, and the ability to hold off creditors while awaiting payment for goods sold. Judging from extant *oficio* accounts of Córdoba and scraps of data on the Buenos Aires *oficio,* it seems that the total volume of goods and money handled by *oficios* in the eighteenth century must have made them the first and largest "mail order" purchasing/clearing/credit house combinations in eighteenth-century Latin America. The following brief summary of the transactions of the Office of Córdoba, taken from its general ledger, gives an idea of the scope, nature, and magnitude of its operations.[23]

Office of the Province: the two Jesuit procurators going to Europe in 1750 were given 2,500 pesos dobles to buy a printing press for the College of Córdoba; also supplied with 41,000 pesos for unspecified purchases and expenses.

Office of Buenos Aires: Buenos Aires owes Córdoba 1,669 pesos for hides and eighty-eight mules.

Office of Missions of Buenos Aires: Four thousand pesos owed to Córdoba for tithes paid.

Office of Missions of Santa Fe: bales of salt, tea, and tobacco sent from Santa Fe and sold for 8,811 pesos.

Office of Salta: most recent adjustment of accounts with Salta was in 1747; most business in mules; 9,000 mules sent to Salta from province ranch between 1747 and 1754; 13,721 pesos sent to office via agent; 9,082 pesos sent to office for mules sold in 1753; Salta owes Córdoba 25–26,000 pesos in 1760.

Office of Potosí: Simon Baylina, S.J. was the Jesuit business manager in Potosí until 1754; office owes 1,757 pesos to Córdoba for various transactions; 75 pesos for payment for a tent charged to Potosí; 167 pesos for thirty-three lbs. of cinnamon; travel for missionaries to Chiquitos and Chuquisaca charged although no outstandingly large sums involved.

Office of Santiago de Chile: owes the following to Córdoba— 10,080 pesos for 1,260 arrobas of tea; 275 pesos for 550 lbs. of wax; 1,522 pesos for 430 arrobas of tea (1757).

Each of the colleges—the Colegio Máximo, Buenos Aires, Belén, Santa Fe, Corrientes, Asunción, La Rioja, Santiago del Estero, Tucumán, Salta, and Tarija—all had small but regular dealings with the Córdoba office. Mules, tea, tobacco, and manufactured goods were the major items charged to colleges. Locally, the Colegio Máximo was supplied and charged with lime, bricks, wine, books from Europe, chalices, and livestock. As might be expected, the Córdoba office also had extensive relations with Jesuit missions in Paraguay. For example, the reduction of Miraflores was credited with 1,200 pesos "for the cattle drive of 1,600 cows at six reales a head from Santa Catalina to Zatasta;"[24] also "with 1,200 pesos sent by Don López who came for the cattle in 1757."

Each of the offices had similar kinds of economic relations with each other and with other colleges, but it is likely that Córdoba, being at the hub of colonial trade, centrally located for reaching Potosí, Chile, or Lima, had the greatest volume of economic activity. In mule transactions alone between Córdoba and Salta the gross sums exchanged between 1762 and 1764 were well in excess of 140,000 pesos.[25] By the same token, the Córdoba office was more likely to fall into awkward debts and financial situations, as happened in 1739.[26] The following year, the Jesuit agent in Potosí, Simon Baylina, wrote anxiously that he had not yet sold the tea crop because of the *horrenda calma,* or work stoppage, by muleteers. An extraordinary dry spell destroyed the pasturage usually used by mule trains journeying between Cuzco and Potosí.[27] The mule drivers refused to expose their mules to such conditions.

A second category or level of trading occurred without using business offices as intermediaries. This was done by colleges trading directly with each other, either locally or long-distance. An example of the former would be the relatively close ties between the Colleges of Buenos Aires and Mendoza.[28] Both exchanged products from their estates. Sales also occurred. In 1731 Córdoba sold La Rioja 500 cows at twelve *reales* each, equivalent to the current market price. And in 1749 the College of Chile bought 212 lbs. of animal fat from Córdoba and also 217 lbs. of wax. Payment was made and arranged through the Jesuit College of Mendoza. These are only a few of the many examples that are recounted in the general ledger of Córdoba.

Both business offices and the colleges used agents or long-distance traders mainly for distributing the yerba acquired from the Jesuit reductions of Paraguay.[29] Simon de Aquinaga and Andrés Loscano were employed as long-distance traders primarily supplying Chile, whereas others were used who dealt mainly with Potosí and Peru. The average turn-around time for Córdoba–Potosí yerba transactions was two years. For example, the 102 bales of yerba de palos sent to Potosí in October 1747 realized 3,500 pesos which entered Córdoba's coffers in August 1749. But both the College of Córdoba and the Jesuit province lost several thousand pesos when the infamous tidal wave of 1745 flooded Callao and the merchandise stored in its *bodegas*. An unknown quantity of tea recently arrived from Córdoba was washed out to sea.[30]

The ledger of Córdoba also indicates that some sort of financial arrangements were made between college and agent traders, the exact nature of which is unknown. Statements such as, "1,000 pesos lent to Don Domingo de Castro on August 26, 1737, for payment of textiles from Chile;" "a debt to Don Gil de Herrera in Potosí for yerba caamini, for which Fr. Juan Francisco de Aguilar posted bond for 1,100 pesos;" or "1,107 pesos handed over by Simón de Aquinaga in textiles from Quito, leather jackets, and other goods and 400 pesos he left in Chile last year," all point to commercial relationships with agents trading in Chile and Peru.[31] It seems that the more common arrangement was to entrust merchandise to a trusted trader who would sell the goods at commission; but there is some evidence that the Colleges of Córdoba and Buenos Aires, at least, actually lent money or advanced credit to merchants even when the college's goods were not involved.

Commercial relations between the Jesuit Colleges of Tucumán, Río de la Plata and colleges in Europe are even less well known. There is no question that such relations in the form of permanent and periodic investments existed. Their specific form, nature, and arrangements are unknown. Shipping silver to Europe from America was a major economic activity but meaningful data on this activity are scarce. In 1609, when all Jesuit houses subsisted on alms with no ranches or farms as sources of income, the superior general in Rome, Claudio Acquaviva, prohibited the transportation of American silver to Europe.[32] Apparently Jesuits returning to Spain acted as couriers for merchants in Córdoba and Buenos Aires. In cases where local superiors permitted individual Jesuits to bring silver to Europe, lists of owners were to be sent to the Rome office. Towards the end of the century, the local Jesuit administration argued that the province could not survive without European investments, which required trips to Spain and the continent every six years. In 1687 colleges were just barely meeting the expenses that usually totalled 30,000 pesos annually. The income from mule sales of the ranch of Santa Catalina fluctuated each year sometimes wildly, so no reliable estimate of income was possible. The conclusion to the argument was that the superior general should allow the shipment of silver from the Paraguay Province to continue.[33] He did. The list of silver shipped from Paraguay to Spain in 1687 was as follows:

20,000p.	expenses of P. Cristobal de Grijalva, given to him in Seville
3,856	*oficios,* alms, sepulchre of Ignatius Loyola in Rome
3,400	given to Vergara for passage
2,520	given to Vergara at 8 percent and *indueto* [?] at 1 percent
985	*deposito* of the seminary
291	increased value of silver *(plata blanca)* in Spain
31,052	TOTAL

It is difficult to know exactly how much of the above was actually invested for a return. It seems likely that part of the 20,000 pesos in expenses and the 2,520 given to Vergara were investments. Other data for 1687 reveal that Diego de Altamirano brought 18,637 pesos to Spain "to pay certain debts there"; 14,000 pesos were shipped to Lima and 12,300 pesos were in the "ships of Retana."[34] In the following five-year period at least 16,000 pesos were borrowed in Madrid at twelve percent interest. In 1693 Lauro Nuñez, the provincial superior of the Jesuits in Paraguay, suggested that the Jesuits returning to America that year from Europe use what silver they had left over to purchase manufactured goods that could be sold at a profit in Buenos Aires.[35] It was this type of activity that caused a great deal of opposition both outside of and within the Society of Jesus. In 1736 the superior general in Rome, Francisco Retz, put his foot down. The year before, Guillermo Herrán and Antonio Machoni had returned to Buenos Aires with 35,000 pesos in goods which were promptly sold at considerable profit. "I am saddened," wrote Retz, "and I am not surprised at the bad reputation we have. To see two Jesuits leave for Europe in order to collect missionaries to convert the heathen, and have them return as merchants loaded with goods bought in Europe!"[36] Retz thought that he would shut the door to such "disorder and scandal" by forbidding, under Holy Obedience, that anything brought from Europe be sold to seculars, and ordering that goods sold to colleges and missions should have no increase over purchase price, "with only a little added for shipping." It is unlikely that Retz's prohibitions actually stopped the silver/merchandise activity. It may have made it more clandestine, but the exchange was too engrained and it involved too many commitments to be done away with by simple fiat. The College of Asunción could always argue that it needed the income it derived from the salt mines of Andalucía. And the provincial's office would continually argue that the province would collapse, with all sorts of the dire consequences ensuing, if the silver trade were not permitted, to say nothing of the large number of local investments that the business managers of Córdoba and Buenos Aires handled, much like investment brokers.[37] The ring of the bureaucrat's self-perpetuation is no doubt present. They could hardly have been expected to see that the tail was beginning to wag the dog.

Controversy

In 1609, soon after the Jesuits arrived in Tucumán, all of their houses subsisted on alms. They had no farms, ranches, or vineyards as yet. The Jesuit rector of Santiago del Estero, Juan Dario, reported the lack of income, the poor quality of clothing that his colleagues possessed. "They suffer great want," he wrote.[38] A century-and-a-half later the situation had changed dramatically. Over the intervening years, Jesuit colleges in Tucumán and Paraguay had acquired land, developed farms and ranches, and established trade relations. They became an economic power in the region. But not without cost.

From as early as 1645 the Jesuit superior general in Rome was warning the Jesuits of Paraguay about excessive commercial dealings. In 1713 Miguel Angel Tamburini actually stopped all construction work on the College of Córdoba because: "its magnificence serves only an ostentation inappropriate to the houses in which we should live and work."[39] And the next year Tamburini was back pounding again. "The only goal of superiors seems to be construction, money, and banking. . .a pitiful subversion of ends and means which God will punish."[40] The local provincial, Juan Baptista Zea, repeated much the same to the province in 1719. "There is too much time spent on temporal matters, superfluous building and costly churches all constructed with the sweat of the Indian's brow. . ."[41] Over a decade later superiors were saying the same. Jaime Aguilar wrote of the "discredit and the reputation for being merchants" that the Jesuits of Asunción had acquired, and Francis Retz, the superior general, wrote in 1734 of the common aversion in which the Society was held because of "costly and useless purchase of haciendas and possessions which the colleges acquired solely out of the vainest ostentation of wealth or to prevent someone else buying them."[42] Again in 1735 the provincial forbid individuals to sell or exchange college goods; only the products of haciendas and slaves could be sold by the appropriate business manager. It is clear that in the eighteenth century both Rome and the local superiors were hoisting the warning signals.

Local government officials were equally explicit in warning and criticizing the Jesuits for their involvement in trade and commerce. The criticism became especially acute in the 1670s and 1680s when a flurry of royal orders from Madrid attempted to stop the Jesuits from dealing in tea and in manufactured goods from Spain. In 1679 a royal order to the bishop of Buenos Aires encouraged the prelate to have observed the brief forbidding ecclesiastics from trading. But even the royal order conceded that a repetition of the brief was impractical because "everyone did it and it was tolerated."[43] The Jesuits in Paraguay were singled out for their involvement in the yerba trade. What especially irked local government officials was Jesuit exemption from any type of sales tax, *alcabala* included. The Jesuits on their part argued that they were not buying goods for the purpose of reselling but simply selling the fruits of their estates in order to support their activities. And 9,000 pesos was annually turned over to the crown from yerba sales to pay the tribute of the Guaraní Indians.[44] What was particularly curious about the criticism and reaction of the Jesuits was the ambivalence exhibited by both critics and Jesuits. The governor of Buenos Aires, José de Ibarra, was at one time a staunch defender of the Jesuits. While admitting their suspect reputation for trading and acting against canon law, he offered several explanations in their defense. For one, wrote Ibarra, there was a critical shortage of coin currency and goods were used in exchanges. Through their business manager, the Jesuits had to buy quantities of supplies and goods for missions and parishes that for a layman would appear enormous.[45] But divided among so many, supplies were really quite modest in size. Ibarra was more than generous to the Jesuits and what he said was true, as far as it went. Supplying parishes and missions required enormous quantities of goods from thread to printing presses, all of which were stored in the College of Buenos Aires. But the other side of the coin was the sale of estate goods and purchase and sale of goods from Europe. The crux of the matter really lay here. But even in this the Jesuits had defenders in very high places. The governor of Buenos Aires, Fernando de Mendoza, wrote in 1682:

> Although many calumniate the Jesuits for being traders and covetous, it is said through ignorance. It is absolutely certain that they administer prudently and economically the fruits of their haciendas solely with a view to maintaining their colleges and houses. This they do by exchanging estate products for other goods they need. It cannot be done otherwise because there is here an acute shortage of silver coinage. . . .[46]

As I have argued elsewhere, the main issue for merchants who regularly marked prices up 200 percent was not whether the Jesuits violated canon law.[47] They may have said so but in reality the antagonism was fueled by the competition offered by the Jesuits. The town council of Córdoba admitted as much in 1769, two years after the expulsion of the Jesuits. The council wrote: "The backwardness of the Province of Tucumán during the existence of the Society of Jesus was due to the order's numerous haciendas and slaves which produced goods for sale at a low price. Other producers did not have such assets as numerous slaves and mule herds."[48] What the town council was saying was that Jesuit enterprises produced goods at low cost, which savings they were able to pass on to consumers. This decreased competition and allowed the Jesuits to corner the market on certain goods. This was what hurt.

In 1683–1684 the Jesuits dealt yearly with over 50,000 arrobas of yerba and tobacco produced in the mission reductions, and they had royal permission to sell 12,000 *arrobas* of yerba. However, only about 6,000 *arrobas* a year arrived in Buenos Aires from the reductions, and much of this was used as tender to buy goods from Spain.[49] If it were simply a matter of selling or exchanging yerba or exporting hides to Europe, it is unlikely that there would have been any flap over Jesuit commercial activity. Clerical involvement in trade was tolerated by ecclesiastical officials and winked at by the civil. But what disturbed the secular yerba farmers and merchants was the dominant, not to say monopolistic, position the Jesuits enjoyed. When the Jesuits began selling Indian-produced yerba because Spanish purchasers in Santa Fe and Buenos Aires paid ludicrously low prices, the day was not too far off when they would store and distribute it themselves. When this day came in the late seventeenth century, enough laymen were pushed out of the commercial picture to raise and continue raising a steady protest. Crown reaction was ambivalent. It slapped clerical wrists for participating in commerce, while knowing full well that 9,000 pesos a year were generated from yerba to pay Indian tribute. At the same time the government placated Asunción merchants by reducing official Jesuit yerba trading to 12,000 *arrobas* a year; and probably secretly applauded when informed that a good number of merchants were eliminated from the yerba trade by Jesuit warehouses and distribution activity.[50] The Council of the Indies put a final stamp of approval on the Jesuit tea trade in 1743, hearing the customary complaints but deciding that the trade should continue *sin novedad.*[51] And continue it did quite successfully for another two decades.

The local Jesuit superiors were sensitive to the criticism. Some of the questions listed in Appendix A reveal how ideally circumspect the local procurators were expected to be, but the ideal was out of reach of most, or easily rationalized. The *animo lucrandi,* or profit incentive, was considered a major factor in determining whether a transaction was "business" to be avoided or not.[52] And major emphasis was placed on whether goods were produced by hired personnel or by the farm's slaves, and whether the raw materials used were estate products or purchased for the purpose of manufacture. If made by hired personnel or produced from purchased material, a shadow of business hung over the procedure and hence it was to be avoided. But this was a transition period, a time when the medieval notions of business and usury were gradually giving way to a more modern view; when questions were raised about the appropriateness of former censures. The procurator whose assigned task it was to produce funds by intelligent business procedures would not have been very successful if he had to pause before each transaction and consciously eliminate any "desire for profit." Many of the judgments or declarations in Appendix A were properly products of a seminary classroom and probably found little acceptance on the ranch, farm, or procurator's office. The most widely accepted business guideline was *decencia,* appropriateness or propriety. This appeared frequently as a touchstone, "appropriate to our state." Of course, it was left to the individual to determine in each case what was or was not appropriate.

The European and American criticism of the economic activities of the Jesuits had its roots in the early medieval notion that certain trades were by nature illicit. Usurers, of course, and by extension anyone who handled money, were tainted. To a society living within the bounds of a natural economy—an agricultural framework—the invasion of the monetary economy represented a threat to existing society.[53] The Jesuits seemed to disregard this ancient taboo. They took advantage of price fluctuations to gain increased returns; they constructed a solid trading infrastructure that even included commercial listening posts; they lent money, borrowed for business and construction purposes, accumulated debts; in brief they did all that medieval society had branded as questionable. The Jesuits clung to the justification that good intentions (financial support of a religious institution) and not a bad one (an eye to profit, *lucri causa*) dominated their activity. But the issues were wider. Not only were they faced with byzantine-like European politics but also with the more basic problem of constructing an economic base for apostolic activities without depending exclusively on almsgiving. In attempting to construct such a base, to be totally independent economically, the Jesuits ran afoul of both lay- and churchmen. To the former they had become too powerful, too worldly; to the latter, too arrogant and successful.

Only in 1767 was the criticism silenced. Obeying a royal order of expulsion, thirty-four wagons and ten carts left Córdoba on July 23, 1767, at 2 a.m., loaded with 132 Jesuits and essential supplies bound for Buenos Aires where ships would transport the exiles to Europe. The scene was repeated in all Jesuit colleges and houses throughout Paraguay Province. The government office placed in charge of former Jesuit property (the *Junta de Temporalidades)* rented and then sold the Society's ranches and farms, auctioned off its slaves, and disposed of liquid assets. Silver was sent to Madrid and written records (account books and the like) were minutely examined for incriminating evidence. In the meantime, the carefully-developed libraries were sacked and creditors of the Jesuits caught by surprise knocked long and hard at the door of the *Junta de Temporalidades* demanding payments for mules, the use of wintering quarters, and for a variety of services and goods.[54] Some were never paid, caught in the interminable web of Spanish government bureaucracy. There was a touch of irony in the fact that the properties that had been so controversial under Jesuit ownership continued to be so even after their departure.

CHAPTER 8

Conclusion

The leap from the specificity of Jesuit rural activity to generalizations about the rural economics of colonial Latin America appears to be hazardous to say the least. How does one relate data from a localized to a macro-level context? Perhaps the most that can be expected from the data presented here and in my other two books *(Lords of the Land* and *Farm and Factory)* is a certain approach to the economic role of the large estate and an approximation of what life was like on as well as the business mentality of the large private or institutional ranch or farm. Despite the inexactitude, some generalizations can be attempted and implications explored. The focus of these three studies has been the relationship between the urban-based Jesuit educational institution and rural economic organization. Because no tuition was collected and funds from overseas or local financial markets limited, each of the universities and colleges that the Society of Jesus operated in the cities and towns of colonial Latin America was supported primarily by large rural farms, cattle ranches, or textile mills. The preeminent regional role of these lands and associated economic activities helps us understand rural agrarian organization as well as the commercial and financial activity of the period. These economic activities also help us understand more comprehensively the institutional role of a religious order in the colonial structure. The division of society into fighters, workers, and prayers explains why the religious institution (the prayers who prayed for the fighters) in medieval times received government grants of land as well as bequests, gifts, and inheritances from private sources.[1] In colonial Latin America the faint outline of this medieval heritage was present. Conquest society viewed the church as a stable institution representing shared traditional values in a new world of uncertain allegiances. Just as the monastery was perceived in the Dark Ages as the preserver and protector of Western Civilization, so too the religious order in Latin America was perceived as a major vehicle for preserving, defending, and propagating Spanish cultural values. In recognition of this essential service, the government provided stipends and land as sources of support. Lay society also contributed financially not only to achieve increased status but because it was considered to be the appropriately pious thing to do. Such support linked the religious to the values and aspirations of the new society. Funds and properties so acquired became the basis for the financial well-being of the religious establishment. Farms thrived. Ranches expanded. Real estate was rented and sold. Mortgages were collected. The religious orders in America were thus introduced into civic and political responsibility and integrated into the secular life of society.

The Society of Jesus was a major beneficiary of such government and private largesse coming primarily in the form of the period's major source of wealth, land. The nucleus of Jesuit landownership in Spanish America formed two triangles: the Santa Fe de Bogotá, Lima, Cuzco triangle, cutting through the Quito basins, and the Tucumán, Río de la Plata, Asunción triangle. On the periphery of these two zones were Chile, coastal New Granada, and Brazil. (The coastal *fazendas* of the Jesuit colleges of Brazil were of considerable local and international significance.)[2] Outside of the interior borders of the triangles and the Brazilian strip were Jesuit missions—to the Mojos, Llanos, the Amazon interior, and Mainas. The total number of Jesuit estate units found within the triangles is far less significant than the quality of the specific estate land and the productivity of the farm or ranch. The gradual acquisition and ownership of the major and most fertile parts of Peruvian coastal valleys, like Huaura, or Los Chillos in the Quito basin, was of far more social and economic significance than the claimed ownership and even working of frontier land. The key point is not so much the size of the estate but the efficiency and productivity of operation. A level of productivity greater than surrounding units meant greater influence on the supply of labor, on wages, and on prices. Thus, the estates controlled by the Jesuits had impact both on the prices of commodities and on the supply of labor. It was the level of production rather than acreage which explains the impact of Jesuit estates on the regional and local economy.

Given the major objective of these enterprises, the support of city-based educational institutions, these estates were money-making enterprises and not primarily self-contained, self-sufficient, quasi-monastic units. By design, these estates were located adjacent to supply routes which gave ready access to intermediate gathering points and major markets. Information about a potential land purchase always included assessment of market access.

The method of acquiring land units varied. Where town plots had not already been completely distributed among the conquerors, portions were reserved by the city council for religious institutions. Sizeable rural plots were distributed in a similar way, provided arable lands were available. But by and large the most extensive rural holdings were obtained by purchase. The general pattern was that the university or college acquired through grant or endowment funds an extensive piece of rural property. Adjacent or contiguous additions were made to the nuclear farm or ranch, and other properties were acquired as supportive or totally independent of the major enterprise.

The colleges were not merely passive recipients of property. Prior to acquisition of land there was usually a lengthy discussion concerning its utility. Even potential town council grants made early on were carefully examined before the institution made a request for the land. The discussion of the usefulness of the property was focused on a committee report called a *Razón de Utilidad* that outlined the benefits and disadvantages that might accrue. The exposition usually stated the major reasons why the property or enterprise should be purchased (or accepted as a donation), buttressed by empirical data. Factors of size, location, mortgage payments, past and projected income, capital needs, and investment potential were frequently examined.

Once it was agreed that a purchase or donation would be appropriate and useful, the process of actual acquisition began. This usually kept public scribes busy for weeks. Wills had to be drawn up, verified, or copied; titles to land had to be re-examined and triplicated; even maps were drawn. One transfer of land might involve a complicated series of documents involving prior endowment donation, land purchases, mortgage defaults, bankruptcy charges, and public auctions.

Jesuit acquisition of farm and ranch land in Asunción, Paraguay, and Tucumán assumed different characteristics from that of coastal Peru or Interandine Quito. Unoccupied land was much more abundant in Tucumán. Original generous grants followed by additional purchases and private donations contributed to the amassing of large estates in Córdoba, Paraguay, and the Río de la Plata, likewise on the frontier of New Granada. Even the surrounding legalities were more relaxed. Boundaries were hazy, often unfixed, and the land itself was even measured in three-mile units, leagues, rather than by the *fanegada* or three-hectare units.

The pattern of administration of Jesuit landholdings was similar throughout Latin America. The corporate owner, either the individual college or the Jesuit province as a corporate body, usually administered the landholding through a permanently resident majordomo. However, the largest of the Jesuit estates had resident Jesuit administrators and chaplains. This represented a departure of the Latin America Jesuits from European tradition. Latin American Jesuits actually managed the day-to-day operations of farms and ranches, and not merely collected farm rents, probably because originally the infrastructure could not supply efficient, honest majordomos. Directly overseeing the college's estates were the college business manager and the rector. They were advised by the general rules to visit their holdings frequently. In addition, the provincial superior, accompanied by the province business manager, also visited colleges estates every few years. The provincial interviewed resident Jesuits, inspected the farm and its operations, the financial books, and sometimes talked with laborers about their working and living conditions. The Jesuit provincial administration reported every three years to the central Jesuit office in Rome on the economic status of the colleges, residences, missions and their supporting landholdings. These were sometimes glowing reports that painted statistically favorable pictures. Problems with the actual running of rural enterprises are revealed only in the provincial's correspondence with the owner-college. The chain of command, roles, and responsibilities were clear. They stretched from the rural farm to the urban college and across oceans to Seville, Madrid, and to Rome.

It was significant that not only were Jesuit estates rationally managed, in the economic sense of maximizing or attempting to maximize returns, but also on an administrative level vertically integrated. In some degree this may have enhanced technical efficiency by shared methodology. It might also be noted that this overseeing function characteristic of Jesuit farms was an extension of the common practice with colleges and other houses of the Society. Such communication, indicative of centralized management, was a characteristic of Spanish colonial policy perhaps reflecting the "communication become management" syndrome.

Labor forms on Jesuit agricultural enterprises reflected local regional practices. However, one major difference between Jesuit and other estates was the increased reliance on black slave labor. Jesuit estates in general were characterized by massive investment in slave labor in the late seventeenth and eighteenth centuries. Major sugar haciendas of coastal Peru, Quito's mills and farms, and Tucumán's ranches all received major increases in slave laborers. This was not coincidental but the result of conscious decision-making based on economic motives. The black African slave became particularly connected with the large Jesuit sugar plantation or vineyard with economically rational agricultural production. The slave laborer became a commodity par excellence. Labor was capitalized; it became "appropriate" and therefore "moral."

The income generated from rural farming and ranching was correlated to the size of the supported institution. In general, income was used for maintenance and expansion of the physical plant, for the support of both students and faculty, and also for capital reinvestment in the form of farm construction and the purchase of new lands, equipment, and slave laborers. Income and expenditures are important because they can explain rates of return from rural enterprises, but for our purposes they are of special importance because it was precisely here that the ecclesiastical institution was linked with the wider commercial world, where the rural world interacted with the urban market. Estates sold their products locally; credit activity flourished for long-distance trading; rental agreements were signed. By the very nature of these activities colleges became involved in the secular aspects of society and politics.

The leap from the specificity of Jesuit rural activity to generalizations about rural economics is indeed hazardous. The differences between the private and the institutional rancher or landowner seem more significant than the similarities.[3] At the root of the differences were radically different financial bases characterized by access to credit or lack thereof. This affected the type and mode of agro-pastoral activity engaged in by either private or institutional landholder. The financial base of Jesuit economic activity was initially formed from donated endowment funds, public or private donations of land, and from additional land purchases that generated capital. Capital expenses such as buildings, herds, and slave laborers were made out of this original financial base. Since the major focus of the Jesuits was the local college or university, a civic and cultural symbol, the increased bequests, donations, and gifts permitted a gradual increase in the institution's economic activity. The stability of the institution also inspired confidence in sources of credit. In a society in which there were institutional and religious inducements for bequests to religious institutions and where Jesuits were running tuition-free quality educational institutions—and in cities where many of the rich with rural holdings lived—there was a continual flow of interest from capital available to Jesuits but not available to some degree to private ranchers and farmers. There were two different capital markets.

A second major difference was the attitude of the landholder or rancher toward his holdings. The institution did not engage in farming or ranching because it thought such activity had a value in itself, be-

160

cause such activity provided a meaningful "way of life." For the institution the farm and ranch were only a source providing the wherewithal to engage in the "real" work of the Society, urban education. Raising wheat or cattle was a means to an end. Farms were used as summer retreats or vacation spots where Jesuit scholastics swam and rode horses but they were never thought of as places to live permanently. Most Spanish Jesuits were products of the urban educational centers of Spain and the same was true of the American-born Jesuits who were in fact in the majority. They brought with them into the Society an urban bias that imaged a rural world of ignorance, stolid tradition, a poor but proud peasantry, and a sector of landless agricultural workers. This image created a context within which the institution set relationships with its workers, and it was eminently capitalistic in nature. Absentee ownership made for rational, efficient operations but also less humane. An owner-resident to some degree may be more the traditional farmer, seeking long-term stability rather than short-term maximization.

In another very important way the religious institutional owner differed from lay colleagues. By a twist of baroque (or medieval) logic, goods produced by ecclesiastical owners or their slaves, but not by wage laborers, could be legitimately sold.[4] Slaves were part of the household, the *familiari,* whereas hired workers were not. This resulted in massive slave purchases to reduce or eliminate the need to employ temporary workers. One result was that the Jesuits became the largest institutional slave owner in colonial Spanish America. But just how far ecclesiastical restrictions and limitations inhibited other Jesuit economic activity is difficult to say. The jurists of the university frequently cited *animo lucrandi,* the profit-making motive, as a major factor determining an economic activity's canonical legitimacy. The identification of attitudes and motives is a complicated if not impossible process. How was a college business manager to determine whether he was guided by a "profit-making motive" or a desire to bale his college out of a financial hole?

While it is difficult to say how closely the very complicated principles laid down by moralists and jurists were followed, there is ample evidence showing that price and profit limits were adhered to. A markup of 200 percent, common among many merchants in Tucumán, was considered excessive. Also the fact that Jesuit ranches and farms paid workers in goods that were assigned the current lowest market price indicates that a capitalist spirit was not wholly pervasive. The just price was not considered that which the consumer would pay but a figure dependent on a number of variables, the most important one of which was the *decencia de nuestro estado,* or appropriateness to the religious state. The lay merchant was not thus hampered, so the attempt by the cleric or religious to understand canon law in traditional Spanish fashion, as an onerous burden to be avoided, was often interpreted as simple hypocrisy. The "appearance of things" might strike the modern as hypocritical but it played an extremely important role in Latin behavior patterns. It was part of a given set of circumstances, the cultural environment that had to be respected.

Thus, the major differences between the institutional (Jesuit) owner and its lay counterpart revolved around finance, prices, and attitude toward the nature of buying and selling. But while differences certainly existed, similarities were present as well and it is these that encourage one to generalize, to make the leap from the specific to the more universal; or at the very least, to identify certain patterns suggesting that a rural economy developed along certain lines.

While colonial agricultural land for farming and grazing was abundant, more so in Tucumán and less so in Interandine Quito and coastal Peru, lack of available laborers restricted the size and development of farms. Moreover, markets were distant and the population, such as it was, limited demand for perishable commodities. Ranching was sometimes a feasible alternative. One suspects that a major factor in the rise of ranching in Tucumán was the absence of sizeable regional markets for foodstuffs.

Labor or the lack thereof was the perennial problem, in Peru in the sixteenth century and in Tucumán after Juan de Alfaro promulgated his ordinances in 1612. According to the governor, Luís de Quiñones, these measures "caused the Indian to flee to the mountains; he would no longer sow corn or wheat, and hunger, pestilence and the plague of Egypt descended on Indian and Spaniard alike."[5] The city of Córdoba complained that it did not have enough slaves to work the fields or bring in the harvests. They were all purchased by farmers and ranchers in Buenos Aires and Asunción. These are exaggerations, but with more than a kernel of truth. It is possible that lack of laborers was a major factor that made ranching more desirable. Far fewer hands were needed to tend herds of cattle and mules than to prepare, sow, and harvest a crop and keep the fields in order. Shortage of labor affected land use, and inclined many owners to engage in less labor intensive enterprises. Those with the capital available and willing to invest in a slave labor force were at an enormous advantage for they could engage in cereal production and cattle raising at the same time, one acting as a hedge against the other. If herd and cereal production were large enough, prices could be affected as the governor accused the Jesuits in Tucumán of doing.

The peculiar relationship between college and rural enterprise was similar to that between private owner and rural enterprise. Just as the farm and ranch furnished goods and services to the college, so it did to the private owner. The ecclesiastical institution developed its rural holdings within the parameters of perceived need. Time and again the phrase "whether necessary for our haciendas" appeared as the measure of legitimacy and appropriateness. The Spanish Jesuits were especially sensitive to the "appearance" of things, so they were intensely concerned with whether their activity had even the "appearance of business dealings." But one wonders whether the preoccupation with the "appearance of things" should be the subject of criticism. The Italian "bella figura" is not so much hypocrisy as the direction by way of which one approaches the appraisal of things. If so, the layman worked with a similar restraint. Both Jesuit and layman were driven by a profit-making motive. If profit is taken as a net surplus, then any enterprise seeks at least a modicum of such in the long run or it collapses. The question is whether this profit was at a conventional, appropriate level characteristic of a traditional enterprise, or "profit-maximization" which is at once the rational element of capitalism. Perhaps it was the perception of this rational element that was singled out as "the appearance of business dealings."

It is unlikely that the revenues acquired by Jesuit ranches such as Santa Catalina or Candelaria in Tucumán, or Vilcahuaura in Peru were ever achieved except by the largest of the privately-owned enterprises. The more modest farms owned by the smaller Jesuit colleges ranked in size with local farms. But until more detail is known about non-institutional farms and ranches, comparison is difficult. The same general enterprises were developed: cattle raising (mules and cows) and farming (wheat, corn, and some barley) but the degree of reinvestment, the rate of return on the enterprises, the number of slaves possessed, and the degree of reliance on hired labor are all key variables that must enter into a meaningful comparison.

Credit in the form of *censos* and loans was available to both institution and private owner, but the institution had the edge if only because of its stability. The major loan sources of the Jesuits were other religious institutions. These sources were available to laymen but perhaps neither at the same interest rate nor size.

A major advantage was held by the Jesuits in product distribution. The system of business offices, scattered throughout the Jesuit province and throughout Latin America, enabled colleges to store, ship, and distribute goods with fewer complications and with much less of the anxiety usually accompanying long-distance commerce.[6] Nonperishable goods could be stored until the price was right. Goods could be exchanged at a distance with college business managers confident that the rate of exchange was fair. Listening posts were thereby available in key centers to inform a college of prices, the business climate, or of sudden market changes. None of this was as rapidly available to the average distributor. What the Jesuits in fact enjoyed was a vertically integrated business that produced, stored, and distributed its product with the most up-to-date business information available.

Can the economic experience of the Jesuits in Tucumán, Peru, and Quito tell something about the religious institution's role in and effect on the society in which it existed? Within the past few years a number of historians have studied large European monastic institutions with this in view.[7] The results have offered not only new insights into the organization and operation of a religious institution, but also new approaches to the study of the social ecology of the region where they were located. Although the inferior quality data with which historians of similar Latin American topics must deal prevent a richly detailed analysis of all major aspects of the problem, nevertheless, a tentative general assessment based on solid data can be made. But even this is useful, given the paucity of appraisals of the colonial Latin American rural scene.

In the three regions about which I have written (Peru, Quito, and Tucumán), the Jesuits were part of a quasi "gift economy." As the medieval monasteries of an earlier period, they received gifts, bequests, and endowment funds frequently in the form of land. This was a major source of wealth. In return for these gifts the recipients were obligated to bestow spiritual favors on the donor; they were to intercede with the deity in their behalf. But these gifts were only a part of the source that generated income. The institution made many other land purchases and associated business transactions that generated income. Since the institutions involved conducted business, whether cattle, vegetable, supply purchases of related estate sales, to support entire colleges that held sometimes 300–400 individuals (students, faculty, and workers), the volume of these transactions was frequently large. This entire process and complex of interrelationships continued the late medieval ecclesiastical tradition of rural enterprise supporting urban activities. And the rural enterprise provided more than food and lodging. The urban college was frequently, and especially in colonial centers, a social focus. Religious and civic celebrations were often handled at least in part by the local college. This was an added expenditure, besides the food, clothing, medical expenses, building repair, alms, wages, and travel provided for by the rural enterprise. Within the restricted regional Latin American context, this represented a massive flow of goods and services. It also represented the perceived inferiority of rural vis-a-vis urban.

Perhaps inferiority is an inappropriate word. To the city dweller, to the Spaniard with a strong urban bias, the rural world was that of the country bumpkin.[8] It was half-civilized. Life was scarcely worth living unless accompanied by a significant urban linkage. For the Jesuit as well, the perception of and attitude toward the countryside was decidedly negative. Rural assignments were viewed with disdain, a place for the untrained, a dumping ground for those unfit for the urban college, the incompetent, or for those who had fallen out of favor with provincial superiors. The rural world furnished food for the urban dweller. It supplied land and produce which was sold or exchanged for other needed goods. The rural world was looked on as a means to an end. This is not to deny that the rural world possessed a dynamic of its own; a rhythm that synchronized its seasons with the movements of the urban word. It only meant that the major activities of a complicated society, those of government and its political decisions that affected the masses, those of commerce and business, and those cultural activities revolving around education and mores, were identified with the urban and not rural world. Urban society had its differentiated ranks and classes based on a variety of determinants. Rural society, whether Spanish, Indian, or mestizo, tended to be lumped together. One very real effect of this was to impede the development of a genuinely humane outlook toward the rural workers who labored on Jesuit estates. The tour of inspection undertaken by provincial superiors occurred every three to five years which meant that care of slaves and hired laborers was left to a local supervisor or overseer. He was more of a quality assurance specialist inspecting and organizing the labor force. As a result, a genuine rural spirituality never developed in the areas of Jesuit ranches and farms. Instead, periodic missions or sweeps through the countryside were undertaken by one or two fathers. Unlike an earlier time when the great monasteries of Europe were focal points of rural social, cultural, and religious innovation, the large ecclesiastical estate of rural Latin America served only as an economic entity interacting but little with lay society. I submit that this is because the rural estate was considered principally as a means to an end with value only insofar as it pumped financial life into the urban enterprise.

Another major role of the religious institution in rural Latin America was its sanction, support, and in some places construction, of land use patterns and agrarian structures. By their very size, Jesuit rural enterprises provided an enormous bulwark of support for a land use pattern that produced for the urban rather than the rural market, for a market at some distance from where the products originated. The sugarcane and vines grown on the haciendas of coastal Peru, the large flocks of sheep that provided wool for the mills of Interandine Quito, and the mules and *yerba mate* of Paraguay were features of an early capitalistic mentality concerned with profit. This was the forerunner of nineteenth-century cash crop production which by creating the plantation forced some countries to import grains and food. The religious institution did not create new land tenure relations but participated in a system whereby accumulation of smaller holdings to create a large hacienda was the accepted norm. The result was the incongruous situation of the religious institution (in this case the Society of Jesus), professing a vow of poverty but possessing the largest amount of land, the largest number of slaves, and the most prosperous rural enterprises.

Because the Latin American estate was not like the autonomous European Benedictine monastery, the agriculture was market-oriented, inducing particular patterns of land use and ownership. For the most part, it was an agriculture directed towards a Spanish market. This type of crop specialization (like sugarcane on coastal Peru) imposed specific patterns of ownership. The type of agriculture engaged in by Jesuit estates also reflected a strong environmental influence. Sugarcane readily adopted to the subtropical Peruvian coast; viticulture flourished on the coastal plateaus of southern Peru; barley was a major Andean grain because of its short growing season; the mountain grasses abundantly fed the sheep of Quito, and the fertile plains of Tucumán and the river valleys of the Paraná and Uruguay produced a variety of leaves, cereals, and cattle foods. These types of activity restricted to specific zones created certain types of farms, more or less large, that also were restricted in ownership to the Spanish elite. This is not to say that all Spanish-owned farms were immense—they were not—but only that the great majority of large farms (ranches) that did exist were Spanish-owned. Nor do I mean to say that the economic basis of agrarian society was the Spanish-owned large farm or ranch. Further research into the land tenure patterns of colonial Latin America might well reveal that the large landed estate was the economic base of limited, distinct zones of rural Latin America. The smaller Indian-owned farm might well have been not only more numerous (and undoubtedly they were before 1750) but also more active and vibrant on the rural scene than has hitherto been supposed. The type of agriculture engaged in by Jesuit estates with their attendant social and organizational features, clearly indicates that farm specialization existed very early in colonial Latin America.

The ownership features of these Jesuit farms and ranches likewise buttressed the colonial agrarian structure. The rural enterprises were based on an abundance of land and the availability of labor. These were the two essential features required to produce a high value good necessary to support the urban institution. Large amounts of land, absolute or relative, were obtained by Jesuit colleges either through donation or purchase. Black slaves were bought to provide the stable labor force. In 1767, over 7,000 black slaves worked on Jesuit farms, ranches, and colleges of Spanish America. The absolute numbers alone on these ecclesiastical lands reinforced the perception that black slavery was a totally moral and ethical entity in no way at variance with Christian beliefs. The large estate, then, with a hierarchy of paid and unpaid workers, occupying a fairly large expanse of land, became an accepted feature of the rural landscape. The relationship between the large farm or ranch and the small or contiguous native-owned farm is still in general poorly understood. How great the pull was from the small farm to the urban center or to paid labor on the large estate has not yet been measured. Where large estates did exist on the rural scene, with few exceptions their economic and social impact on surrounding Indian villages has not been assessed.[9]

How, in fact, does one measure and assess the impact of Jesuit rural activity on a locality? What effect did a major enterprise or group of enterprises have on the flow of the total quantity of produce? What percentage was the farms' and how did their production affect prices and labor? To assess adequately the economic impact of Jesuit production in Córdoba, there would be necessary a careful analysis over time of the level of production, the role of competitors, prices, wages, and available labor. Until this is done we must be content with some hazy qualitative judgments that perhaps can serve as the basis for hypotheses for further investigation.

As alluded to previously, the city council of Tucumán believed that the Jesuit estates of the region retarded economic growth because their superior infrastructure and production kept prices low and competition in check. In this case, the council might have been echoing the arguments of the Jesuits' economic rivals. But low prices are not necessarily a bad thing. Only if the Jesuit estates with their vertically integrated operation played the role of a modern supermarket which drove the smaller competitors out of business could there have been occasion for serious concern. This hardly could have occurred in the

Tucumán mule market since the Jesuits controlled only a small fraction of the mules shipped to Peru. And the *yerba mate* controversy involved the merchants of Paraguay. The council could only have had in mind farm products and textiles produced on college land and looms with the massive slave labor force concentrated on college enterprises. Added to this was the local business in yerba from the Paraguay missions. This whole complex of producing, selling, and shipping represented an enormous flow of goods.

The city council's statement is one of the few we have about the wider economic effect of Jesuit enterprises in Tucumán. Most commentators of the period restricted themselves to statements on the quantity and quality of holdings. While the council may not have been trying to curry favor with his Madrid superiors, it may have been consciously siding with the local economic elite. Some of their number stood to gain the most from the sale of Jesuit property and goods after the expulsion.

The religious institutional landowner played a major role in changing the agrarian life of colonial Latin America. Crop specialization, settlement patterns, and the landholding structure were altered. Indian systems of farming were affected, more profoundly in some places than others, but nevertheless affected.[10] These major changes took place within a century-and-a-half after the initial Spanish conquest. Of course, they were not solely due to the Jesuit landowner, and in most places changes in agrarian structure were accomplished without their presence. However, where Jesuits were present, especially in coastal Peru, Andean Quito, and Tucumán, their ranches and farms were preeminent in quality and quantity. Therefore, their effect on the rights and obligations governing ownership and control of land and on the political, economic, and social aspects of agricultural production could have been nothing if not profound.

APPENDIX A

The Morality of Business Transactions

The following document is the articulation by the Jesuit theology faculty of the College of Córdoba of what they perceived to be business activity permitted to their fellow Jesuits in Tucumán. They were not writing for laymen but for their clerical brethren who approached them with a series of questions about the canonical legitimacy and appropriateness of certain types of contractual activity. The document is important for several reasons.

The responses were written in 1711, during a transition period when finance capitalism was still under a shadow—confused and associated with the practice of usury. Lending money for a profit, hardly reprehensible today, was despised in centuries past as immoral and unjust. By extension the business-man or merchant was also suspect, much as we suspect "the used car dealer" of today. All the more reprehensible was the activity when practiced by religious or priests. There was a dual fault, if you will, one in the nature of the tainted activity and the other in the person who performed it. The dilemma, therefore, was clear: how was the business manager of a college supposed to provide and develop the economic base of the institution and at the same time not engage in "business activity," *negotiatio.* How was this tightrope to be walked when the only sources of finance were cattle, agriculture, or land, each of which required business acumen and expertise not usually acquired in seminaries?

The proposed solution was to make enough money from these activities to cover costs, and no more. But there's the rub. "Cost" was a very flexible term. Those costs incurred by the Colleges of Córdoba or Buenos Aires were far greater than those incurred by Catamarca or Salta. Church facades and rural structures varied considerably. And the person delegated to find and administer funds for these costs was the college business manager.

Several points should be underlined. One is the distinction made in the document between business and the species of business. Apparently what was intended was that there was not to be given even the remotest occasion for accusing the Jesuits of business dealings. So both were treated with equal rigor. Secondly, the key criteria to be used by colleges were the desire for gain *(animo lucrandi)* by which the business activity was totally tainted, and *decencia,* appropriateness to the religious state. It was not appropriate to sell wine to inns or deal with liquor. Even if an activity were neither business nor the species thereof, it had to be "decent," "appropriate" to the religious state. Thirdly, the intriguing idea that goods made by slave labor were legitimately saleable as products of the religious community's estates while those made by hired hands were not and were considered products of "business" activity reveals an almost medieval concept of slavery—the black slave was part of the larger estate family, a member of the medieval *familiari*. Of course, the idea was never taken too far but it was held and apparently justified the purchase of large numbers of black slaves for the Jesuit colleges of Paraguay.

But of course all of these distinctions were summarily dismissed as casuistry and hypocrisy. The careful distinctions made by the moral theologians often fell on deaf ears. The large houses, immense ranches and herds, far-flung vineyards and wheat fields were symbols of wealth and power. And they could not be explained away.

The translation of this document and that of Appendix B is on the literal side. Hopefully, some of the original Spanish flavor will thereby be retained.

Some doubts about certain contracts are resolved according to the opinion of missionary fathers of the College of Córdoba, Province of Paraguay.

Since it was our obligation not only to abstain from business dealings but also from whatever has the appearance of business, according to Canon 25 of the Second General Congregation that stated: "All activity that has the appearance of secular business, for example, selling farm products and other things in a public market, is understood to be forbidden to ours," it was asked in the Seventh General Congregation what precisely were those things that had the appearance of business. Because there were so many examples, the Congregation felt that to enumerate them all was impossible and so contented itself with expressing Decree 84 of the Seventh Congregation.

It is not possible to enumerate all examples of the appearance of business dealings, but necessity obliges us to inquire if some contracts which are common in this province are in reality business or at least give the appearance of business or if these two things are separable. To this end the following doubts or questions are proposed to which concise answers are required either affirming or denying with the necessary distinctions whether there is present business or only the appearance of such or whether neither is present.

Doubts about some contracts

1. It is doubted whether it be business or the species thereof if one buys a number of two-year-old mules from traders under pretext of completing the herd already purchased under contract but then selling those mules purchased. It is alleged that this is done because some of the mules escape, are lost, or die in wintering quarters. The same is asked about mares, cows, horses, and other cattle.

Answer: Ordinarily it would be a business transaction because always some cattle are lost or die and for this reason a sufficient number of cattle should be available according to the calculation of usual loss. But if in some fortuitous case more cattle than usual are lost òr die, it would not be business or the species thereof unless they are sold at a higher price than purchased.

2. Would it be business or the species thereof to buy mules, cows, mares, oxen, horses, and without changing or fattening them on our lands to fatten the herd and sell it at a higher price on the pretext of thereby paying salaries and transportation costs? It happens frequently that costs so increase that not even half of the proceeds is sufficient to cover them.

Answer: This is clearly business even though one buys to sell merely to cover costs of salaries and transportation because always in this kind of transaction is the desire for profit.

3. Would it be business or the species thereof to buy some mules even though they are not needed by our haciendas with the sole intention of having them a few months without need of fattening or improving them and then sell them at a higher price in Salta or Peru? The same doubt is raised about other kinds of cattle.

Answer: This is surely business.

4. Would it be business or the species thereof to fatten the cattle of others on rented pasturage? The cattle would then be sold by its owner at a higher price.

Answer: This has the appearance of business.

5. Would it be business or the species thereof to clear a pasturage for twenty of our mules then learn that the pasture can take forty, and in order not to lose the pasturage buy twenty more mules to sell them after they are pastured in said rented lands?

Answer: This has the species of business. This is especially true if there were another way of fattening the cattle without having to spend money on more land rentals with greater carrying capacity and consequently more expensive.

6. Would it be business or the species thereof given that there is available rented pasturage on which to fatten our cattle to leave these lands for others of greater size and capacity and in order not to waste the pasturage to buy more mules and then sell them at a higher price?

Answer: This has the appearance of business.

7. Would it be business or the species thereof to sell surplus church jewelry in exchange for mules (the buyer claiming he has no silver) at a low price and then sell them at a higher price without fattening the mules?

Answer: It would be business if it is done with the desire for gain. Even if another buyer is found who would use silver at a just price, the transaction would still have the appearance of business even though it is alleged that it is accomplished without the desire for gain.

8. Would it be business or the species thereof to sell, as is sold, mules receiving payment in textiles, silverware, or other precious metals that pass for coin and selling these precious goods in our missions in exchange for yerba, tobacco, and linen, selling said goods at a high price and receiving linen at four

171

reales a vara, yerba at two pesos an arroba and tobacco at a moderate price; and afterwards selling these products at current prices which are higher?

Answer: It is a species of business if there is someone available who can buy in silver or in goods that the college needs and still the products of mule sales are sold to the missions for goods the college does not need, being present the intention of resale. If this last condition were lacking, it is neither business nor species thereof. However, there might be a question of injustice if goods at such excessively high prices are sold to the missions.

9. Would it be business or the species thereof to buy cows and without fattening them on our own haciendas in order to slaughter them for soap, grease, and jerked beef?

Answer: It would be the species of business if said products were not made principally by hacienda slaves but by hired labor.

10. Would it be business or the species thereof if out of grave necessity when the diezmos are purchased, mules also are bought (as all know the mules are not necessary but must be sold) in case it might be possible to buy the diezmo and not the diezmo of the mules?

Answer: It is neither business nor the species thereof if the mules are changed or fattened on our pasturage. But it would be if they are fattened or changed on rented pasturage.

11. Would it be business or the species thereof to order not our slaves but hired laborers to sew and weave wool or cotton?

Answer: It would be the species of business if such goods were bought and acquired by contract in order to benefit from and sell them for a profit.

12. Would it be business or the species thereof to give what is grown on our college lands, e.g., wheat, to laymen so that they knead it in their own house and sell it as their own, paying these people for their work?

Answer: It would not be business or the species thereof but it would be against province regulations which state that this could not be done in accordance with the decency of our religious state.

13. Would it be business or the species thereof to have made saddles, carriages, bricks, tiles, reins, spurs, etc., not by our own slaves but by paid laborers?

Answer: It would be the species thereof if the raw materials were bought and were not from our haciendas.

14. Would it be business or the species thereof to have made belts or sashes by laymen or buy them made with the intention of sending a portion to the port of Buenos Aires and there to buy ruan, clothing material, etc., or send them to Paraguay there to buy yerba, tobacco, sugar, and transport these products and sell them at a higher price and make much more money than what they were worth?

Answer: It is business if done with the desire for gain.

15. Would it be business or the species thereof for the prefect of a *cofradía* to take alms given to his group (if given in goods) and send them someplace else for sale or exchange where they have better exchange values and prices

and thus exchanged for other goods sell them where they have a good sale price in order to advance the economic base of the *cofradía*?

Answer: It would be the species of business.

16. Would it be business or the species thereof to invest the alms received in goods and send them in several trips to haciendas and ranches gaining twenty pesos a trip and even more for the *cofradía*?

Answer: This is business.

17. Would it be business or the species thereof if the rector of a college residence used the silver that the residents gave for their food to exchange for goods that were not going to be used in the college and thus keep exchanging to the profit of the college?

Answer: This is business.

18. Would it be business or the species thereof for a rector or procurator of a college to invest the silver from sales of hacienda products in goods which he knows will not be used in the college, e.g., if he needs only ten varas of linen, he buys four arrobas, and needing only 200 arrobas of yerba or tobacco, more is purchased?

Answer: It is business if it was bought with the implicit or explicit intention of selling later at a profit and absolutely speaking it would be the species of business if excessive quantity (according to prudent judgment) were always obtained either because the goods were lacking or because it could happen, morally speaking, that more would have to be purchased at a higher price.

19. Would it be business or the species thereof to buy with silver goods in order to pay for or buy what was needed, with this difference: that by paying or buying with silver and then the silver is used up, but by paying or buying with goods, the principal remains intact or even increases?

Answer: It would be business or at least the species thereof if one can pay in silver or if one can easily buy goods that one needs with silver.

20. Would it be business or the species thereof if one could sell the products of the college or community for silver at a just price current in the city but instead one sells them for other goods which in turn have to be resold at higher prices?

Answer: This is business.

21. Would it be business or the species thereof to sell products or goods of a college and in exchange buy at a lower price what the college needs?

Answer: It would not be business nor the species thereof *secundum* [quid] because according to some there has been repeated exchanges; but there is a precept in the province of not selling purchased goods without permission of the provincial, and only goods acquired in payment for the fruits of our haciendas are exempt, and this exemption is because these goods could not have been sold for silver nor could they have had a good sale except through exchange.

22. Would it be business or the species thereof to buy necessary wine or aguardiente under pretext that wine sours and keeping aside what is necessary for community use put the rest in an inn owned by a layman so that the latter

could sell it as his own product as long as the principal cost of the wine is deducted and what is used in the house is free and without cost?

Answer: It is business if it is purchased with the intention of selling for a profit no matter how it is colored by a pretext. But if there was no implicit or explicit intention at the time of purchase then it was neither business nor the species thereof. However, it would be against the precept of the province since such activity with wine is not appropriate to our religious state.

23. Would it be business or the species thereof to buy wax, linen, yerba, or tobacco in order to sell the same wax and buy with the proceeds more linens, yerba, or tobacco at considerable gain?

Answer: It would be business.

24. Would it be business or the species thereof to lend a layman silver or some other goods that he needs and in return the college receive goods that it does not need and then sell these said goods at a much higher price in order to obtain silver and retain the profits?

Answer: At the least it is the species of business if the loan is made with the intention of profiting from the sale of the goods given as a substitute for what is left, but it is not a species of business if this object were not intended.

25. Would it be business or the species thereof to buy ruan, cambray, cottons, yerba, tobacco or anything else in great quantity on credit, greater than what the college needed, and then sell half in order to recoup the original sum spent or most of it and so to pay off legitimate college needs and in the process acquire profit little by little?

Answer: This is business if purchase is made with intent to sell at a greater price for a profit and always such contracts have the species of business.

26. Would it be business or the species thereof given the fact that merchants do not like to sell retail to a Fr. procurator of a college just what the college needs but wholesale in bulk or various kinds of linens, iron, paper, wax, silks, woolens, with a selection called *listoneria*, combs, thread, hats, silk stockings, etc.? What if a procurator buys all of this and being able to retain what the college needs and sell what it doesn't at cost price, he does not do this but he sells piece by piece for a profit?

Answer. It is not business nor the species thereof to sell the whole lot or a considerable part of it even though it be at a higher price than the purchase; however, it still has the species of business if it is sold piece by piece given that the lot could be sold in bulk.

27. Would it be business or the species thereof to obtain a profit of 100 or 200 percent as do laymen for the goods mentioned in the previous doubt?

Answer: To sell at such high prices the goods mentioned in the previous doubt would or would not be a species of business according to the distinctions made above; but it is ordered in this province that goods given as salaries are given at the lowest price current in the city and it should be kept in mind that not only goods but even products should be sold at the lowest price since this is more in conformity with good example.

28. Would it be business or the species thereof for a college to sell to others goods at 100 or 200 percent profit as said in the above doubt?

Answer: The same response is in order. But keep in mind that there is an order in this province that when a college sells some goods to another college, they are sold at cost price.

29. Would it be business or the species thereof to buy salt with goods for sale in Santa Fe then resell these at a higher price for a considerable profit?

Answer: It is business.

30. Would it be business or the species thereof to collect common salt in Las Salinas not with slaves but with hired labor then sell it in Santa Fe, returning to the Province with goods for sale a good profit?

Answer: It would be business if done with the desire to buy with the said salt goods for resale at a higher price.

31. Would it be business or the species thereof to buy fat for soap not for ordinary college use but to sell it when said soap is made by hired labor and not by college slaves?

Answer: It is business and the species thereof.

32. Would it be business or the species thereof to continually transport goods from one city to another and sell them at increasing profits, e.g., eight to ten reales, to twelve reales for a vara of linen purchased at four reales, and in the same way yerba, salt, wax, sugar, and tobacco?

Answer: At the very least this is the species of business if these goods are not products of one's hacienda and if said goods are purchased or exchanged with the intention of selling them at a higher price, it is certainly business.

33. Would it be business or the species thereof to buy clothing in Buenos Aires, for example, and afterwards give it as payment in Corrientes to hired workers who round up cattle in *vaquerías* because of the lack of silver coinage?

Answer: It is neither business nor the species thereof to buy clothing for such a reason if done without the desire of profit and because Corrientes does not have other kinds of goods acceptable to hired workers.

34. Would it be business or the species thereof to give goods at such high prices as salaries to salaried workers who collect cattle in Las Corrientes as said above in the same way that merchants do who bring goods for sale at high profits?

Answer: Purchasing such goods as mentioned above is at least the species of business because of the excessive prices which the merchants in Las Corrientes are accustomed to charge (more than 200 percent markup).

35. Would it be business or the species thereof to make so much profit on goods in Las Corrientes, e.g., bought for 1,747 pesos in Santa Fe or Buenos Aires and sold in Las Corrientes for 8,627 pesos not for silver but for *pesos huecos* or in goods of the land as they say here?

Answer: It is business if the goods were bought with the intention of selling or exchanging them in Corrientes but if they were purchased without this intention and in good faith, having been judged that they were necessary for the ordinary use of the college, and afterwards they were sold or exchanged at such high profits, then it would not be business; however, there remains a serious reason for suspecting that there is a species of business present and even of judging that with such excessive profits proper edification, example and even justice was lacking.

These resolutions which were given concerning these thirty-five doubts conform to the opinion of the Fathers Professors of the Colegio Máximo de Córdoba and are to be observed in practice as long as Fr. General does not dispose otherwise. And so I order seriously that no one of ours do anything that seems censurious of business or the species thereof according to these resolutions. Córdoba, March 1, 1711. Antonio Garriga.

SOURCE: BS, in bound volume titled "Paraguay."

APPENDIX B

Directives to the
Office of the Missions
on Business Activity, 1738

The general and specific principles given in Appendix A applied for the most part to goods produced on Jesuit farms and ranches. In 1738 the provincial, Jaime Aguilar, pointed out two areas of acute concern that did not involve Jesuit-produced goods. Apparently, the mission office in Buenos Aires handled goods produced by laymen and also gold and silver owned by others. This raises several questions. Why were the activities of buying and selling performed by the Jesuit office? For friends, for those who were in some way connected to the office by previous dealings, or for future considerations? And why did they go through the Jesuit office at all? What advantages accrued? Trust, reliability, convenience. Apparently Aguilar thought that the province had enough to handle with criticism about selling its own produce let alone compounding the problem by acting as agent for others. So he put his foot down. The first sentence of the letter has an almost fatalistic ring. The phrase, "greater discredit is feared in the future," gives the sense of bracing for a battle soon to come. Aguilar was correct. There were more and fatal criticisms of the Society in the future that eventually led to its expulsion from Spanish America in 1767.

Precepts of Father Provincial Jaime Aguilar for the Office of Missions in the College of Buenos Aires.

In order to eliminate the disorders and the great discredit that the Society of Jesus has begun to experience (and greater ones are feared for the future), I order the Father Procurators or whoever is in their place in the Office of the Missions in virtue of Holy Obedience under pain of mortal sin that they do not perform any act of buying for the purpose of selling nor any other act of business even though the goods involved belong to Indians, laymen, or clerics. Only those acts are licit and allowed that involve goods owned by the Society as long as they conform to the common precepts of the province and those specifically given to the Office of the Missions.

I order these same procurators and their replacements as well as all members of the Society in the College and Hospital of Our Lady of Belén under Holy Obedience that gold or silver (minted or not) not belonging to the Society or its missions, even though it arrive labeled or with letters for any of ours, be not admitted as belonging to us but it be manifested that it has another owner. The effect of this will be to dispel the notion that we or the Indians are rich and that a great deal of treasure passes through our hands.

These two precepts are to be included among those of the other provincials and read to the community once a year. Buenos Aires, August 24, 1738. Jaime Aguilar.

SOURCE: AGBA, Compañía IX, 6-9-7.

Notes

Introduction

1. Nicholas P. Cushner, *Lords of the Land. Sugar, Wine, and Jesuit Estates of Coastal Peru* (Albany: SUNY Press, 1980).

2. Nicholas P. Cushner, *Farm and Factory. The Jesuits and the Development of Agrarian Capitalism in Colonial Quito* (Albany: SUNY Press, 1982).

3. For Mexican background to Jesuit estate development see Herman W. Konrad, *A Jesuit Hacienda in Colonial Mexico. Santa Lucía, 1576–1767* (Stanford: Stanford University Press, 1980), pp. 31–45.

4. Two fairly recent and revealing studies of Indian warfare are Alfred J. Tapson, "Indian Warfare on the Pampas during the Colonial Period," *Hispanic American Historical Review* 42 (1962): 1–28; and Robert Ryall Miller, "The Fake Inca of Tucumán: Don Pedro de Bohorques," *Americas* 23 (1975): 196–210.

5. Report of October 25, 1581, AGI, Charcas 34.

6. Ibid., Charcas 26.

7. AGI, Charcas 26, 34 and Buenos Aires 37 and 39 contain several sixteenth- and seventeenth-century accounts of battles with Indians and reports of expenditures made to resist incursions.

8. AGI, Buenos Aires 49.

9. See the detailed account of battles, especially one near Santa Fe around 1760 when 120 Indians were killed, 124 captured and 325 horses taken, in AGI, Buenos Aires 37.

10. Report of August 2, 1777, Ibid., Buenos Aires 49.

11. Report of July 25, 1682, AGI, Charcas 26.

12. In 1638 the Mexican provincial pointed out to the viceroy that most of the cattle raised on the mission ranches of Sinaloa were slaughtered for the fiesta celebrations of the Indians. The object was to render the Indians benevolent before catechizing them. ARSI, FG 1467/5, fol. 4.

1. The Lay of the Land

1. The physical geography described in this chapter is a combination of Preston James, *Latin America* (New York: Odyssey Press, 1959), pp. 324–31; Ione S. Wright and Lisa M. Neckhorn, *Historical Dictionary of Argentina* (Metuchen, N.J.; Scarecrow Press, 1978), pp. 218–19; T. E. Weil, *Area Handbook*

for Argentina (Washington, D.C.: U.S. Government Printing Office, 1974), pp. 31–37; and Antonio Ortells, *Manual de geografía de la provincia de Córdoba* (Buenos Aires, 1906) pp. 10–11.

2. José Torre Revello (ed.), *Documentos históricos y geográficos relativos a la conquista y colonización rioplatense. I.* (Buenos Aires: Casa Jacobo Peuser, 1941), 84.

3. Ibid., pp. 174, 285.

4. Roberto Levillier, *Descubrimiento y población del Norte Argentina por españoles del Perú* (Buenos Aires: Espasa-Calpe, 1943.)

5. "Relación de Pedro Sotelo Narbaez," in Torre Revello, *Documentos históricos,* 84.

6. Pedro Greñón, *Documentos históricos. El Libro de Mercedes.* (Córdoba: Talleres Gráficos de la Penitenciaria, 1930).

7. Pedro Greñón, *Documentos históricos. Los Pampas.* (Córdoba: Talleres Gráficos de la Penitenciaria, 1927), p. 16.

8. Ibid., pp. 29–30.

9. Ibid., pp. 33–37.

10. Ibid., pp. 43–44.

11. Greñón, *Documentos históricos. El Libro de Mercedes,* p. 206.

12. "Relación de la tierra, (1573)," Torre Revello, *Documentos históricos,* pp. 69–70.

13. Jane Pyle, "A Reexamination of Aboriginal Population Estimates for Argentina," in William M. Denevan (ed.), *The Native Population of the Americas in 1492* (Madison: University of Wisconsin Press, 1976), pp. 181–204.

14. The best general survey of the Jesuits in Tucumán is Joaquín Gracia, *Los jesuitas en Córdoba* (Buenos Aires: Espasa-Calpe, 1940).

15. Ibid., p. 226.

16.. Ibid., p. 232; a detailed manuscript description of novitiate holdings is in AGBA, Jesuitas IX, 47–8–2.

17. CA, 2, 65–66.

18. AGBA, Temporalidades de Córdoba, IX, 29–9–3, fols. 241–54.

19. Oscar Dreidemie, "La estancia jesuitica de Jesús María," *Boletín de la Comisión Nacional de Museos y Monumentos Históricos* 9 (1948): 13; the documentation for many of these transactions is in MJM.

20. Hernando de Torreblana to Rector of Córdoba, La Rioja, September 18, 1637, MJM.

21. AHC, Escribania 2, 7–2.

22. Guillermo Furlong, *Historia del Colegio de la Inmaculada de la ciudad de Santa Fe, 1610–1692* (Buenos Aires, 1962), p. 382.

23. Ibid., pp. 398–406.

24. College lands are described in detail in "Relación de las tierras," AGBA, Jesuitas 45–3–13. What is said below about Asunción's holdings is for the most part based on this account.

25. CA, 2, 202.

26. Ibid., p. 256.

27. AGBA, Jesuitas 47–8–9.

28. CA, 2, 512, 572, 397–398.

29. Aroaz to Hidalgo, Nonagasta, c. 1700, AGBA, Compañía IX, 7–1–2.

30. Catalogus Rerum Prov. Paraq., Colegio de la Rioja, ARSI, Paraq. 6.

31. Documents on foundation covering 1739–1746 are in AGI, Charcas 396.

32. AGBA, Compañía IX, 6–10–1.
33. CA, 2, 199.
34. AGBA, IX, 7–3–7.
35. Ibid., and IX, 6–10–6, docs. 270–73.
36. Letter from Frias written around 1700 is in BNC, Jesuítas 203, doc. 101.
37. Horacio C. E. Giberti, *Historia económica de la ganadería argentina* (Buenos Aires: Solar/Hachette, 1970), p. 16.
38. "Relación de la tierra, (1573)," Torre Revello, *Documentos históricos,* 69–70.
39. Ibid., p. 170.
40. Same as note 36.
41. Antonio de la Tijera to king, Jujuy, September 30, 1702, BNC, Jesuítas 199.
42. AHC, Escribanía 2, 2/19.
43. MJM, 1660.
44. "Litigio judicial, 6 mayo 1666," MJM.
45. Case of September 7, 1732, AGBA, Compañía IX, 6–9–6, fols. 702–703; also case of Areco vs. Don Pascual de Zarate who kept cattle on college land, April 15, 1749, Ibid., Jesuítas 45–3–13.
46. AHC, Escribanía 2, 4/10.
47. AHC, Escribanía 2, 12/14.
48. Ibid., fols. 19–20.
49. See also AHC, Escribanía 1, 222/8; and Escribanía 2, 2/3; 4/10.

2. Farmsteads and Ranches

1. For architectural comparison see Pál Kelemen, *Baroque and Rococo in Latin America* (New York: Dover Press, 1967).
2. Photographs in *La Prensa* (Buenos Aires), July 8, 1973 *(Secciones Ilustradas).*
3. Kelemen, *Baroque and Rococo,* pp. 43, 195.
4. A note on an eighteenth-century map showing major towns says that the houses of the Spanish rural and urban poor scarcely differed from those of the Indians. Guillermo Furlong, *Cartografía jesuítica del Río de la Plata* (Buenos Aires: Casa Jacobo Peuser, 1936), Map XXII; for construction materials used in Córdoba see Juan Kronfuss, *Arquitectura colonial en Córdoba,* (Córdoba: A. Biffignanchi, n.d.), pp. 52–53, 63–69, 82–89.
5. Kelemen, *Baroque and Rococo,* p. 193.
6. Ibid. Also personal inspection of this and other hacienda structures by author in 1973–1974.
7. David Mitchell, *The Jesuits. A History* (London: Macdonald, 1980), pp. 135, 139.
8. Mark Girouard, *Life in the English Country House. A Social and Architectural History* (New Haven and London: Yale University Press, 1978), pp. 2–3.
9. "Preceptos, 1710," in BS.
10. See these ideas developed in Cushner, *Lords of the Land,* pp. 175–80.
11. Economic report of Francisco Urbano de Zarate, October 14, 1644, FG 1483/3/5.
12. Most of what is said here is based on the entries and inventories in LCC.

13. AGBA, Temporalidades de Córdoba, IX, 21–9–3.

14. Carlos Storni, *Descripción de viñedos que se cultivan en Argentina desde la época colonial* (Córdoba: Alianza, 1927), p. 15.

15. Ibid., pp. 47–48.

16. Memorandum of Miguel López, June 16, 1736, AGBA, IX, 6–9–7.

17. Visit of La Rioja, July 20, 1754, AGBA, IX, 6–10–1, doc. 748.

18. AGBA, Temporalidades de La Rioja, IX, 22–7–1.

19. Accounts of August 4, 1757, AGBA, IX, 6–10–7; and Razón año de 1765, Mendoza, Ibid., 6–10–6.

20. LCC, fol. 408.

21. Memorandum of February 2, 1739, AGBA, IX, 6–9–7.

22. See Appendix A, numbers 22 and 28.

23. Gracia, *Los jesuítas,* p. 378.

24. Antonio de Castillo to José Rodriguez, Córdoba, December 22, 1762, AGBA, Compañía IX, 6–10–5.

25. AGBA, Compañía IX, 6–10–5.

26. Thyrso Gonzalez to Simón de San Miguel, Rome, April 12, 1699, APA.

27. Catalogues in ARSI, Paraq. 6.

28. AGBA, Compañía IX, 7–1–1; other collections of directives written by Jesuit provincials in the seventeenth and eighteenth centuries are in "Paraguay," BS.

29. See especially his letters of December 13, 1736 and April 1, 1734, APA.

30. European monastic establishments with extensive agricultural holdings bear comparison. See Colin Platt, *The Monastic Grange in Medieval England. A Reassessment* (New York: Fordham University Press, 1969), pp. 11–12.

31. Barbara Harvey, *Westminster Abbey and Its Estates in the Middle Ages* (Oxford: At the Clarendon Press, 1977), p. 3.

32. Ibid., pp. 11–12.

3. The Mule Trade

1. Memorandum to Altagracia, December 28, 1747, AGBA, Compañía 6-10-1, doc. 130.

2. Theodore H. Savory, "The Mule," *Scientific American.* #223 (1970): p.103.

3. Ibid., p. 104.

4. Most of what follows is based on Estela B. Toledo, "El comercio de mulas en Salta, 1657–1698 "*Anuario del Instituto de Investigaciones Históricas* (Rosario, Argentina), 6 (1962–1963): 165–190; also Nicolás Sánchez Albornoz, "Extracción de mulas de Jujuy al Peru. Fuentes, volumen, y negociantes," *Estudios de historia social* (Octubre, 1965): 107-20; (with Patricia Ottolenghi de Frankmann, Manuel Urbina, and Dorothy Webb), "La saca de mulas de Salta al Peru, 1778–1808," *Anuario del Instituto de Investigaciones Históricas* (1965): 261-312; also the "Entrada y saca de mulas de esta estancia desde Marzo 1718," APA.

5. Concolorcorvo. *El Lazarillo de ciegos caminantes desde Buenes Aires hasta Lima, 1773* (Buenos Aires: Ediciones Argentinas Solar, 1942), pp.

112–13; and the translation of this colorful travel description: Concolorcorvo. *El Lazarillo. A Guide for Inexperienced Travelers between Buenos Aires and Lima, 1773* translated by Walter K. Kline (Bloomington: Indiana University Press, 1965).

6. Statement of Francisco Ortiz, 1674, AHC, Escribanía 2, 3/4.

7. LC.

8. Report of Manuel Rodríguez, in Pedro Greñón, *Alta Gracia. Documentos Históricos* (Córdoba, 1929), p. 102.

9. Ibid., p. 103.

10. April 10, 1734, AGBA, Compañía, IX, 6-9-6, doc. 919.

11. AGBA, Temporalidades de Córdoba IX, 21-9-3.

12. "Entrada y saca de mulas de esta estancia desde marzo 1718," APA, fol. 270.

13. In 1736 Areco sold 2,194 mules and Paraquari had 2,500 in 1720. AGBA, Compañía IX, 6-9-7; also see 6-10-1.

14. Report in AGBA, Compañía IX, 6-9-3.

15. "Instrucción," AGBA, Temporalidades de Salta IX, 22-1-1.

16. AGBA, Compañía IX, 7-1-2.

17. Ibid., 6-10-5.

18. Ibid., 6-9-7, doc. 454.

19. LCC, fol. 94.

20. In 1741 the cost of driving a herd from Tafi to Salta was 620 pesos, LCC, fol. 363; in 1748, 18 *peones* and a foreman were paid 425 pesos for a mule drive, LCC, fol. 419. The usual cost of driving mules was six reales per head.

21. "Razón de las mulas," AGBA, Compañía IX, 7-1-1.

22. AGBA, Compañía IX, 6-10-1, doc. 1003.

23. "Poder otorgado, 4 set. 1745," AGBA, Compañía IX, 6-9-7.

24. AGBA, Compañía IX, 6-9-3, fol. 900.

25. Parodi to Morales, Salta, October 24, 1743, AGBA, Compañía IX, 6-9-7.

26. Baylina to Juan de Echaneque, Salta, February 27, 1734, AGBA, Compañía IX, 6-9-6, doc. 916.

27. Baylina to Machoni, Potosí, July 23, 1742, ACBA, Compañía IX, 6-9-7.

28. Miranda to Aruel, Córdoba, December 8, 1766, AGNBA, Compañía IX, 6-10-7.

29. Concolorcorvo. *Lazarillo. A Guide,* p. 122.

30. See Peter Bakewell's figures in Herbert S. Klein, *Bolivia. The Evolution of a Multi-Ethnic Society* (New York: Oxford University Press, 1982), p. 289.

31. Ibid., pp. 56, 57.

4. Works and Days: The Functioning Farm

1. Walter Larden, *Estancia Life. Agricultural, Economic, and Cultural Aspects of Argentine Farming* (London: Unwin, 1911), republished Detroit: Blaine Ethridge Books, 1974.

2. For standard accounts of the period see James R. Scobie, *Argentina. A City and a Nation* (New York: Oxford University Press, 1971); and Jonathan Brown, *A Socioeconomic History of Argentina, 1776-1860* (Cambridge: Cambridge University Press, 1979).

3. Scobie, *Argentina,* pp. 57–58.

4. Produced here means shipped to the College of Córdoba from the vineyard. This included almost all of the wine and aguardiente; little was kept on the estate for sale in view of the Jesuits' decision not to sell it for public consumption. See Appendix A, number 22.

5. "Método y instrucción para el arreglo de capataces y mayordomos, 1768," excerpted in Orestes de Lullio, *La estancia jesuítica de San Ignacio* (Santiago del Estero, 1954), pp. 77-84.

6. AGBA, IX, 22-7-1.

7. Ibid. 6-10-6.

8. See the catalogues of economic data, Catalogus Rerum, in ARSI, Paraq. 6; and visita report of July 26, 1754, AGBA, IX, 6-10-1, doc. 748.

9. Machoni's memorandum is in AGBA, Compañía IX, 6-9-7.

10. See the memoranda of Bernard Nusdorfer, 1745, AGBA, IX 6-9-7, fol. 1029; Lorenzo Rillo 1726, Ibid., 6-9-6, doc. 447; and Antonio Machoni, 1739, Ibid., 6-9-7.

11. See, for example, the letters of Antonio de Castillo, Córdoba, February 22, 1762, AGBA, IX 6-10-5, and the Governor of Tucumán, March 18, 1671, Pablo Pastells, *Historia de la Compañía de Jesús en la Provincia del Paraguay (Argentina, Paraguay, Uruguay, Peru, Bolivia y Brasil) según los documentos originales del Archivo General de Indias* (Madrid: Libreria General de Victoriano Suárez, 1912–1948), III, 29-30.

12. ARSI, Paraq. 2, fols. 74–75, (SL, 151). Payment of salaries in kind to estate workers lasted well into the nineteenth century. See articles given as wages on the estate of Las Vacas, in Jonathan C. Brown, *A Socioeconomic History,* p. 43.

13. LCC, fol. 406.

14. Morton Winsberg, *Modern Cattle Breeds in Argentina. Origins, Diffusion, and Change* (Lawrence: University of Kansas, Center of Latin American Studies Occasional Papers, 13, 1968), p. 5.

15. Laura Randall, *A Comparative Economic History of Latin America, 1500-1914. Vol. 2, Argentina* (Ann Arbor: Published for the Institute of Latin American Studies, Columbia University, by University Microfilms, 1977), pp. 3–4.

16. *Actas Capitulares. Libro Quinto* (Córdoba: Archivo Municipal de Córdoba, 1900), 367–68.

17. See sales contract in AGBA, Compañía IX, 6-9-3, doc. 71.

18. Memorandum of Antonio Machoni, August 28, 1740, Ibid., 6-9-7.

19. Memorandum of Antonio Machoni, October 27, 1940, Ibid.

20. LCC, fol. 480.

21. Orders of Andrés de Rada to Novitiate, 1665, FG 1404, (SL, 229).

22. Emilio Coni, *Argricultura, comercio, y industria coloniales: siglos XVI–XVIII.* (Buenos Aires: El Ateneo, 1941).

23. "Factura de los efectos," AGBA, Compañía IX, 7-1-1, doc. 236.

24. Ibid., Compañía IX, 6-10-4.

25. Ibid., Compañía IX, 7-1-2.

26. "Razón de las estancias," AGBA, Compañía IX, 7-1-2.

27. See eighteenth-century rental agreements and contracts in AGBA, Compañía IX, 6-9-4, 45-3-11, and 6-10-7.

28. AGBA, Compañía IX, 6-10-5.
29. Cayetano Bruno, *Historia de la iglesia en la Argentina* (Buenos Aires: Editorial Don Bosco, 1967–1968), II, 74, 80.
30. CA, 38, 199.
31. "Estado en que se hallaron. . .las haziendas," AGBA, Compañía IX, 6-10-5.
32. Torre Revello, Documentos históricos, 217–18.
33. See Cushner, *Lords of the Land,* pp. 156–80.
34. Concolorcorvo. *Lazarillo. A Guide,* pp. 90–92.
35. LCC, fol. 231.
36. LCC, fol. 378.
37. Tijera to King, Jujuy, September 30, 1702, BNC, Jesuítas 199/318.
38. Pastells, *Historia,* VI, 41–46.
39. Rector to Verlo, AGBA, Compañía IX, 7-1-2.
40. Memorandum of Aguilar, February 16, 1735, Ibid., 6-9-7.
41. See war references in Ibid., 6-9-7, fol. 1040; 6-10-1.
42. Pastells, *Historia,* VIII(1), 112–13; and Spanish reprisals recounted in VII, 611.
43. Pastells, *Historia,* VI, 144.
44. Jane Pyle, "A Reexamination of Aboriginal Population Estimates for Argentina," in William M. Denevan (ed.), *The Native Population of the Americas in 1492,* p. 187.
45. Ibid., pp. 203–204.

5. Labor

1. By the nineteenth century the definitions were reversed. The *peon* was the long-term worker.
2. Carlos Mayo, "Los pobleros del Tucumán Colonial. Contribución al estudio de los mayordomos y administradores de encomienda en América," *Revista de historia de América* 85 (1978): 27-57; AHC, Escribanía 1.
3. For Alfaro's position and acts while visitor of Tucumán see Enrique de Gandía, *Francisco de Alfaro y la condición social de los indios. Río de la Plata, Paraguay, Tucumán, y Peru, siglos XVI y XVII* (Buenos Aires: Editorial La Facultad, 1939).
4. Luis de Quiñones, governor, May 10, 1614, AGI, Charcas 26.
5. See the letters of the city council of August 23, 1631 and 1633, AGI, Charcas 34.
6. "Algunas de las razones. . .," ARSI, Paraq. 11 (SL, 155).
7. "Ordenaciones del P. Francisco Vásquez Trujillo," FG 1483/3/13.
8. Carrafa's letter of November 30, 1645 and Tamburini's of January 1, 1707 are in APA.
9. Ibid.
10. Santa Fe, May 3, 1754, AGBA, Compañía 6-10-1, doc. 723.
11. The continual complaint of rural enterprises, both farms and ranches, was the scarcity of labor. José Luis Mora Merida, *Historia social del Paraguay (1600-1650),* p. 73.
12. Juan Muhn, (ed.), *La Argentina vista por viajeros del siglo XVIII* (Buenos Aires, 1946), pp. 41–42.

13. Ibid., p. 22; and Mario J. Buschiazzo (ed.), *Buenos Aires y Córdoba en 1729. Según cartas de los padres C. Cattaneo y C. Gervasoni, S.J.* (Buenos Aires, 1941) p. 144.

14. March 10, 1692, AGBA, Compañía IX, 6-9-4.

15. See this relationship in Ibid., 7-1-2, for the years around 1700.

16. February 5, 1682, AHC, Escribanía 2, 5/11.

17. January 6, 1713, AHC, Escribanía 2, 12/21.

18. AGBA, Compañía IX, 6-10-7.

19. Ibid., 7-1-2.

20. Rodríguez's statements are in Greñón, *Alta Gracia,* pp. 109–110.

21. Ibid., p. 100.

22. AGBA, Compañía IX, 6-10-6.

23. See the incisive comments of Arnold J. Bauer, "Debt Peonage in Colonial Economy: A Brief Historiographical Discussion," to appear shortly in the Acts of the 43rd International Congress of Americanists, Vancouver, August 11–17, 1979, cited with permission of author.

24. "Libro de conchabados de la estancia de san Ignacio de los Exercicios, y de los deudores de ella cuyo indice está al fin (1736-1750)," APA.

25. Bauer, "Debt Peonage," p. 5.

26. Conchabado books in AGBA, Compañía IX, 6-10-6.

27. Ibid., 7-1-1, docs. 644, 645.

28. "Razón de los oficiales y peones," Ibid., 6-10-1, doc. 666.

29. BNC, Jesuítas Ms. 6104.

30. Ibid., 6-10-1, doc. 132; and 6-10-5.

31. See memorials left after provincial visits of 1742 and 1745 in AGBA, Compañía IX, 6-9-5, 6-9-7.

32. Supplementary food was regularly given to conchabados on Corrientes, Ibid., 3-9-6, doc. 96.

33. AHC, Escribanía 1, 57/14.

34. Carlos Sempat Assadourián, *El tráfico de esclavos en Córdoba de Angola a Potosí. Siglos XVI–XVII* (Córdoba: Universidad Nacional, 1966), pp. 28, 33.

35. Elena F. S. de Studer, *La trata de negros en el Río de la Plata durante el siglo XVIII* (Buenos Aires: Universidad de Buenos Aires, 1958), p. 212.

36. José Torre Revello, "Negros esclavos introducidos en América por la South Sea Company," 128.

37. David G. Sweet, "Black Robes and 'Black Destiny': Jesuit Views of African Slavery in 17th Century Latin América," *Revista de historia de América* 86 (July–December, 1978): 133.

38. ARSI, Paraq. 11, fol. 419 (SL, 155).

39. Studer, *La trata de negros,* Appendix, Cuadro 17.

40. AGBA, Compañía IX, 6-9-6, doc. 126.

41. See the example in Ibid., 6-9-6, docs. 915, 765.

42. Ibid., 6-9-6, doc. 922.

43. Memorandum of March 20, 1745, AGBA, Compañía IX, 7-1-2; also that of 1734, Ibid., 6-9-6, doc. 922.

44. Rolando Mellafe, *Negro Slavery in Latin America* (Berkeley and Los Angeles: University of California Press, 1975) p. 140, misreads and misinterprets his source, Concolorcorvo. *El Lazarillo,* p. 71, and makes the Jesuits guilty of slave breeding. The reason for insistence on purchasing female slaves

was not breeding purposes but providing wives for male slaves. Thus, extramarital sex would be lessened and the wrath of God averted.

45. AGBA, Compañía IX, 6-9-3, fol. 436.

46. See Appendix A, number 13.

47. See letter of Juan Claussner, March 19, 1719, in Juan Muhn, ed., *La Argentina vista por viajeros del siglo XVIII,* p. 20.

48. Catalogues in ARSI, Paraq. 6.

49. Ceferino Garzón Maceda, *Economia del Tucumán; economía natural y economía monetaria. Siglos XVI–XVII–XVIII.* (Córdoba: Universidad Nacional, 1968).

50. George Reid Andrews, *The Afro-Argentines of Buenos Aires, 1800–1900,* (Madison: University of Wisconsin Press, 1980), p. 27.

51. Memorandum of Luís de la Roca, October 20, 1714, AGBA, Compañía IX, 6-9-5.

52. Memorandum of Juan Baptista de Zea, July 28, 1718, Ibid.

53. "Cathálogo de los esclavos de este colegio," AGBA, Compañía IX, 7-1-2.

54. Memorandum of April 18, 1745, AGBA, Compañía IX, 6-9-7, fol. 1101.

55. Memoradum of July 11, 1740, Ibid.

56. Memorandum of December 9, 1714, Ibid., 6-9-5.

57. See, for example, Bernard Nusdorfer's memorandum to Santa Fe College, 1745, Ibid., 6-9-7, Luís de la Roca's in 6-9-5.

58. See the account book for slaves for 1762–1765 in AGBA, Compañía IX, 7-1-2.

59. Memorandum of Antonio Machoni to College of Santiago del Estero, August 22, 1739, Ibid. 6-9-7.

60. Memorandum of September 24, 1721, Ibid., 6-9-5, fol. 881.

61. Memorandum of July 28, 1718, Ibid.

62. Ibid., 6-9-7.

63. Herrán to rector of Buenos Aires, 1745, AGBA, Compañía IX, 7-1-2.

64. "Copia de órdenes del P. Provincial Joseph de Barreda,'¹ AGBA, Compañía IX, 7-1-1.

65. Ibid.

66. Contract for manumission is in AGBA, Compañía IX, 6-10-5.

67. Examples of freed slaves are in Ibid., fol. 87; and also see Emilano Endrek, *El mestizaje en Córdoba. Siglo XVIII y principios del XIX* (Córdoba: Universidad Nacional, 1966), p. 7.

68. Calculated from costs and purchases of clothing for slaves in LCC.

69. Gonzalez to Núñez, Rome. January 31, 1696, APA.

70. October 27, 1691 and January 31, 1696, APA.

71. FG, 1483/3/13.

72. January 11, 1722, APA.

73. Matias Stroebel to governor, Concepción, December 26, 1746, AGBA, Compañía IX, 6-10-1, doc. 55.

74. Ibid.

75. Memorandum to College of Santa Fe, February 13, 1721, Ibid., 6-9-5.

76. Frank B. Costello, *The Political Philosophy of Luís de Molina, S.J. (1535–1600)* (Rome: Institutum Historicum S.I., Gonzaga University Press, 1974), p. 192.

77. Alonso de Sandoval, *De Instauranda Aethiopum Salute. El mundo de*

la esclavitud negra en América (Bogotá: Empresa nacional de publicaciones, 1956), pp. 26–27. See also Sweet, "Black Robes," 95-101; Vincent P. Franklin, "Alonso de Sandoval and the Jesuit Conception of the Negro," *Journal of Negro History* 58 (1973); 353-54; and G. E. M. de Ste. Croix, "Early Christian Attitudes to Property and Slavery," p. 21, in Derek Baker (ed.), *Church, Society and Politics* (Oxford: Basil Blackwell, 1975).

78. Sweet, "Black Robes," p. 101.

79. Sandoval, *De Instauranda,* p. 189; Franklin, "Alonso de Sandoval," pp. 356-57.

80. G. E. M. de Ste. Croix, "Early Christian Attitudes to Property and Slavery," pp. 18-19, in Derek Baker (ed.), *Church, Society and Politics* (Oxford: Basis Blackwell, 1975).

6. Finance

1. "Catalogus Tertius," ARSI, Paraq. 6.

2. Dionysius Fernández Zapico, (ed.), *Regulae Societatis Iesu* (Romae: Apud "Monumenta Historica Societatis Iesu, 1948), pp. 416–20.

3. LC, fol. 231, and for May 1755, fol. 228.

4. LC, fol. 208.

5. LC, fol. 270.

6. This account book has been abbreviated as LCC throughout these notes.

7. Tamburini to Parodi, Rome, May 1, 1716, APA; LCC, fol. 20.

8. LCC, fol. 303.

9. LCC, fols. 342–43.

10. See LCC, fols. 79, 99, and 120 for increasing quantity of goods.

11. Catalogus Triennalis, ARSI, Paraq. 6; also visita record of 1668 in AGBA, Compañía IX, 6–10–7; and Tirso Gonzalez to Lauro Núñez. Rome, July 31, 1696, APA.

12. Catalogus in ARSI, Paraq. 6.

13. Andrés de Rada's visita memorandum of 1668 in AGBA, Compañía IX, 6-10-7 and also accounts of 1669 in FG 1486/3/16; and comments to Lauro Núñez on financial state of the province, January 31, 1696, APA.

14. LCC, fol. 16.

15. Retz to Aguilar, December 13, 1732, APA.

16. LCC, fol. 5, and unpaginated summary.

17. The total value of Santa Catalina's buildings, slaves, and land was set at 161,743 pesos in 1767. AGBA, Temporalidades de Córdoba 21-9-3, and 21-9-2, fols. 105-213.

18. Report of Francisco Lupercio de Zurbano, Córdoba, October 14, 1644, FB 1483/3/5.

19. Report of Jaime Aguilar, Potosí, September 10, 1736, AGBA, Compañía IX, 6-9-7., fol. 191.

20. AGBA, Compañía IX, 6-10-5.

21. Ibid., 6-10-6.

22. Each missionary in the Paraguay reductions was budgeted at 169 pesos. Ibid., 6-10-5.

23. Andrés Aztina to Vicente Nicolás Contucci, Salta, May 14, 1764, AGBA, Compañía IX, 6-10-6.

24. "San Miguel Relación," AGBA, Compañía IX, 6-10-1, doc. 1009; for Asunción see Ibid., doc. 651; and for Tucumán, Ibid., doc. 734.
25. Investment sum is based for the most part on values assigned to Jesuit property after the expulsion in 1767. AGBA, Temporalidades de Córdoba, 21-9-3.
26. AGBA, Compañía IX, 7-3-7.
27. Inventories of 1768 are in APA; and "Estado del Colegio de Tucumán," AGBA, Compañía IX, 6-10-1, doc. 734. Ranches in nineteenth-century Argentina apparently had similar rates of return. Calculating rates could be tricky business because ledger books frequently put capital investments alongside of daily expenses. See Jonathan C. Brown, "A Nineteenth-Century Cattle Empire," pp. 176–177.
28. LCC, fol. 462.
29. "Razón de lo que se a edificado, 1758," AGBA, Compañía IX, 6-10-5.
30. See references to tithe payments in Ibid., IX 6-10-5, 6-10-6, and 6-10-7.

7. Credit, Money, and Colonial Trade

1. LCC, fol. 319.
2. Garzón Maceda, *Economía del Tucumán,* 7, 8.
3. Ibid.
4. *Actas Capitulares. Libro Octavo* (Córdoba: Archivo Municipal, 1900), 119.
5. Learte to Delgado, Córdoba, September 16, 1762, AGBA, 6-10-5.
6. "Memoria de géneros de almacén, 1727," Ibid., 6-9-6, doc. 360.
7. AGI, Buenos Aires 21.
8. October 1796, Ibid.
9. John T. Noonan, *The Scholastic Analysis of Usury* (Cambridge, Mass.: Harvard University Press, 1957), pp. 154–64, 230–48.
10. AHC, Escribanía 2, 4/29.
11. LCC, fol. 81.
12. LCC, fol. 177.
13. ARSI, Paraq. 6.
14. Ibid.
15. LCC, fols. 47–48.
16. Ibid., fol. 79.
17. These debts are listed in the triennial economic reports in ARSI, Paraq. 6.
18. AGBA, Compañía IX, 6-10-6.
19. García to Arnol, Santa Fe, June 16, 1767, AGBA, Compañía IX, 6-10-7 .
20. See "Liquidación de cuentas, 1721," AGBA, Compañía IX, 6-9-5, fol. 899, and 6-10-1, docs. 271, 690.
21. See accounts for 1751, 1756 in Ibid., 6-10-1, doc. 922.
22. Ibid., 6-9-7, fol. 348.
23. AHC, Hacienda 3.
24. Ibid., fol. 142.
25. "Extracto, cuenta, 1762–1764, September 13, 1764," AGBA, Compañía IX, 6-10-6.
26. Memorandum of Antonio Machoni to Simon Baylina, June 29, 1739, Ibid., 6-9-7, fol. 414.

27. Baylina to Machoni, Potosí, October 24, 1740, Ibid., 6-9-7.
28. "Ajuste de cuentas de este colegio de Buenos Aires," Ibid., 7-1-2.
29. This trading is discussed in Cushner, *Lords of the Land,* pp. 158–62.
30. LCC, fol. 90.
31. Ibid., fol. 49.
32. "Ordenaciones particulares," Rome, November 10, 1609, MSS. Biblioteca Nacional (Lima), Ms. 5, fol. 386.
33. "Razón de la Plata, 1687," ARSI, Paraq. 11, fol. 483 (SL, 155).
34. Ibid.
35. Report of Lauro Núñez, Córdoba, January 23, 1693, ARSI, Paraq. 11, fol. 499 (SL, 155).
36. Rome, January 15, 1736, APA.
37. See the large quantity of *libranzos* or drafts sent to and from Jesuit procurators in AGBA, Compañía IX, 6-9-7, and 6-10-6 just for the years 1735 and 1736.
38. Pastells, *Historia,* I, 155–56.
39. April 14, 1713, APA.
40. April 28, 1714, APA.
41. AGBA, Compañía IX, 45-3-12.
42. See Appendix B; Retz's letter in APA.
43. Pastells, *Historia,* III, 225.
44. AGBA, Compañía IX, 47-8-7, fols. 92–94 for tax exemptions and 47-8-5 fols. 1–10 for payment of Guaraní tribute.
45. Letter from Buenos Aires, January 9, 1683, AGI, Charcas 26.
46. AGI, Charcas 26.
47. Cushner, *Lords of the Land,* pp. 174–80.
48. City Council to Governor of Tucumán, Córdoba, November 11, 1769, AGI, Buenos Aires 49.
49. Memorandum of Altamirano of 1684 in Pastells, *Historia,* IX, 17–18, 45, 54.
50. See cédulas in Pastells, *Historia,* III, 101; VII, 491. The rivalry between Jesuit and lay growers is discussed in Adalberto López, "The Economics of Yerba Mate in Seventeenth-Century South America," *Agricultural History* 48 (1974): 506–509.
51. Ibid.
52. Appendix A, number 7.
53. "Lista General de los Jesuítas, 1767," AGBA, Compañía IX, 6-10-7; Pastells, *Historia,* VIII (2), 1252–1253.
54. "Autos de los robos," AGBA, Compañía IX, 21-9-2.

8. Conclusion

1. J.A. Raftis, "Western Monasticism and Economic Organization," *Comparative Studies in Society and History* 3 (1961): 453–454.
2. Dauril Alden of the University of Washington is preparing a comprehensive work on Jesuit economic activity throughout the Portuguese empire. An important segment of this study will focus on the Jesuits in Brazil.
3. A good comparison between institutional and private estates is B. E. S. Trueman, "Corporate Estate Management: Guy's Hospital Agricultural Estates, 1726-1815," *Agricultural History Review* 28 (1980): 31–44.

4. See Appendix A, numbers 9 and 11.

5. AGI, Charcas 26.

6. Although describing the late eighteenth century, see the general business practices of the Buenos Aires merchants in Susan Migden Socolow, *The Merchants of Buenos Aires, 1778–1810. Family and Commerce* (Cambridge: Cambridge University Press, 1978), pp. 54–70.

7. I have in mind here Penelope D. Johnson, *Prayer, Patronage, and Power. The Abbey of la Trinité, Vendôme, 1032–1187* (New York: New York University Press, 1981); Maarten Ultee. *The Abbey of St. Germain des Prés in the Seventeenth Century* (New Haven and London: Yale University Press, 1981); Edmund King, *Peterborough Abbey, 1086–1310. A Study in the Land Market* (Cambridge: Cambridge University Press, 1973); and Barbara Harvey, *Westminster Abbey and its Estates in the Middle Ages* (Oxford: Oxford University Press, 1977).

8. The urban-rural dichotomy has shifted emphases over time. See W.H.C. Friend, "Town and Countryside in Early Christianity," pp. 25–42, and Michael Richter, "Urbanitas-Rusticitas: Linguistic Aspects of a Medieval Dichotomy," pp. 149–157, in Derek Baker (ed.), *The Church in Town and Countryside* (Oxford: Basil Blackwell, 1979); and Jacques Le Goff, *Time, Work, and Culture in the Middle Ages.* trans. by Arthur Goldhammer (Chicago: University of Chicago Press, 1980), pp. 87–97.

9. The notable exceptions to this deal with Mexico: Konrad, *A Jesuit Hacienda in Colonial Mexico;* David Brading, *Haciendas and Ranchos in the Mexican Bajio. León, 1700–1860.* (Cambridge: Cambridge University Press, 1978).

10. Harold Blakemore and Clifford T. Smith, *Latin America: Geographical Perspectives* (London: Methuen and Co., 1971), pp. 277–282.

Glossary of Spanish Terms

Alcance: account balance; remainder
Almacén: warehouse
Bodega: warehouse; storage room
Capatas: foreman; master herdsman
Casco: nucleus of estate structures
Censo: mortgage imposed on property yielding an interest
Cepa: stock of a vine
Chácara (chacra): vegetable garden or farm
Cofradía: parish organization of laypersons
Conchabado: wage worker contracted by ranch, farm, or mill for a period of
  time
Cría de mulas: range and associated building for raising mules
Cuba: wine cask
Cuero: hide
Dependencia: auxiliary business or place of activity
Domador: ranch hand caring for animals; horse tamer
Ejido: grazing land reserved for communal use
Encomendero: holder of an *encomienda*
Encomienda: grant of natives, mainly as taxpayers; area of the natives
  granted
Estancia: cattle ranch
Estanciero: ranch administrator
Fanega: unit of weight equivalent to about 1½ bushels
Fanegada: areal measure equivalent to about three hectares
Fresada: blanket, shawl
Fundación: endowment; money or property donated to found a college or
  institution
Gañán: hired worker
Gente de la estancia: estate workers
Grasa: grease, fat, softer than *sebo*
Hacienda: large farm or estate
Huerta: fruit or vegetable garden; orchard

Invernada: wintering grounds
Jerga: coarse woolen cloth
Mayordomo: estate manager, either Indian or Spanish
Merced: reward for services rendered
Obraje: textile mill
Oficio: business office
Paraje: same as *puesto;* corral and hut on a cattle range
Peón: general worker
Peonada: group of *peones*
Poblero: foreman of mill or workhouse
Procurador: business manager; representative sent periodically to Rome
Puesto: see *paraje*
Quinta: fruit orchard
Ranchería: bunk house or workers' quarters
Rancho: individual worker's or slave's hut
Rector: local superior of a college
Ropa de la tierra: coarse frieze; material used for Indian clothing
Sayal: sackcloth
Sebo: tallow, animal fat
Sementera: farmland for grains
Solar: houseplot
Suela: sole leather
Suerte de tierra: plots of land of equal size
Tajamar: reservoir
Vaquería: organized hunt for wild cattle
Vara: unit of length, about a meter
Yanacona: Indian agricultural worker
Yerba (Yerba Mate): Jesuit tea

Bibliography

Sources

The hard data for much of what is written in this book are found in the central Jesuit archives in Rome (ARSI) and in the national and Jesuit archives in Buenos Aires. The Jesuit records preserved in ARSI are especially valuable for throwing much needed light on the social and economic history of colonial Argentina, and more specifically on the economic enterprises of the Society of Jesus. These data are to be distinguished from those relating to the Jesuit reductions of Paraguay, much of which are now found in the form of population records, memoranda, cattle sales receipts, and mate distribution in AGBA. ARSI economic data are found for the most part in the triennial economic reports and in the yearly *Catalogus Rerum*. The catalogues for Argentina are all classified under ARSI, Paraq. 6. Outside of Rome the only copies of these catalogues seen by this writer were in the possession of SL and of the late Fr. Guillermo Furlong, S.J. They formed part of Furlong's personal library and perhaps they are now on deposit in the library of the Universidad Salvador where Furlong resided for so many years.

Letters and reports sent from provincials and rank-and-file Jesuits to Rome are gathered in seven volumes titled *Litterae* and *Historiae* spanning the years 1608 to 1767. This material is composed of general reports sent from the provincial superior in Córdoba on the state of the province, reports on the operations of the reductions of Paraguay, and letters from individual Jesuits on a variety of topics. Some of the material found in this section has been published by Carlos Leonhardt, *Documentos para la historia argentina. Cartas Anuas de la Provincia del Paraguay,* Buenos Aires, 1927–1929, and also used by Magnus Mörner, *The Political and Economic Activity of the Jesuits in the La Plata Region,* Stockholm, 1953. The *Fondo Gesuítico* section of ARSI is concerned solely with the economic aspect of Jesuit colleges in Europe, Asia, and America. It contains bundles of documents on Jesuit colleges in Argentina and here are found bills of sale for urban and rural properties, litigation, and economic reports. Of less importance for the history of Argentina but of great importance for the history of the Jesuits were meetings held every few years to discuss policy and problems. The minutes and reports of these meetings, called Provincial Congregations, are found in ARSI under the title *Congregationum Provinciarum*. All of the Jesuit archive material is in SL. The Jesuit Archive in Rome is located in the Curia Generalis, Borgo Sancto Spiritu, Casella

Postale 9084, Rome, Italy 00100. It contains two well-lighted reading rooms and provides xerox and microfilm service at a reasonable cost. It is a private archive but its material is made available to any responsible scholar.

The documents in ARSI must be complemented by several other depositories of documents dealing with the Jesuits in Argentina. The largest are the *Compañía de Jesús* and *Temporalidades* sections of the Archivo General de la Nación, Buenos Aires. The present Jesuit Archives in San Miguel, outside of Buenos Aires, is notable not so much for quantity but for quality. Two bundles worth noting are the account books of the College of Córdoba (of which I and SL have microfilm copies), and letters sent by the Jesuit superior generals in Rome to the provincials of Paraguay from roughly 1700 to 1760. Frequently one can be misled by rosy reports sent by local provincials to Rome on the state and activities of the province. The generals' letters are often critical and to the point. The Archivo General de Indias, Seville, the Archivo Histórico Nacional, Madrid, the Academia Nacional de la Historia, Madrid, and the National Library of Santiago de Chile also have holdings of Jesuit material. Santiago is especially strong on the Jesuit troubles with the bishop of Asunción in 1648 and the problems relating to the Treaty of Demarcation of 1750. Pastells, *Historia* has packed into his seven-volume work many complete AGI documents. Hopefully, Hugo Storni, S.J. will collect the most important documents in these widely scattered sources for publication in the projected *Monumenta Historica Societatis Iesu* volumes on the Jesuits in Argentina.

Actas Capitulares. Córdoba: Archivo Municipal (various years).

Andrews, George Reid. *The Afro-Argentines of Buenos Aires, 1800–1900.* Madison: University of Wisconsin Press, 1980.

Arcondo, Anibal B. *La agricultura en Córdoba, 1870–1880.* Córdoba: Universidad Nacional, 1965.

_____. "Los precios en una economía de transición: Córdoba durante el siglo XVIII." *Revista de economía y estadística* 15 (1971):7–32.

Baker, Derek, ed. *The Church in Town and Countryside.* Oxford: Basil Blackwell, 1979.

_____. *Church, Society and Politics.* Oxford: Basil Blackwell, 1975.

Ball, J. N. *Merchants and Merchandise. The Expansion of Trade in Europe, 1500–1630.* New York: St. Martin's Press, 1977.

Bishko, Charles J. "The Peninsular Background of Latin American Cattle Ranching." *Hispanic American Historical Review* 32 (1952): 491–515.

Blakemore, Harold, and Clifford T. Smith, eds. *Latin America. Geographical Perspectives.* London: Methuen, 1971.

Blanco, E. *La viña y los vinos en Mendoza.* Buenos Aires, 1884.

Boxer, C. R. *The Church Militant and Iberian Expansion, 1440–1770.* Baltimore and London: Johns Hopkins University Press, 1978.

Brading, David. *Haciendas and Ranchos in the Mexican Bajio. León, 1700–1860.* Cambridge: Cambridge University Press, 1978.

Brown, Jonathan C. "A Nineteenth-Century Argentine Cattle Empire." *Agricultural History* 52 (1978): 160–178.

_____. *A Socioeconomic History of Argentina, 1776–1860.* Cambridge: Cambridge University Press, 1979.

Bruno, Cayetano. *Historia de la Iglesia en la Argentina. Vol. 2. 1600–1632.* Buenos Aires: Editorial Don Bosco, 1967. Vol. 3. 1632–1686. 1968.

Buschiazzo, Mario J. ed. *Buenos Aires y Córdoba en 1729. Según cartas de los Padres C. Cattaneo y C. Gervasoni, S.J.* Buenos Aires, 1941.

_____. *Argentina: Monumentos históricos y arqueológicos.* Mexico: Ed. Fournier, 1959.

_____. *Estancias jesuíticas de Córdoba.* Buenos Aires, 1969.

Caraman, Philip. *The Lost Paradise. The Jesuit Republic in South America.* New York: Seabury, 1976.

Carrio de la Vandera, Alonso. See: Concolorcorvo.

(Cartas Anuas). *Documentos para la Historia Argentina. Tomo XIX. Iglesia. Cartas Anuas de la Provincia del Paraguay. Chile, y Tucumán, de la Compañía de Jesús, (1609–1614).* Buenos Aires: Jacobo Peuser, 1927.

_____. (1615–1637). Tomo XX. Buenos Aires: Jacobo Peuser, 1929.

Concolorcorvo. *El Lazarillo. A Guide for Inexperienced Travelers between Buenos Aires and Lima, 1773.* Translated by Walter D. Kline. Bloomington: Indiana University Press, 1965.

_____. *El Lazarillo de ciegos caminantes desde Buenos Aires hasta Lima, 1773.* Buenos Aires: Ediciones Argentinas Solar, 1942.

Coni, Emilio A. *Agricultura, comercio y industria coloniales: siglos XVI–XVIII.* Buenos Aires, 1941.

_____. *Historia de las vaquerías del Río de la Plata, 1555–1750.* Buenos Aires, 1950.

_____. *Antecedentes para la historia del desarrollo agrícola y ganadero argentino.* Buenos Aires, 1964.

Chatfield, Michael. *A History of Accounting Thought.* Hillsdale, IL: Dryden Press, 1974.

Costello, Frank B. *The Political Philosophy of Luis de Molina, S.J. (1535–1600).* Rome–Spokane: Institutum Historicum S.I., Gonzaga University Press, 1974.

Cushner, Nicholas P. "Slave Mortality and Reproduction on Jesuit Haciendas in Colonial Peru." *Hispanic American Historical Review* 55 (1975): 177–99.

_____. *Landed Estates in the Colonial Philippines.* New Haven: Yale University Southeast Asia Studies, 1976.

_____. *Lords of the Land: Sugar, Wine and Jesuit Estates of Coastal Peru, 1600–1767.* Albany: State University of New York Press, 1980.

_____. *Farm and Factory. The Jesuits and the Development of Agrarian Capitalism in Colonial Quito, 1600–1767.* Albany: State University of New York Press, 1982.

Denevan, William M., ed. *The Native Population of the Americas in 1492.* Madison: University of Wisconsin Press, 1976.

DeRoover, Raymond. *Money, Banking and Credit in Mediaeval Bruges.* Cambridge, Mass.: Mediaeval Academy of America, 1948.

Dobson, Richard B. *Durham Priory, 1400–1450.* Cambridge: Cambridge University Press, 1973.

Documentos históricos y geográficos relativos a la conquista y colonización rioplatense. (Tomo Primero: Memorias y Relaciones históricas y geográficas, con introducción de José Torre Revello). 5 vols. Buenos Aires: Talleres S. A. Casa Jacobo Peuser, 1941.

Dreidemie, Oscar. "La estancia jesuítica de Jesús María." reprint, Buenos Aires: 1948. (Originally published in *Boletín de la Comisión Nacional de Museos y Monumentos Históricos,* Año IX, no.9), 33–69.

Endrek, Emiliano. *El mestizaje en Córdoba. Siglo XVIII y principios del XIX.* Córdoba: Universidad Nacional de Córdoba, 1966.

Franklin, Vincent P. "Alonso de Sandoval and the Jesuit Conception of the Negro." *Journal of Negro History* 58 (1973): 349–360.

Friend, W. H. C. "Town and Countryside in Early Christianity," pp. 25–42, in Derek Baker, ed., *The Church in Town and Countryside.*

Furlong, Guillermo. *"The Jesuit Contribution to Agriculture and Stock Raising in the Argentine." Historical Bulletin 11 (May, 1933): 66–68.*

_____. *Cartografía jesuítica de Río de la Plata.* Buenos Aires: Talleres S. A. Casa Jacobo Peuser, 1936.

_____. *Pedro Juan Andreu y su carta a Mateo Andreu, 1750.* Buenos Aires: Librería de la Plata, 1953.

_____. *Misiones y sus pueblos de Guaraníes.* Buenos Aires, 1962.

_____. *Historia del Colegio de la Inmaculada de la Ciudad de Santa Fe, 1610–1962.* 6 vols. Buenos Aires, 1962–1963.

_____. *Antonio Sepp y su "Gobierno Temporal," 1732.* Buenos Aires: Ediciones Theoría, 1962.

_____. *Manuel Quirini, S.J. y sus "Informes al Rey," 1747–1750.* Buenos Aires: Ediciones Theoría, 1967.

_____. *Historia Social y Cultural del Río de la Plata, 1536–1810.* 3 vols. Buenos Aires, 1969.

_____. *Historia social y cultural del Río de la Plata, 1536–1810.* Buenos Aires, 1969.

Gandía, Enrique de. *Historia de la conquista del Río de la Plata y del Paraguay, 1535–1556.* Buenos Aires: Librería de A. García Santos, 1932.

_____. *Francisco de Alfaro y la condición social de los indios. Río de la Plata, Paraguay, Tucumán, y Perú, siglos XVI y XVII.* Buenos Aires, 1939.

Garzón Maceda, Ceferino. *Economía del Tucumán; Economía natural y economía monetaria. Siglos XVI–XVII–XVIII.* Córdoba: Universidad Nacional, 1968.

Garzón Maceda, Ceferino and J. W. Dorflinger. "Esclavos y mulatos en un dominio rural del siglo XVIII en Córdoba." *Revista de la Universidad Nacional de Córdoba* 2 serie, 2 (1961): 625–640.

Gies, Joseph and Frances. *Merchants and Moneymen. The Commercial Revolution, 1000–1500.* New York: Thomas Y. Crowell, 1972.

Girouard, Mark. *Life in the English Country House. A Social and Architectural History.* New Haven and London: Yale University Press, 1978.

Gracia, Joaquín. *Los jesuitas en Córdoba.* Buenos Aires, 1940.

Greñón, Pedro. *Documentos Históricos. Los Pampas.* Córdoba, 1927.

_____. *Documentos históricos. El Libro de Mercedes.* Córdoba, 1930.

_____. *Alta Gracia. Documentos Históricos.* Córdoba, 1929.

_____. *La Compañía de Jesús en Córdoba. Documentación de su establecimiento.* Córdoba, 1938.

Grigg, David. *The Harsh Lands. A Study in Agricultural Development.* London: Macmillan, 1970.

_____. *The Agricultural Systems of the World. An Evolutionary Approach.* Cambridge: Cambridge University Press, 1974.

_____. "Agricultural Geography." *Progress in Human Geography* V (1981): 268–76.

Harvey, Barbara. *Westminster Abbey and its Estates in the Middle Ages.* Oxford: At the Clarendon Press, 1977.

Horn, Walter and Ernest Born. *The Barns of the Abbey of Beaulieu at its Granges of Great Coxwell and Beaulieu–St. Leonards.* Berkeley and Los Angeles: University of California Press, 1965.

Jaimes Freyre, Ricardo. *El Tucumán del Siglo XVI (bajo el gobierno de Juan Ramírez de Velasco).* Buenos Aires: Imprenta de Coni Hermanos, 1914.

James, Preston E. *Latin America.* New York: Odyssey Press, 1959.

Johnson, Penelope D. *Prayer, Patronage, and Power. The Abbey of la Trinité Vendôme, 1032–1187.* New York: New York University Press, 1981.

Kelemen, Pál. *Baroque and Rococo in Latin America.* Second edition, 2 vols. New York: Dover Publications, 1967.

King, Edmund. *Peterborough Abbey, 1086–1310: A Study in the Land Market.* Cambridge: Cambridge University Press, 1973.

Klein, Herbert S. *Bolivia. The Evolution of a Multi-Ethnic Society.* New York: Oxford University Press, 1982.

Konrad, Herman W. *A Jesuit Hacienda in Colonial Mexico. Santa Lucía, 1576–1767.* Stanford: Stanford University Press, 1980.

Kronfuss, Juan. *Arquitectura colonial en Argentina.* Córdoba: A. Biffignanchi, n.d.

Larden, Walter. *Estancia Life. Agricultural, Economic, and Cultural Aspects of Argentine Farming.* London: T. Fisher Unwin, 1911 (republished by Blaine Ethridge Books, Detroit, 1974.

Le Goff, Jacques. *Time, Work, and Culture in the Middle Ages.* Translated by Arthur Goldhammer. Chicago: University of Chicago Press, 1980.

Leonhardt, Carlos. *See:* Cartas Anuas.

Levene, Ricardo. *Documentos para la Historia Argentina. Tomo V. Comercio de Indias. Antecedentes legales (1713–1778).* Buenos Aires: Compañía Sud-Americana de Billetes de Banco, 1915.

_____. *Historia de la Provincia de Buenos Aires y formación de sus pueblos.* 2 vols. La Plata: Archivo Histórico, 1940–1941.

_____. *A History of Argentina.* Translated and edited by William Spence Robertson. New York: Russell and Russell, 1963.

Levillier, Roberto. *Antecedentes de política económica en el Río de la Plata. Documentos originales de los siglos XVI al XIX. . . . 2 vols.* Madrid: Suc. de Rivadeneyra, 1915.

_____. *La Audiencia de Charcas. Correspondencia de Presidentes y Oidores. Documentos del Archivo de Indias.* 3 vols. Madrid: Imprenta de Juan Pueyo, 1918–1922.

_____. *Gobernación de Tucumán. Correspondencia de los Cabildos en el siglo XVI. Documentos del Archivo de Indias. . .* Madrid: Suc. de Rivadeneyra, 1918.

_____. *Gobernación de Tucumán. Papeles de Gobernadores en el siglo XVI. Documentos del Archivo de Indias.* Madrid: Imp. de Juan Pueyo, 1920.

_____. *El Tucumán. Papeles de los gobernadores. (Colección de Publicaciones Históricas de la Biblioteca del Congreso Argentino).* Tomo I. Madrid, 1920.

_____. *Papeles eclesiásticos de Tucumán. Documentos originales del Archivo de Indias.* 2 vols. Madrid: Imp. Juan Pueyo, 1926.

_____. *Descubrimiento y población del Norte Argentino por españoles del Perú*. Buenos Aires: Espasa-Calpe, 1943.

_____. *Guerras y conquistas en Tucumán y Cuyo . . . 1554–1574*. Buenos Aires: Espasa–Calpe, 1945.

Little, Lester K. *Religious Poverty and the Profit Economy in Medieval Europe*. Ithaca: Cornell University Press, 1978.

López, Adalberto. "The Economics of Yerba Mate in Seventeenth-Century South America." *Agricultural History* 48 (1974): 493–509.

Lullio, Orestes de. *La estancia jesuítica de San Ignacio*. Santiago del Estero, 1954.

Marianetti, Benito. *El racimo y su aventura. La cuestión vitivinícola*. Buenos Aires: Editorial Platina, 1965.

Martínez, Pedro S. "La mano de obra, el artesanado y la organización del trabajo en el Virreinato Rioplatense." *Historia* 13 (1967): 68–77.

Martiníere, Guy. *Les Ameriques latines. Une histoire économique*. Grenoble: Presses Universitaires de Grenoble, 1978.

Mayo, Carlos. "Los pobleros del Tucumán colonial. Contribución al estudio de los mayordomos y administradores de encomienda en América." *Revista de historia de América* 85 (Jan.–June, 1978): 27–57.

McCusker, John J. *Money and Exchange in Europe and America, 1600–1775: A Handbook*. Chapel Hill: University of North Carolina Press, 1978.

Mellafe, Rolando. *Negro Slavery in Latin America*. Berkeley and Los Angeles: University of California Press, 1975.

Mille, Andrés. *Derrotero de la Compañía de Jesús en la conquista del Perú, Tucumán y Paraguay, y sus iglesias del Antiguo Buenos Aires, 1567–1768*. Buenos Aires, 1968.

Miller, Elbert E. "The Frontier and the Development of Argentine Culture." *Revista Geográfica* (1979): 183–198.

Miller, Robert Ryal. "The Fake Inca of Tucumán: Don Pedro de Bohorques." *The Americas* 23 (1975): 196–210.

Mitchell, David. *The Jesuits: A History*. New York: Franklin Watts, Inc., 1981.

Mora Merida, José Luís. *Historia Social del Paraguay (1600–1650)*. Sevilla: Escuela de Estudios Hispano-Americanos, 1973.

_____. *Iglesia y Sociedad en Paraguay en el siglo XVIII*. Sevilla: Escuela de Estudios Hispano-Americanos, 1976.

Morgan, W. B. and R. J. C. Munton. *Agricultural Geography*. London: Methuen, 1971.

Mörner, Magnus. *The Economic and Political Activities of the Jesuits in the La Plata Region. The Hapsburg Era*. Stockholm: Institute of Ibero-American Studies, 1953.

Muhn, Juan, ed. *La argentina vista por viajeros del siglo XVIII*. Buenos Aires, 1946.

Nider, Joannes. *On the Contracts of Merchants*. Translated by Charles H. Reeves; edited by Ronald B. Schuman. Norman: University of Oklahoma Press, 1966.

Odell, Peter R. and David A. Preston. *Economies and Societies in Latin America: A Geographical Interpretation*. New York: John Wiley and Sons, 1978.

Ortells, Antonio. *Manual de Geografía de la Provincia de Córdoba*. Buenos Aires, 1906.

Pastells, Pablo. *Historia de la Compañía de Jesús en la Provincia del Paraguay (Argentina, Paraguay, Uruguay, Peru, Bolivia y Brasil) según los documentos originales del Archivo General de Indias.* 7 vols., Madrid: Librería General de Victoriano Suarez, 1912–1948.

Peña, Roberto I. *Vitoria y Sepúlveda y el problema del Indio en la antigua gobernación de Tucumán.* Cuadernos de Historia, XVI. Córdoba: Universidad Nacional de Córdoba, 1951.

Peragallo, Edward. *Origin and Evolution of Double Entry Bookkeeping. A Study of Italian Practice from the Fourteenth Century.* New York: American Institute Publishing Co., 1938.

Plá, Josefina. "Los talleres misioneros (1609–1767). Su organización y funcionamiento." *Revista de Historia de América* 75–76 (1973): 9–56.

Platt, Colin. *The Monastic Grange in Medieval England. A Reassessment.* New York: Fordham University Press, 1969.

Puiggros, Rodolfo. *Historia económica del Río de la Plata.* Buenos Aires, 1945.

Raftis, J. A. "Western Monasticism and Economic Organization." *Comparative Studies in Society and History* 3 (1961): 452–469.

Randall, Laura, *A Comparative Economic History of Latin America, 1500–1914. Vol. 2, Argentina.* Published for Institute of Latin American Studies, Columbia University by University Microfilms, Ann Arbor, 1977.

Reales Cédulas y provisiones. Epoca colonial, 1517–1662. Tomo I. Buenos Aires: Archivo de la Nación Argentina, 1911.

Richter, Michael. "Urbanitas-Rusticitas: Linguistic Aspects of a Medieval Dichotomy," pp. 149–157, in Derek Baker ed., *The Church in Town and Countryside.* Oxford: Basil Blackwell, 1979.

Rout, Leslie. *The African Experience in Spanish America, 1502 to the Present Day.* Cambridge: Cambridge University Press, 1976.

Sabsay, Fernando L. *Historia económica y social argentina. España y Río de la Plata.* Buenos Aires: Bibliográfica Omeba, 1967.

Sánchez-Albornoz, Nicholás with Patricia Ottolenghi de Frankmann, Manuel Urbina, and Dorothy Webb. "La saca de mulas de Salta al Peru, 1778–1808." *Annuario de Instituto de Investigaciones Históricas* (1965): 261–312.

_____. "Extracción de mulas de Jujuy al Peru. Fuentes, volumen, y negociantes." *Estudios de historia social* (October, 1965): 107–120.

_____. *The Population of Latin America.* Translated by W. A. R. Richardson. Berkeley: University of California Press, 1974.

Sandoval, P. Alonso de. *De Instauranda Aethiopum Salute. El mundo de la esclavitud negra en América.* Bogotá: Empresa nacional de publicaciones, 1956.

(Santa Catalina). *La estancia jesuítica de Santa Catalina. Documentos de Arte Argentina, Cuaderno IX.* Buenos Aires: Academia Nacional de Bellas Artes, 1940.

Savory, Theodore H. "The Mule." *Scientific American* 223 (1970): 102–108.

Scobie, James R. *Argentina. A City and a Nation.* New York: Oxford University Press, 1971.

Sempat Assadourián, Carlos. *El tráfico de esclavos en Córdoba, 1588–1610.* Córdoba: Universidad Nacional, 1965.

_____. *El tráfico de esclavos en Córdoba de Angola á Potosí. Siglos*

XVI–XVII. Córdoba: Universidad Nacional, 1966.

Simon, Andre L., ed. *Wines of the World.* New York: McGraw-Hill, 1967.

Socolow, Susan Migden, *The Merchants of Buenos Aires, 1778–1810. Family and Commerce.* Cambridge: Cambridge University Press, 1978.

Ste. Croix, G. E. M. de. "Early Christian Attitudes to Property and Slavery," pp. 1–38, in Derek Baker, ed., *Church, Society and Politics.* Oxford: Basil Blackwell, 1975.

Storni, Carlos. *Descripción de viñedos que se cultivan en Argentina desde la época colonial.* Córdoba, 1927.

Storni, Hugo. "Jesuitas italianos en el Río de la Plata (antigua provincia del Paraguay, 1585–1768)." *Archivum Historicum Societatis Iesu* 48 (1979): 3–64.

Studer, Elena F.S. de. *La trata de negros en el Río de la Plata durante el siglo XVIII.* Buenos Aires: Universidad de Buenos Aires, 1958.

Sweet, David G. "Black Robes and 'Black Destiny': Jesuit Views of African Slavery in 17th–Century Latin America." *Revista de historia de America* 86 (July–Dec., 1978): 87–133.

Tapson, Alfred J. "Indian Warfare on the Pampas during the Colonial Period." *Hispanic American Historical Review* 42 (1962): 1–28.

Toledo, Estela B. "El Comercio de Mulas en Salta: 1657–1698." *Anuario del Instituto de Investigaciones Históricas* (Rosario, Argentina) 6 (1962–1963): 165–190.

Torre Revello, José. "Negros esclavos introducidos en América por la South Sea Company." *Historia* 14 (1938): 128.

_____. "Sociedad colonial, las clases sociales, la ciudad y la campaña," in *Historia de la Nación Argentina* (2nd ed.) Vol. IV, Buenos Aires, 1940.

_____. *Documentos Históricos y Geográficos relativos a la conquista y colonización rioplatense. I.* Buenos Aires: Casa Jacobo Peuser, 1941.

Trueman, B. E. S. "Corporate Estate Management: Guy's Hospital Agricultural Estates, 1726–1815." *Agricultural History Review* 28 (1980): 31–44.

Ultee, Maarten. *The Abbey of St. Germain des Prés in the Seventeenth Century.* New Haven and London: Yale University Press, 1981.

Weil, T. E. et. al. *Area Handbook for Argentina.* Washington, D.C.: U. S. Government Printing Office, 1974.

Wethey, Harold E. *Colonial Architecture and Sculpture in Peru.* Cambridge: Harvard University Press, 1949.

White, Richard Allen. "The Political Economy of Paraguay and the Impoverishment of the Missions. Classical Colonial Dependence." *The Americas* 31 (1975): 417–433.

Wilson, Thomas. *A Discourse upon Usury. With an historical introduction by R. H. Tawney.* New York: Augustus M. Kelly, 1963.

Winsberg, Morton. *Modern Cattle Breeds in Argentina: Origins, Diffusion, and Change.* University of Kansas. Center of Latin American Studies. Occasional Papers, 13. Lawrence: 1968.

Wright, Ione S. and Lisa M. Nekhom. *Historical Dictionary of Argentina.* Metuchen, N.J.: Scarecrow Press, 1978.

Zavala, Silvio. *Orígenes de la colonización en el Río de la Plata.* Mexico: Editorial de el Colegio Nacional, 1977.

Zorraquín Becú, Ricardo. *La organización política argentina en el período hispánico.* Buenos Aires: Editorial Perrot, 1962.

Index